WITHDRAWN

The Blue Demons

The Blue Demons
Great DePaul Teams and Traditions

Tim Stephens

co-published by Bonus Books, Inc., Chicago and DePaul University

Bonus Books, Inc.

©1991 by Bonus Books, Inc.
All rights reserved

Except for appropriate use in critical reviews or works of scholarship, the reproduction or use of this work in any form or by any electronic, Mechanical or other means now known or hereafter invented, including photocopying and recording, and in any information storage and retrieval system is forbidden without the written permission of the publisher.

95   94   93   92   91   5   4   3   2   1

Library of Congress Catalog Card Number: 91-75661

International Standard Book Number: 0-929387-56-2

Bonus Books, Inc.
160 East Illinois Street
Chicago, Illinois 60611

Printed in the United States of America

For my mother, Peggy, who taught me to work with passion.
For my father, Steve, who taught me to work with diligence.
And most of all, for my wife, Susan, who has to put up with the strange combination of passionate diligence.

Gone but not forgotten...
JJL—She never wrote any books or became famous, but she could grow flowers in rock.
LEL—He had $59 and one winch truck, and he left his name on this world.

Contents

Foreword ix

I In the Beginning

1. A Team Is Born 3
2. The New Era 7
3. Continuing the Success 13

II The Ray Meyer Years

4. The M&M Boys 21
5. Success After the Mikans 35
6. Closing ''The Barn'' Door 47
7. Guarding the Tradition 55
8. Hard Times 65
9. The Chicago Gang 73
10. Final Four Time 85
11. A New Home 99
12. A Fond Farewell 119

III The Joey Meyer Era

13. The Second Coach Meyer 129
14. A Perfect Fit 143
15. Fast Forwards to the Future 161
16. A Family Business 177

Year-by-Year Results 179

Foreword

In many ways, a history of the DePaul University men's basketball program reads like the history of the Meyer family. The 1991-92 season marks the 50th year our family has been part of the program.

It seems hard to believe now, but when I signed my first contract to become head coach at DePaul, I only signed a one-year deal. I wasn't sure if I'd like coaching here, and I didn't want to be tied down. Well, I guess I liked it!

A lot of people still come up to me and recognize me. Most of them associate my face with DePaul basketball. That's really a tribute to the power of television. I coached here for about thirty-five years before the TV cameras started coming around. Very few people recognized me until our games started being televised regularly.

While its nice to be recognized, I really can't take the credit for the success our basketball team knew during my days as head coach. There's only so much you can do as a coach. Ultimately, the players make the plays that win or lose the game. I was fortunate to have some outstanding young men play for me.

Three of those players were my sons: Tom, Joey, and Bob. There is no greater thrill, yet no bigger challenge as a coach, than having your children play for you. Trying to separate your parental side from your coaching side in dealing with your own children is almost impossible. And both you and the child are targets of criticism.

If you play your child, regardless of how good they are, people are going to say you're showing favoritism. It's even harder on the player. No matter how good they are, or how hard they work, some people will always say they are playing just because they're the coaches kid.

I think I learned better how to deal with that as the three boys came through DePaul. I probably should have played Tom more than I did. He was a good player. He worked hard. He deserved it. By the time Joey came along, I was better.

Even today, I continue to deal with that same kind of challenge. But now, it's as a retired coach being followed by his son. Although seven years have passed since I retired, I still have a lot of people ask me how the program is doing.

I believe we are headed in the right direction. Over these past seven years, Joey has proven himself as a coach and a recruiter. I think the best years for him are still ahead.

He's bringing young men into DePaul who are not only good players but good people as well. It's a pleasure to be around the team in my role as a radio announcer. I still travel with the team and attend some of the practices.

It's great to see the tradition of DePaul basketball continue in the Meyer family. So much of our history is intertwined with DePaul basketball. It's hard to see where the program stops and we end sometimes.

I've received great pleasure being part of this program. There are so many fond memories, so many wonderful people, and so many thrilling games. And so much more is still to come.

Ray Meyer
September 1991

I

In the Beginning

1

A Team Is Born

Chuck Murphy took the ball and began dribbling up the left side of the floor. As he approached midcourt, the final horn sounded and Murphy let fly with a high arching prayer of a shot that hit the glass just to the right of the rim.

Glancing upward at the scoreboard, head coach Joey Meyer walked stiffly to center court. As Meyer shook hands with Georgia Tech mentor Bobby Cremins, he glanced again at the final verdict displayed in patterned lights on the end of the University of Dayton Arena: GEORGIA TECH 87, DEPAUL 70.

Meyer turned and headed off the floor. The 1991 season was over and the stiffness from moments earlier was replaced by disappointment in his slumped shoulders. Meyer reached the end of the floor, turned to his left and disappeared down the tunnel to visit with his players for a few moments before heading to a postgame press conference.

Eventually, Meyer and his team would return to the Radisson Inn on Dayton's north side and begin to write the postscripts for another season. They would call it a success, pointing to twenty wins and an NCAA tournament berth. But success is a relative term. To be fully appreciated, success must be measured in relation to other years. At DePaul, successes have outnumbered the failures.

During the decade of the 1980s, DePaul's program was one of the most successful in college basketball. The Blue Demon's 1991 NCAA tournament bid was their thirteenth in fifteen years. DePaul played before more than three million fans during the 1980s as college basketball grew to be one of the biggest spectator attractions in all of sports.

Time was, things were different. Long before Meyer and his Blue Demons lost to Georgia Tech before 13,055 in Dayton and a national television audience on CBS, DePaul was looking for a winter activity to bridge the time between football in the fall and baseball in the spring. Basketball seemed a natural. The game, invented in a Springfield, Massachusetts, YMCA by Dr. James Naismith, was beginning to develop a following. So, as the country began to rebound from World War I, DePaul began to play basketball.

Coached by Tex Kirschten, DePaul met with success from the beginning. By the 1921-22 season, DePaul, then considered a western team, was notching victories against basketball powers Valparaiso, St. Louis, Monmouth, and Lake Forest. Its lone resounding defeat came at the hands of the University of Chicago, the first college basketball team in the area after Amos Alonzo Stagg brought the game back with him from Massachusetts after working with Dr. Naismith.

The first great DePaul team was the 1922-23 squad. Led by freshman "Big" Joe Hoban and still coached by Kirschten, the Blue Demons went 16-1 and handed Loyola an overwhelming defeat in that burgeoning rivalry.

Hoban, emerging as the first big star in DePaul basketball history, continued his solid play in the 1923-24 season, leading DePaul to an 8-6 record.

When basketball practice began in December 1924, the site was the seminary gymnasium (now known as Hayes-Healey). But new coach Harry Adams and his team moved to their new home, DePaul Auditorium, on Sheffield Avenue between Belden and Webster.

The DePaul Auditorium, later known simply as "The Barn," was to become the site of some of DePaul's greatest successes. From 1938 to 1956, the Blue Demons won 113 consecutive games in their home facility.

That magic was not evident in the early stages of the building's existence. Off to a 1-1 start, following a win at Illinois State Teachers College (now Northern Illinois) and a loss at Valparaiso, DePaul readied to christen "The Barn" on January 16, 1925. The result was not magical, as DePaul fell to St. Louis, 23-11.

But things quickly turned around. DePaul took on St. Thomas, the Minnesota state champions, and defeated them 24-16. Their next opponent, the Wisconsin champions from LaCrosse Normal (now Wisconsin-LaCrosse), nearly felt the sting of "The Barn," but escaped with a 25-23 win.

A pair of road trips, both of which were trouble for DePaul, highlighted the rest of the campaign. The Blue Demons lost 29-17 at St. Louis and 35-29 at Concordia (Mo.) before allowing a then school record 42 points in a 42-41 defeat by Lombard to conclude the trip.

Returning home, DePaul lost a close one to Columbia (now Loras) before posting a 40-19 win over Kent, the first 40-point performance in school history. The homestand ended with the second loss of the season to Lombard.

The second road trip went little better for the Blue Demons than the first. Columbia, LaCrosse Normal, and St. Mary's (Minn.) all earned wins at the expense of DePaul. But DePaul was much more competitive on this trip than the first. The margin of defeat for all three games was kept to single digits as they lost 33-27 at Columbia, 20-17 at LaCrosse Normal, and 24-20 to St. Mary's.

Despite the losses, DePaul's momentum seemed to be building — but it would have to wait to have an effect. YMCA College forfeited to the Blue Demons, leaving coach Harry Adams just one final game in his lone season with the team.

St. Mary's made the return trip to Chicago and jumped to an early 15-6 lead. But Hoban and the Blue Demons would not be denied. Battling back, the Blue Demons closed the season with their second straight victory. With veterans Hoban, Joe McInerney, and Timothy Callahan returning, the foundation appeared set for bigger things.

While the nucleus of players returned for the 1925-26 season, there was one significant change. Joe Hoban, a team captain for two years, took the position of team manager, something of a mix between assistant coach and player who helped the head coach with administrative duties. Hoban was succeeded as captain by Joe McInerney.

The shortest player on the team, McInerney

was an outstanding leader. As quarterback of the football team, he had helped DePaul to a 4-2-1 season in 1925. It was McInerney who kicked the winning extra point in a 7-6 victory over Fort Sheridan in the season opener, and who hit Pat Dowling with the conversion pass to beat Valparaiso, 7-6, late in the year. McInerney brought that same winning spirit onto the basketball court.

The Blue Demons started the 1925-26 season under new head coach Eddie Anderson with two straight home games, and two straight victories. Their first victory was a 33-18 thrashing of St. Mary's, followed by a 37-26 win over Loras. Off to a 2-0 start, the Blue Demons were set for their first road challenge of the season.

The challenge came in St. Louis as the Blue Demons tackled the St. Louis University Billikens. Sporting new road uniforms, DePaul set a pair of school scoring records in its 43-37 win. The 43 points were the most ever by a DePaul team, a record which stood until the last game of the 1930-31 season. The big gun for DePaul was center Bjarnes Varnes, who scored a school record 19 points.

Wins over Concordia and Valparaiso pushed its mark to 5-0, and set DePaul up for another major road test at Illinois State Teachers College in DeKalb. The Blue Demons entered the game at less than full strength; freshman guard Thomas Cunningham was out with an injury. And when McInerney was saddled with foul trouble, the Blue Demons found themselves limited in the backcourt. Despite solid performances by Varnes, Joseph Gannon and John Bordes, DePaul was stung for its first loss of the season, 32-21.

DePaul snapped right back with a 24-19 win over YMCA College to set up a Chicago rematch with ISTC. DePaul came out hot, rolling to a 24-11 halftime lead, and never looked back. When the final buzzer sounded, they had avenged their only defeat with a 34-19 decision.

A win over St. Viator's gave DePaul an 8-1 record and put the Blue Demons in the driver's seat in the race for the championship of the Western Interstate Conference. That was, however, a championship that would not come easily. For despite their gaudy record, DePaul had played only three games away from home. And the schedule called for a season ending five-game road trip.

A pair of home games preceded that swing. St. Louis exacted revenge for its earlier home-court loss with a 38-22 win in Chicago. The Blue Demons again bounced back from defeat with a 25-21 win over the American College of Physical Education in the season's final home game.

The five-game road swing started on a bad note with a 45-22 loss at St. Viator's. And after losing 33-31 at Loras, the Blue Demons found themselves 9-4 with their first two-game losing streak in fifteen games.

Again the team rebounded. A 26-21 win over Wisconsin-LaCrosse righted the ship and a 36-20 win over St. Mary's put the Blue Demons over the top. Despite a 33-26 loss at Valparaiso to close the campaign, DePaul claimed the conference championship and placed five players on the all-conference teams.

Varnes led the league in scoring with 151 points and earned first-team all-conference honors along with Hoban. Gannon, who scored 146 points, was second team, while Bordes and Cunningham were selected third team.

The success Eddie Anderson and the Blue Demons knew in 1925-26 was not quickly repeated. The 1926-27 season opened with promise with DePaul winning six of its first seven games. And after its second victory of the season over St. Louis, DePaul appeared headed for another outstanding campaign. But then the bottom dropped out. DePaul closed out the season with six consecutive losses, including an eight-point loss to Loras in which DePaul scored only twelve points, to finish the season at 7-7.

The next two seasons were abbreviated ones due to the length of the football season. After playing an average of sixteen games the previous three seasons, DePaul played just seven contests in 1927-28 and nine in 1928-29.

The 1927-28 season still stands as the low mark for DePaul basketball. The Blue Demons went 2-5 that season, although one of the victories was a 31-14 hammering of storied rival St. Louis.

A 5-4 season followed in 1928-29 with two of the wins over the Illinois "B" team. DePaul also played its first game ever against Dayton, losing 22-18.

At the end of the season, Eddie Anderson left the basketball team to concentrate on his duties as football coach. The basketball reins were handed to Jim Kelly, the school's director of athletics since 1927. A new era was to begin.

2

The New Era

When Jim Kelly stepped in as head basketball coach at DePaul for the 1929-30 season, he inherited a program that in the last five years had posted a 31-34 record. Included in the period before his arrival were two seasons in which DePaul posted its lowest single season winning percentages in history (.286 in 1927-28 and .316 in 1924-25).

By the time Kelly was to leave DePaul in 1936, the Blue Demons were on the national map. They had won at least 60 percent of their games every year in his tenure, averaged over fourteen wins per year, and reached the Olympic Finals. A little known fact for trivia fans: Kelly still stands as the DePaul coach with the best winning percentage in school history (100-22, .820).

One of Kelly's first moves was to make the Blue Demons a national team. Just as Ray and Joey Meyer would do in the 1970s, Kelly scheduled his team against the best teams in the country.

Kelly, who came to DePaul from Buena Vista College in Storm Lake, Iowa, led the Blue Demons out of the local Western Interstate Conference and launched them on the path of independence. And he started quickly. While the country looked to rebound from the stock market crash of October 1929, and as the Great Depression was beginning, Kelly began building his program. He put together the most ambitious schedule in school history. The Blue Demons played twenty games, including sixteen in a single road trip through the West, during the 1929-30 season.

Kelly's new era of Blue Demons basketball began with four home games and one familiar opponent. DePaul opened the campaign with a 34-21 win over Valparaiso as Clarence "Heine" Coan scored 11 points and team captain Manning "Stix" Powers provided floor leadership.

A 22-14 win over North Dakota was followed by a 38-19 win over a South Dakota team which had just beaten Iowa. The homestand, and the

Manning "Stix" Powers
Guard — 1928-31

College basketball during the Great Depression era was much different than the game millions of fans are familiar with today.

A jump ball was used to restart play after each made basket. Teams routinely scored only twenty-five to forty points per game. But though the big man's role in the game has increased in importance, one thing has remained the same: a team must have guards that can score from the perimeter.

At DePaul, the first guard to supply the outside punch was Manning Powers. Nicknamed "Stix" because of his slender build, Powers was an early star during his three years of varsity basketball with the Blue Demons. He was the team captain on the 1929-30 squad that first year coach Jim Kelly took on a fifteen-game road trip out West. The first extended journey outside the Midwest for DePaul put them on the college basketball map, as they posted a 15-5 record for the season.

The trip also allowed people from across the country to see Powers in action. An adept ballhandler and pinpoint passer, Powers also had the ability to score the big points when needed.

When Powers graduated following the 1930-31 season, he had played on three teams with a combined 33-12 record. His junior and senior seasons were the first back-to-back 10-plus victory seasons in Blue Demon history. Though his name is no longer prominent in the Blue Demon record book, it was Stix Powers who helped basketball become an important sport at DePaul.

---

entire home season, ended with a 21-17 win over Detroit before a then record crowd at the DePaul Auditorium.

DePaul's first venture to the West began in a familiar place — Dubuque, Iowa — against a familiar opponent — former conference rival Loras. A hard fought 27-25 win made DePaul 5-0 for the first time in five years. Their record went to 6-0 the next night as DePaul handled Colorado College, 34-22. Coan, a forward, was the scoring star with 21 points.

Kelly experienced his first defeat, in game seven, as Wyoming downed the Blue Demons 33-25. It did not take long for the second loss, as Utah defeated DePaul the next night, 46-41.

Their second meeting with the Utes would be different. Utah was unbeaten and rated as the best team in the West, but DePaul prevailed 35-32 in the rematch.

The trip, and the string of close games, continued for DePaul as two out of their next three games went into overtime. The one game that did finish in regulation was a tough battle against Nevada. DePaul, trailing 24-21 with five minutes remaining, managed two long-range baskets to take the victory, 25-24. In their next game it was DePaul who squandered a late lead, to Young Men's Institute of San Francisco (now the University of San Francisco), before winning in overtime, 37-33. Overtime wasn't as kind the next night as St. Ignatius defeated DePaul 33-31 despite Coan's 11 points.

Coan and Powers combined for 23 points in the next game as the Blue Demons rebounded with a 35-31 win over the Olympic Club. A 21-20 loss to the Athens Athletic Club dropped DePaul to 10-4, but also set up a five-game winning streak.

DePaul won three-straight games in the Los Angeles area, the most impressive being a 35-14 trouncing of Santa Barbara. Kelly's crew then left California and started their swing back toward home. A stop in Tucson netted a 29-16 win over the University of Arizona as Babe Ascher scored 10 points. The winning streak moved to five with a 38-29 win in El

Paso over the Texas School of Mines (later Texas Western and now Texas-El Paso).

DePaul headed for New Mexico with a 15-4 record and a shot at tying the school record of 16 wins posted by the 1922-23 squad. They fell short. Playing their third game in three nights, the Blue Demons ran out of gas as they lost to New Mexico after leading most of the way.

As the team loaded into the train to return to Chicago, the book closed on the season. But rather than just an end to a successful season, it was the beginning of the national rise of DePaul basketball.

Long road trips were not part of the plan in 1930-31, but head coach Jim Kelly continued his magical touch. A 9-1 start was highlighted by a pair of wins over the Illinois "B" team and victories over Southern Illinois, Rice, and Centenary.

The 1930-31 season marked the reappearance of city rival Loyola on the schedule for the first time since 1922-23. The two teams each won a game in the series; DePaul won the first, 22-15, while Loyola returned the favor by winning 24-20.

The final contest of the season was a fitting way to end a 13-3 season. DePaul set a school record by scoring 48 points in their 48-15 victory over St. Mary's.

The 1930-31 season marked the end of the playing days for one of DePaul's great pioneer players — Manning "Stix" Powers. The guard capped his college career by earning honorable mention all-tournament at the National AAU Tournament in Kansas City, Missouri, and first-team all-tourney at the Examiner-Central AAU Tournament in Chicago.

Stix Powers was the first of DePaul's many great point guards. Though he could score, his 9 points sparked the Blue Demons to their first victory of the season, a 40-27 victory over Illinois "B," it was his defensive effort and passing ability that drew the most praise.

Jim Kelly started the 1931-32 season, his third as head coach of DePaul, with a 28-8 career record. The season contained some of the same elements as Kelly's first on the job — a

Manning "Stix" Powers.

western flavor returned to the schedule and the Blue Demons took a lengthy road trip.

The Blue Demons opened the season against their first opponent from California since 1929-30. But this time, the West was coming to them. Playing before a packed house of about 2,500 at Loyola's Alumni Gymnasium, DePaul and the Southern California Trojans traded baskets the entire game with neither team able to garner more than a two-point lead.

The game was tied at 14 in the final minutes when Heine Coan stepped up and drilled a long shot. The Trojans came right back and hit a pair of free throws to knot the score again, 16-16. Tony Lauritis gave the Blue Demons another two-point lead, but USC again responded. Els Weston, the tallest Blue Demon, became the hero in the final seconds as he scored to give DePaul a 20-18 win and make Kelly 3-0 in season opening games.

DePaul won four out of its next five games. Two of those victories came over St. Viator's, which had handed DePaul two of its three losses the previous season. Heading into the first extended road trip since Kelly's first year, the Blue Demons were 5-1.

The first stop on the trip resulted in DePaul's fourth straight win, a 31-22 win over Catholic University. But George Washington University ended the winning ways with a 35-28 decision and started DePaul's first real losing streak in Kelly's tenure.

Playing in New York City for the first time, the Blue Demons were swamped by St. John's, 35-21. Losses at Niagara and Detroit pushed the losing streak to four games and had DePaul looking for the end of the trip. DePaul righted themselves against Detroit City College, but just barely, 33-32. A rematch against Detroit brought a second straight win and an end to the road excursion.

Up next for DePaul was an old nemesis. Looking to make it three in a row over St. Viator's, the Blue Demons had the game tied with five seconds left before a free throw gave St. Viator's the victory. DePaul bounced back for a win in the final game of the season for a 9-6 record. The six losses were the most the Blue Demons would amass in one season with Kelly at the helm.

As in the three previous seasons under Kelly, DePaul got off to another quick start in 1932-33, opening with three straight home wins. A road win at St. Viator's and a home-court victory over Beloit pushed their record to 5-0. Tony Lauritis pumped in 15 points in the Blue Demons' sixth victory, a 38-28 win over St. Thomas, and Els Weston and Peter Barskis were the heroes in an overtime victory over Western Michigan.

The hope of DePaul's first unbeaten season ended in Naperville, Illinois. North Central, taking advantage of some late free throw misses by DePaul, dropped the Blue Demons to 7-1 with a 26-25 victory. But the team bounced back with four straight victories. The only game that was close was against, you guessed it, St. Viator's — 26-23.

DePaul took their 11-1 record on a two-game road trip, and the road wasn't kind. Western Michigan, playing before a homecoming crowd, avenged a previous loss by taking a lopsided 46-27 victory from DePaul. A 35-24 loss to Detroit followed, but the Blue Demons snapped from the slump in the final game of the season to beat Detroit 25-19. The win left the Blue Demons with a 12-3 record, and Kelly with a 49-17 record.

Though the 1932-33 Blue Demons had failed to go unbeaten, the 1933-34 team accomplished the goal. With a 17-0 record, this is the only DePaul team to ever go undefeated and was the first DePaul team to claim a share of the national championship.

When the previous year's team was 7-0, it was North Central that ended the unbeaten dream. No such thing would happen in 1933-34. DePaul handled North Central 33-24 in the season opener and 30-24 in a return engagement later in the season.

Other notable wins included a 35-11 mauling of Nebraska, a 22-14 win over Minnesota, a 37-26 win over Arizona and a pair of victories over St. Louis, the first games against the Billikens in six seasons. By far the closest DePaul came to losing was an overtime win over Armour Tech (now Illinois Tech). Having faced the Engineers in the fifth game of the season at home, a 43-35 victory, the Blue Demons were expecting a challenge. And a challenge they got. Pete Barskis hit a basket late in the game to force the overtime, and it was nip and tuck throughout the remainder of the game. DePaul finally came away with a 43-41 victory and a 13-0 record.

The final opponent of the season was Detroit, a team DePaul had split with in each of the last two seasons. Only seven points had separated them in their first meeting, but, behind Ray Adams' 19 points, the Blue Demons closed their unbeaten campaign with a 50-41 win. It marked the first time DePaul had hit the fifty mark, a mark that was soon to be topped regularly.

When the basketballs began bouncing at DePaul in the winter of 1934-35, the Blue Demons were on top. DePaul owned an 18-game winning streak, was fresh from a 17-0 season the year before and held great promise with players such as captain Frank Linskey.

The streak figured to be severely tested early as DePaul opened against Illinois. The game was the first between the Blue Demons and the Illini varsity team, and DePaul led from tip to horn and emerged with a 29-26 win. Wins over Kalamazoo College, Valparaiso, Missouri State, and Beliot pushed the season mark to 5-0 and the winning streak to 23 games. The streak was on the line New Year's Night as the Blue Demons played Purdue before a crowd of 6,000 in the 132nd Armory. The 4-0 Boilermakers were led by Bob Kessler and Norm Cottom, and ended the season as Big Ten co-champs. On this night they ended the Blue Demons streak with a 48-37 win.

Though the streak had ended, DePaul continued to play great basketball. They finished the season with ten straight victories. The school scoring mark fell twice; first, the Blue Demons scored a 54-33 victory over Detroit, and the next game it was a 60-28 win over Valparaiso. The record was challenged again in a 58-25 win over Detroit to close the season with a 15-1 record.

Kelly and the Blue Demons were squarely on the map. Over a three season period, DePaul owned a 44-4 record and had raised the school scoring record from 48 to 60.

The measure of success was to get even greater.

Long before the opening of the 1935-36 season, DePaul was being mentioned among the nation's elite. The Blue Demons were just one year removed from a claim to the national championship in 1933-34 when they finished 17-0, and the 1934-35 team had finished 15-1. A ten-game streak was on the line as the curtain rose on the 1935-36 performance. Three more wins were quickly added as St. Mary's, Hamline, and the University of Chicago fell. This set up a rematch with Purdue.

The previous season the Boilermakers had ended DePaul's 23-game winning streak. But that game had been on the road, and this time DePaul would be playing before 9,000 fans at the Chicago Stadium. DePaul wanted revenge. It didn't come. Despite a strong performance by Willie Phillips, DePaul fell 28-24.

Illinois, which later tied Purdue for the Big Ten Conference title, also came to Chicago Stadium, and also escaped with a victory. Trailing 26-22 in the final minutes, captain Ray Adams drew DePaul within 26-24. The Blue Demons had a shot at tying the game, but Ed Campion's long-range shot rimmed out at the gun.

Saddled with a two-game losing streak, both Big Ten teams at the Chicago Stadium, the Blue Demons faced Wisconsin. The streak would not go to three. Fred Knez scored the insurance points late as the Blue Demons won their first of the year at the Stadium, a 27-22 win over the Badgers.

With the ice broken, DePaul returned to its winning ways. Victories over Washburn, Drake, Minnesota, Indiana, St. Louis (twice), Western Michigan, and North Central gave DePaul a 13-2 record heading to Western Michigan for a rematch.

Western Michigan, which always played DePaul tough, had the memory of their 53-34 loss to DePaul still fresh in their minds. The game was tight all the way, but WMU nosed out a 35-33 victory.

DePaul rebounded with a 41-29 win over Detroit to close the regular season with a 14-3 mark. They then accepted an invitation by the American Olympic Basketball Committee to enter the Olympic trials. The winner of this national tournament would, as a team, represent the United States in the Olympic Games of 1936 in Berlin, Germany.

Postseason basketball was nothing new to DePaul. After the collegiate season, Kelly regularly kept the team together to play in the Amateur Athletic Union (AAU) tournaments during the spring. DePaul already owned three Cen-

Ray Adams—captain of the 1935-36 squad.

tral District AAU Championships in Kelly's tenure when the invitation for the Olympic trails was extended.

Based on regular season performance, DePaul was seeded in the Fifth District along with Northwestern. A narrow win over Indiana State put DePaul in the sectional final game, but not against Northwestern.

Indiana Central had topped the seeded team the previous game and looked capable of doing the same to the Blue Demons when they had a three-point lead over DePaul at halftime. Nick Yost sparked a second half rally with Ed Campion and Bill Wendt providing the finishing touches to a 41-36 DePaul victory.

As Fifth District champions, DePaul moved on to face Minnesota, the Sixth District champion, in a best of three series. Yost scored 12 points in the first game to lead DePaul to a 36-30 win. Willie Phillips and Ray Adams combined for 16 points in the second game as DePaul finished the sweep with a 33-27 decision.

That victory sent the Blue Demons to New York City for the Olympic Finals, but the run ended there. DePaul played a tough Washington team almost even, but fell 54-53. The loss put a lid on the season, but the team had posted a school record 18-4 final mark.

As much as DePaul won that season, it also lost something big. The 1935-36 season was the last for Jim Kelly as the Blue Demon head coach.

After seven seasons, Kelly left behind a program that was among the best in the country. His Blue Demons were able to regularly compete with the top programs from around the country. His .820 winning percentage still stands as the best among the eight men to serve as DePaul head coach, leading by more than 14 percentage points.

The 1935-36 team, despite its four losses, may have been his best. It certainly was among the best teams ever from Chicago. Every member of the roster was a Chicago native and lived within walking distance of DePaul's North Side campus.

From the time Kelly started as DePaul's basketball coach in 1929 to the early 1970s, DePaul experienced almost uninterrupted success in men's basketball.

Some thirty-five years after Kelly's last game, when Ray Meyer was saddled with a program struggling to win and having a hard time garnering recognition, he would put DePaul back on the map using many of the same methods Kelly pioneered — play a national schedule with a team featuring local players.

3

Continuing the Success

The challenge of following Jim Kelly was a big one, but it was answered quickly. Tom Haggerty, a DePaul graduate in 1927, took over as the Blue Demons' mentor before the 1936-37 season after Kelly left to become track coach at the University of Minnesota. Haggerty brought his own tradition of success to the program.

Following his graduation from DePaul, Haggerty became head coach at the DePaul Academy in 1928, a position he held until moving to the university. As a prep coach, Haggerty twice won a sectional title and once earned the city championship with pony-teams. He later coached a heavyweight team to the city title that then went on to finish third in the National Catholic Tournament.

Haggerty's tenure at DePaul was to be marked by similar success. He left after four seasons with a 64-29 (.688) record, placing him second only to Kelly in winning percentage. As head coach of the 1939-40 team, he was the first man to lead DePaul to postseason play in the National Invitation Tournament (NIT) and coached stars such as Stan Szukala and Bob Neu.

But Haggerty's debut on the DePaul bench was less than spectacular. Playing at home against a veteran squad from North Dakota, Haggerty's Blue Demons lost a close one 36-34. It was the first opening game loss for DePaul since the 1927-28 season.

DePaul righted itself in the next game with a 41-37 overtime win over Pittsburgh in the 132nd Armory. A 27-25 victory over Hamline pushed DePaul to 2-1 and set up a run against Big Ten Conference teams, starting with Illinois.

Things looked bad early against the Illini as DePaul trailed 17-11 at halftime. But Bill Wendt, Nick Yost, and Willie Phillips sparked a furious rally that ended with DePaul on top, 31-25. DePaul had proven their mettle against the eventual Big Ten Conference co-champions.

The outcome wasn't as favorable against Purdue. DePaul led early in this one, but came out on the short end of a 53-45 final. A 33-17 win over Wisconsin came next, sparked by Fred Knez' 12 points. After a 34-25 loss to Minnesota, DePaul stood at 4-3.

Other highlights of the season included a 35-23 whipping of the University of Chicago, then a member of the Big Ten, a pair of victories over St. Louis, and a 23-21 win over Michigan State. DePaul also avenged their loss to St. John's during the 1932-33 season by defeating the Redmen 35-33 before some 12,000 fans at Madison Square Garden.

DePaul went 8-2 in the final ten games of Haggerty's first season. Their 15-6 record kept them among the top teams in the region.

Haggerty's toughest campaign was his second. With only two seniors, co-captains Pat Howlett and Tom Cleland, Haggerty decided to go with his talented younger players to get them experience. Though the results that year were mixed, the groundwork was laid for the coming years.

The season started successfully with a trio of wins over Valparaiso, the University of Chicago, and Illinois Wesleyan. But Hamline brought DePaul back to earth with a 42-28 thrashing.

Wins over Wichita State, St. Louis, Centenary, and St. Joseph's (Pa.) were the highlights of the campaign. The lowlights were yet another loss to Purdue and a three-game losing streak that consisted of losses to Long Island, Loyola, and Western Michigan. The Purdue loss was especially disheartening because it was the first time a team had scored as many as 60 points against the Blue Demons.

Haggerty's second season ended with a 12-10 record and marked the first time since 1924-25 (6-13) that the Blue Demons lost as many as 10 games in a season. It was to be Haggerty's one and only struggling season.

While Jim Kelly had looked west for exposure during the early days of his tenure, Tom Haggerty looked north, south, and east as well

Bob Neu
Forward — 1936-39

Terry Cummings. Mark Aguirre. Stanley Brundy. Bob Neu. Though most DePaul fans will recognize the first three forwards listed, the fourth name may be new to them.

Bob Neu was a basketball pioneeer at DePaul, setting several scoring records in the 1930s. He joined the varsity in 1936 and during his three-year stint, he helped lead the Blue Demons to a 42-23 record.

Joining a veteran team in 1936, Neu excelled in the supporting role. One of his finest games of the season came in a 40-23 victory over St. Louis when he scored 7 points. The victory moved the Blue Demons to 5-3 on their way to a 15-6 record.

Neu played a bigger role in the 12-10 season of 1937-38. Now a team leader, Neu was expected to score more. In the third game of the season, Neu tallied 11 points as DePaul won their third straight game, this time by the score of 35-11. Later in the season he scored 17 in a 46-19 victory over St. Louis. He also scored a school record 24 points in a game that season.

As captain of the team during the 1938-39 season, a lot was expected of Bob Neu. And he usually came through. After a tough loss to Iowa that dropped DePaul to 2-3, Neu scored 14 points to help lead the Blue Demons over Penn State, 31-23. Later in the season Neu broke his school record by scoring 27 points against Illinois Wesleyan. He ended the season with 332 points, a new school record. Neu earned All-America honors for his efforts.

as west. By the end of his reign as coach, Haggerty's squads had played for the first time eastern teams such as St. Joseph's (Pa.), Long Island, Duquesne, and Villanova; western squads such as Santa Clara and Oregon; and southern teams such as Arkansas State and Louisiana State.

The 1938-39 campaign was laced with a definite national flavor, but started with a traditional midwestern foe. The Blue Demons' opener was a success, a 55-32 drubbing of Valparaiso. After a double-overtime loss to the University of Chicago and a 61-32 victory over first-time opponent Arkansas State, DePaul headed into a big contest at Purdue with a 2-1 record.

Playing before a packed house at the Purdue field house, the Blue Demons lost yet another to the Boilermakers, 43-36. DePaul then dropped under .500 with a 34-29 loss to Iowa in Chicago Stadium.

A win over Penn State evened DePaul's record, but a 57-51 loss to Santa Clara in the Madison Street Armory made DePaul 3-4. Wins over Duquesne, Xavier (Ohio), Villanova and St. John's, the latter two on the road, improved DePaul to 7-4 and set up a big match with Butler and coach Tony Hinkle

This was the first matchup between these two Midwest teams. Playing before a big crowd at the Madison Street Armory, DePaul dropped a 39-29 decision as Hinkle's Bulldogs struck late in the first half and pulled away in the second. A win over Toledo set up the Blue Demons for their annual battle against Loyola for city bragging rights. The game was played at the Chicago Stadium and was sponsored by the Chicago Youth Organization to benefit Chicago charities. For the fourth straight time, Rambler fans went away happy, as Loyola won 36-26.

Bob Neu was the story in the next game as DePaul hammered Illinois Wesleyan 58-19 to move to 9-6. Neu scored 27 points, a new school record. The game also started a great run for the Blue Demons

Wins over South Dakota and Creighton gave DePaul a three-game winning streak before a 35-32 loss to Wichita State. DePaul rebounded to close the year with wins over Kansas State, Nebraska, Illinois Wesleyan, and Hamline to finish the season with a 15-7 record. The Blue Demons had won 12 of their last 15 games.

The success of late 1938-39 carried over into the following season. Five more wins were tacked onto the streak as the Blue Demons opened their final campaign under coach Tom Haggerty. Victories over Chicago Normal (now Chicago State), Arkansas State (scoring a school record 65 points), Purdue, Hamline, and Superior State got DePaul off to its best start since 1934-35.

The victory over Purdue was particularly impressive for three reasons. First, it was at Purdue in West Lafayette. Second, it was the first time that the Blue Demons had beaten the Boilermakers. And lastly, Purdue eventually won the Big Ten Conference title that year.

A series of games against western teams provided a new challenge. DePaul opened the run with a 44-42 overtime loss to Southern California, but rebounded with a 39-37 win over Oregon. Oregon was the defending champions of the NCAA tournament, winning the inaugural event in 1939. Southern California went on to finish fourth in the 1940 NIT.

The Oregon win started DePaul on a nine-game winning streak. Highlighting the streak were two victories over Detroit, a 26-point victory over Kansas State, and victories over Santa Clara and the University of Chicago (two teams that had beaten DePaul the previous year).

A crowd of 5,000 packed the Chicago Coliseum to see the 14-1 Blue Demons take on Indiana. What they witnessed was a blowout, and not by DePaul. With Lou Possner limited by an injury, the Blue Demons were crushed 51-30.

Ben Wozny helped DePaul bounce back the next game. Wozny scored 12 points as the Blue Demons rolled to a 53-28 win over Louisiana State. A 21-15 win over Loyola earned DePaul the city title and make the Blue Demons 16-2 heading to a pair of big showdowns.

The first was at home as the Blue Demons challenged an outstanding Bradley team that had finished third in the NIT the previous year. Bradley hit a late field goal to claim a 34-33 win.

Stan Szukala
Guard — 1937-40

One of the brightest stars of DePaul basketball in the late 1930s, Stan Szukala was part of three excellent teams during his varsity career from 1937 to 1940.

As a sophomore, Szukala took little time to show his ability. In the third game of the season, Szukala scored 11 points to lead the Blue Demons to their third straight victory, 35-11 over Illinois Wesleyan. He continued to contribute regularly that season, as the Blue Demons finished at 12-10 under head coach Tom Haggerty.

The 1938-39 season saw the Blue Demons get off to a slow start, going 2-3 in their first five games. Once again it was Szukala turning in an impressive early season performance, this time against Penn State. The junior scored 7 points as DePaul beat the eastern school 31-23. The Blue Demons went 12-4 over the rest of the season to finish at 15-7.

Szukala played an even bigger role in the 1939-40 season. Named team captain, he helped the Blue Demons to a 22-6 record and their first appearance in the National Invitation Tournament. But possibly even more important to the DePaul fans were his 6 points in the 21-15 win over Loyola, breaking a three-year slump against the city rival. Szukala's career ended with him earning All-America honors.

After a win over Toledo, an eastern road swing took the Blue Demons, now 17-3, to Madison Square Garden to challenge coach Clair Bee's Long Island team that had claimed the 1939 NIT championship. A crowd of over 20,000 watched as the Blue Demons led 41-35 with four minutes left. But much to the delight of the huge crowd, Bee's squad rallied in the final minutes to take a 44-43 win.

DePaul moved on to Convention Hall in Philadelphia and a meeting with St. Joseph's. DePaul came out strong early with the help of Ed Norris and claimed a 44-36 win over St. Joseph's.

A rematch with Long Island resulted in a 44-36 win for the Blue Demons and gave DePaul victory number nineteen. That surpassed the school record eighteen the 1935-36 team won in Jim Kelly's final season as head coach.

A win over Concordia set up a regular season finale against Bradley. The Blue Demons, playing in Peoria, Illinois, had already become DePaul's first team to win twenty games, but they wanted more. They got it, a 41-39 win to end the campaign 21-4.

Postseason basketball beckoned as the Blue Demons were invited to New York City to participate in the NIT.

DePaul's first opponent was a familiar one as the Blue Demon's tackled coach Bee and Long Island for a third time. Seven points separated the teams in the first two games. And the difference in the rubber game of the match was seven points, as DePaul claimed a 45-38 decision.

Haggerty's team ran out of luck in the semifinals, losing 51-37 to eventual champion Colorado. DePaul then lost the third-place game 23-22 to Oklahoma A&M (now Oklahoma State), finishing fourth in the tournament with a 22-6 overall record.

The 1939-40 season was Tom Haggerty's last at DePaul, as he was called to active duty in the National Guard. But when Haggerty left the Blue Demons he, like his predecessor Jim Kelly, walked away with the program at the top. Haggerty's final team set a school record with 22 wins. The Blue Demons had won 164 games in eleven seasons with a 164-51 (.763) overall record.

Bill Wendt, like Tom Haggerty who he followed as head coach, was a DePaul graduate who knew success well. A former Blue Demon player, Wendt graduated in 1937 after playing three years of varsity basketball. He was part of teams that went 48-11 and reached the Olympic Finals in 1936.

After graduation, Wendt stayed on as an assistant coach to Haggerty, so the team he took over in 1940 was one that he knew well. Wendt's first team was built on a foundation of co-captains Elmer Gainer and Ed Sachs.

Gainer, a 6-foot-6 center, scored 244 points in 1940-41, his senior year. After his DePaul career was over, Gainer went on to play in the National Basketball League (forerunner of today's National Basketball Association) with six teams, including the Fort Wayne (now Detroit) Pistons.

Sachs, a guard, was a defensive stopper. A good perimeter shooter, Sachs is perhaps best remembered as the defensive stopper who held Loyola star "Wibs" Kautz to 4 points while scoring 8 himself in DePaul's 21-15 win over the Ramblers in 1939-40.

The 1940-41 season that Gainer and Sachs led DePaul through was not as successful as the 1939-40 one, but was marked with some high moments.

Wendt's coaching career opened with seven straight victories. Included in that run was a 30-23 decision over UCLA. The Bruins featured star Jackie Robinson, who later became famous as the first African-American to play major league baseball. DePaul followed the UCLA victory with their second straight against Purdue and their first ever against Butler.

Luck turned quickly as Santa Clara, Bradley, and Long Island took wins from the Blue Demons. Gainer sparked a win over St. Joseph's, 52-50, with 22 points and, after victories over Duquesne and the University of Chicago, it looked like the 10-3 Demons would cruise into the NIT again.

But then the wheels started to come off. DePaul could only muster three victories in their final eight games to finish 13-8. Two of the losses were to Long Island, the eventual winner of the NIT. The season closed with a 43-41 loss to Bradley in Peoria. Paul McCall was the Braves' hero, scoring on a forty footer at the gun for the victory.

Bill Wendt's second season as head coach was to be his last. After opening 5-0, Wendt's team lost twelve of seventeen games to finish 10-12 overall. The losing record was DePaul's first since the 1927-28 team was 2-5. One of the high spots of the season occurred in the fourth game of the season when the Blue Demons scored a school record 72 points in their 72-26 hammering of Arkansas State. The Bill Wendt era had ended quickly. In two seasons, his teams went 23-20. But he will be most remembered for being the last DePaul coach to be named something other than Meyer.

II

The Ray Meyer Years

4

The M&M Boys

From 1923 to 1942, DePaul had seven head coaches in nineteen years. Take away the seven year run of Jim Kelly and the four seasons with Tom Haggerty, and the remaining five mentors averaged less than two seasons each. Put simply, stability wasn't a big factor in coaching at DePaul in the first half of the twentieth century.

That changed in April 1942, when the university took a chance and hired an assistant coach from Notre Dame. His name was Ray Meyer.

Dark haired, thick but slim, and feisty, Ray Meyer was a young and inexperienced twenty-nine-year-old rookie head coach when he took over at DePaul in 1942.

He had coached before, heading the girl's team at St. Agatha's Parish in the Chicago neighborhood where he was raised while attending Quigley Preparatory Seminary. Meyer left Quigley and the pursuit of the priesthood following two years at the school.

Meyer transferred to St. Patrick's High School and played basketball one year, helping his team to the National Catholic High School championship in 1932 under head coach Bjarnes Varnes, the former DePaul player.

After high school, Meyer briefly attended Northwestern before quitting school to work. While laboring as a beer truck driver and later at International Harvester Corporation, Meyer spent his night's coaching basketball at St. Agatha's.

Former Notre Dame star Ed "Moose" Krause heard of Meyer through the grapevine and helped him land an interview with Notre Dame head coach George Keogan. Meyer met Keogan, and backed by Krause's recommendation, earned a place on the Fighting Irish basketball team.

Coach Ray Meyer.

Meyer had a successful career at Notre Dame. He was a member of the team that was named national champions by the Helms Athletic Foundation in 1936, and was team captain two years.

After graduating from Notre Dame in 1938, Meyer returned to Chicago and served as a social worker. There he married Margaret Mary Delaney, a member of the St. Agatha's girl's team he'd coached years before. In 1940, Meyer returned to Notre Dame as an assistant coach.

Although an assistant, Meyer did get head coaching experience during his two years at Notre Dame. Irish mentor Keogan was ill and unable to accompany his team on road trips. On these trips away from home, Meyer served as head coach.

After two years in that capacity, Keogan recommended Meyer for the head coaching posi-

George Mikan.

tion at DePaul. On April 17, 1942, Meyer signed a one-year contract as head coach of the Blue Demons.

Upon arriving on Chicago's North Side, Meyer called for spring practice, which was legal at the time. The eight men that came out were Frank Wiscons, Mel Frailey, Johnny Jorgenson, Tony Kelly, Cliff Lind, Bill Ryan, Jim Cominsky and an extremely tall, gangly kid Meyer had cut at Notre Dame the year before. The big man was George Mikan.

As much as the 1942-43 season marked the beginning of the Meyer era at DePaul, it also marked the beginning of the Mikan era at DePaul. From the start of George's career in 1942 through the end of his brother Ed's playing days in 1948, the Blue Demons were a team headed by the Mikan family.

But that wasn't always so impressive. The George Mikan that Meyer cut during tryouts at Notre Dame was not the same George Mikan who in 1950 was named the greatest player of the first half century, not the same player who was inducted into the Naismith Basketball Hall of Fame as a charter member, and not the same player who had his jersey retired by DePaul

University. That George Mikan was the product of hours of hard work.

In 1942, Meyer was an energetic rookie head coach and Mikan a 6-foot-8, 215-pound, energetic, young player looking to learn. The combination was terrific.

Meyer designed a series of drills to improve Mikan's game. He also studied the rules of college basketball and found ways to use the big man like no other coach had used a big man before.

Among the drills Mikan endured were hours of one-on-one play with 5-foot-4 guard Billy Donato. Mikan jumped rope. He took dancing lessons. He punched a speed bag. He practiced one-handed hook shots with a towel tucked under the arm of his off hand.

Mikan also forced the rule makers to think. Goaltending was legal in those days, so Meyer instructed his center to stand under the basket and swat away shots that appeared to be going in. Meyer also taught him to use the dunk shot, which was legal in those days as well.

Mikan worked on the drills and grew better daily. Meyer, taking advantage of the rules, guided his team toward the big man's skills and built a solid supporting cast.

If Jim Kelly's time as head coach was the beginning of something great, Tom Haggerty's was the prophecy it was coming soon. And Ray Meyer's early years were the fulfillment of that prophecy.

The Meyer/Mikan M&M era started with a flash and a bang in 1942. Two wins over Navy Pier, one over Chicago State and another over the Glenview Naval Training Station gave Meyer a 4-0 record before coaching his first big game at Chicago Stadium.

The matchup was with Purdue and legendary coach Ward "Piggy" Lambert. Though the 1942-43 Purdue team was not of the same caliber as teams of the past, it still was a good test for the young Blue Demons. Mikan led the way for DePaul as it posted a 45-37 win and moved to 5-0 on the season.

DePaul's next two games were against two teams that had had good success against the Blue Demons in the past—USC and Toledo.

Both teams had claimed victories over DePaul during the 1941-42 season and both had winning streaks against DePaul (two games for USC, four games for Toledo). But the Blue Demons met the challenges, beating USC 49-47 and Toledo 49-40.

M&M's first loss together came on the road in the next game. Scoring a season-low 40 points, DePaul fell to Duquesne, 48-40. But the team rebounded with six more wins including two victories over Marquette, one over Loyola, and a 67-20 drubbing of U of C. Next up was Notre Dame at Chicago Stadium. As it turned out, the game would be Meyer's only chance to coach against his mentor, George Keogan. Keogan died in February 1943. The teacher topped the pupil 50-47, and Meyer's first team was 13-2.

DePaul sandwiched two loses to Camp Grant around a 44-40 victory over W. Kentucky St., to stand 14-4 as they readied to host Kentucky and coach Adolph Rupp. With Mikan intercepting the Wildcats perimeter shots, the Blue Demons rolled to a 53-44 win.

The regular season concluded with three more wins, including two against Bradley. Meyer's first team finished with an 18-4 record, good enough to earn the school's first NCAA tournament berth.

DePaul's first game in the eight-team event was against Dartmouth. Relying on the same strategies that had gotten them this far, DePaul defeated Dartmouth, 46-35, to advance to the Final Four. Their opponent would be Georgetown. This would be the second meeting between the schools; the first was the previous year with DePaul winning 34-29. This time the score was again close, but Georgetown finished ahead, 53-49.

Meyer's first season at DePaul had to be considered a success.

Captain Tony Kelly concluded his career, moving on to the professional leagues, but Mikan had three years eligibility remaining. Great things were happening.

Meyer's coaching career almost took a turn after his first season. With World War II raging on two fronts, young men all over the country were enlisting in the armed forces. College coaches were being offered commissions by the Marine Corps, and Meyer volunteered.

But as a player at Notre Dame, Meyer had suffered a knee injury that required surgery. Because of that injury, Meyer was unable to pass his physical and remained as coach of DePaul.

However, as the war continued, many wondered if he'd have a team to coach in 1943-44. There was simply a shortage of healthy young men.

George Mikan was available, being judged too tall for military duty. Dick Triptow was also in the fold, out of military action with a double hernia.

Other candidates followed. Ernie DeBenedetto was out of the service with poor eyesight and Edwin "Whitey" Kachan with a perforated eardrum. Gene Stump, Jack Allen, and Jack Dean were all too young for military duty. Combined, they gave Meyer enough players to field a team.

And what a team it was.

Captained by Triptow, the Blue Demons won their first thirteen games in 1943-44 by an average of over thirty-one points per game. Included in the streak were victories over Nebraska, Indiana, Long Island and Arkansas that established DePaul as one of the country's best teams. This team was DePaul's first to score 80 points in a game, topped by an 88-23 win over Concordia. In all, the Blue Demons would top the 80-mark five times that season.

A loss at Valparaiso, 65-57, made DePaul 13-1 heading into four straight games at Chicago Stadium. The first game was against Marquette, a team DePaul had defeated twice the year before. In a close contest, Marquette proved the better this year, posting a 51-49 victory of the Blue Demons.

DePaul's next opponent was Purdue, owner of a six-game winning streak. The result was a second straight two-point game, but this time DePaul came out ahead, 39-37.

A victory over Notre Dame and a loss to Illinois moved the Blue Demons to 15-3. DePaul closed the regular season with five straight wins that gave the team twenty wins for only the second time in school history. Among the late victories were a 69-38 victory over Valparaiso and a 61-49 overtime victory over Ohio State.

Mikan scored 37 that night against Ohio State, and the victory earned DePaul a second straight berth in the NCAA tournament. But Meyer opted to decline the NCAA berth and play in the NIT. The NIT berth was DePaul's second in five years, and its second postseason trip in as many seasons.

DePaul opened the tournament with a 68-45 win over Muhlenberg at Madison Square Garden, setting up a headlining matchup of Mikan and Oklahoma A&M's 6-foot-11 center Bob Kurland in the second round.

Mikan and DePaul got in early foul trouble and fell behind 15-2 after ten minutes. Mikan eventually fouled out early in the second half, scoring just 9 points. But Oklahoma A&M was also experiencing foul trouble.

Coach Henry Iba's team eventually had to finish with just four players due to injury, fouls, and the substitution limits in effect in college basketball then. DePaul was able to rally for a 41-38 win and headed to the tournament final.

The finals of the tournament pitted DePaul against its Vincentian sister school, St. John's. Mikan again suffered from foul trouble, scoring 13 points before exiting with fourteen minutes to play. This time DePaul was not able to rally for a big comeback, and St. John's earned its second straight NIT crown with a 47-39 win.

The loss sent DePaul home to Chicago with a final record of 22-4. The twenty-two victories tied the school record, and their .846 winning percentage was the highest since the 1934-35 team finished 15-1 (.938).

After the season, Dick Triptow left to sign a professional baseball contract with the Chicago Cubs organization. He would also play professional basketball. But George Mikan was returning for two more years, his younger brother Ed was coming to DePaul, and freshmen Gene Stump and Whitey Kachan were developing as players.

The 1944-45 season brought high expecta-

George Mikan
Center — 1942-46

To say George Mikan was a great college basketball player is an understatement. When the Naismith Basketball Hall of Fame was opened in 1959, Mikan was among the charter inductees, and he was inducted as a college player. It's easy to see why.

When Mikan started his career at DePaul in 1942, he was a lightly regarded gangly 6-foot-8 center. He began playing for a rookie head coach in Ray Meyer, the same man who had cut him from the Notre Dame team earlier. But Mikan was willing to work to become a basketball player. Meyer developed special drills to work on improving Mikan's coordination and basketball skills. And, in time, Meyer made Mikan a star.

Mikan scored 271 points, an 11.3 average, in his freshman year in 1942-43. His offensive production and his defensive intimidation helped lead DePaul to a 19-5 record and an appearance in the NCAA Final Four.

Mikan improved his scoring to 18.7 per game in 1943-44 with 486 total points. This time DePaul rode Mikan all the way to the final game of the National Invitation Tournament and a 22-4 record. For his performance, Mikan was named National Player of the Year and an NIT all-star.

If Mikan was satisfied with his past performances, you couldn't tell by his play during the 1944-45 season. He poured in 558 points, an average of 23.3 per game, to set a pair of school records and helped DePaul to an 18-2 regular season record.

But it was in the NIT that Mikan became a legend. In the opening game against West Virginia, he scored 33 points as the Blue Demons triumphed 76-52. DePaul's second round opponent was Rhode Island. Mikan almost single-handedly destroyed RI, scoring a school record 53 points and a school record 21 field goals. The title game paired DePaul and Bowling Green State. Once again Mikan was a high scorer, this time with a mere 34 points as DePaul won the NIT Championship, 71-54.

Mikan was named the tournament's outstanding player as he averaged 40.0 points per game. He also earned national player of the year honors as well as All-America status. And DePaul finished at 21-3 and had its first NIT Championship.

The question for Mikan's senior season was what would he do for an encore? Answer: score 555 points for a 23.1 points per game average. But the Blue Demons, despite a tough schedule, a 19-5 record and a star player, were not invited to the NCAA tournament or the NIT.

Mikan ended his career with 1,896 points, a school scoring record that stood for thirty years. He also finished with 154 blocked shots, a record that stood for forty years.

Mikan went on to star in the professional basketball league, making his biggest impact as a member of the Minneapolis Lakers. In 1950, he was honored as the greatest basketball player of the first half century.

---

tions. With George Mikan now a polished player and a dominant force, the question wasn't whether or not DePaul would win, it was how often. The answer was very often.

The Blue Demons opened their third year under head coach Ray Meyer with six straight wins, including a 68-29 hammering of Wyoming at Chicago Stadium. The winning streak came to an end in the Stadium, as the Blue Demons lost 43-40 to Illinois. But the next game started DePaul on an eleven-game winning streak.

Among the victories in that run were a 74-47 win over Long Island at Madison Square Garden, and a 63-56 win at Illinois to avenge the earlier loss. Three straight Chicago Stadium games netted wins over Marquette, Notre Dame and Purdue. That set up a rematch of the previous year's NIT semifinal against Oklahoma A&M. The game again featured two of the best

Ray Meyer with his 1944-45 team.

big men in the country, Mikan and Bob Kurland. A&M managed to finish the game with five men on the floor, but the result was the same as the previous year. DePaul won 48-46.

But the winning streak was halted the next game as Great Lakes took a 64-56 decision. A 65-49 win over Western Kentucky ended the regular season with DePaul owning an 18-2 record and receiving another bid to the National Invitation Tournament.

DePaul opened NIT play with a 76-52 win over West Virginia as Mikan scored 33 points. That set up a semifinal match with Rhode Island, perhaps the best running team in college basketball at the time.

Rhode Island coach Frank Keaney talked of running Mikan back to Chicago, but it was Keaney's team that went home. Mikan ended up with a school and NIT record 53 points in a 97-53 win. Both records still stand, and the 97 points was a DePaul single game scoring record that stood for six years.

With that victory in hand, DePaul prepared for the championship matchup with Bowling Green State. Bowling Green featured a 7-foot, 260-pound center named Don Otten, who was expected to provide stiff competition for the 6-foot-9 and 230-pound Mikan. But Mikan proved up to the challenge.

The DePaul center was able to get Otten into foul trouble and held him to just 7 points. Mikan tallied 34 points as the Blue Demons won the NIT championship, 71-54. What a season.

But the season wasn't over. With the war effort draining the coffers of the Red Cross, a special benefit game was arranged pitting the NIT champion against the NCAA tourney winner at Madison Square Garden. DePaul won the NIT title on a Saturday night, but had to stay in New York City through Thursday night to play Oklahoma A&M, the NCAA winner.

The game, and the Kurland-Mikan battle, was diluted by fouls. Mikan, Allen, Stump, and Kachan—four of the starting five—fouled out as DePaul lost 52-44. But over $50,000 was raised from a crowd of 18,158.

Meyer's third season ended with a 21-3 record. He was now 62-12 as a head coach and had been to the NCAA Final Four, finished second in the NIT and won the NIT in three years.

Of the top players on the team, only Kachan,

The 1945 NIT champion DePaul Blue Demons.

who joined the armed forces, was not to return. The 1945-46 season promised to be a great year.

Although the 1945-46 team wasn't able to match the record of the previous two squads, it did have an impressive season. An eight-game winning streak opened the season and once again established DePaul as a power.

Among the victories were a 46-42 win at Oklahoma A&M and a 59-54 victory over Bowling Green State. Other wins came over Washington, Indiana State, and Oregon State.

The unbeaten stretch ended at Illinois in a 56-37 Illini victory. Losses at Minnesota and Notre Dame followed, and DePaul had fallen to 8-3.

The Blue Demons rebounded with five wins in their next six games, making them 13-4 and setting up a rematch with Oklahoma A&M at Chicago Stadium. Mikan scored 19 points, but it wasn't enough as DePaul lost for the fifth time of the season, 46-38.

The winning ways returned quickly thereafter as DePaul closed with six straight. Among the victims were Long Island (twice), Notre Dame, and Bradley.

But the 19-5 record wasn't enough. Following a 65-40 win over Beloit on March 9, 1945, the Blue Demons were not invited to either the NCAA tournament or the National Invitation Tournament.

George Mikan had played his last college game in that Beloit contest, scoring 13. He closed his four seasons with 1,870 points and a 19.1 per-game scoring average. His point total would not be topped for thirty-two years. It was fifteen seasons before a Blue Demon averaged more per game than Mikan.

Mikan graduated from DePaul in 1946 and

George Mikan took his hook shot to the professional leagues after graduation. Here he is shown as a member of the Chicago Gears and the Minneapolis Lakers.

signed a contract with the Chicago Gears of the National Basketball League. After one season, he moved to the Minneapolis Lakers and followed that team to the National Basketball Association in 1948. In the NBA he continued as one of the dominant players ever in basketball.

The departure of George Mikan left a void on the DePaul team. The Blue Demons had rode on Mikan's shoulders to national prominence. Many wondered what a Mikan-less future would hold.

Much was different when DePaul opened its 1946-47 season, but much was the same as well. Ray Meyer was back for his fifth season as head coach, joining Jim Kelly as only the second DePaul mentor with that long a tenure.

Forward Gene Stump was back for his senior season. Guard Edwin "Whitey" Kachan rejoined the team, and veterans Jack Allen and Ernie DiBenedetto were among those who played a major role in the 1945 National Invitation Tournament championship.

And the team wasn't Mikan-less. There was a Mikan starting at center, but it wasn't star George Mikan. It was Ed Mikan, the 6-foot-7 younger brother of George.

For Ed Mikan, the 1946-47 season was a coming out party. He played in George's shadow the previous two seasons, scoring just 41 points in 33 games. Ed played in all 25 games in 1946-47, leading the team with 392 points, an average of 15.7 per game.

As much as things didn't change, some

Edwin "Whitey" Kachan
Guard — 1943-45, 1946-47

When DePaul claimed the championship in the 1945 National Invitation Tournament, star center George Mikan received most of the accolades. Not surprising considering he set a tourney and school record with 53 points in the semifinal round and scored 120 in DePaul's three victories over Western Virginia, Rhode Island, and Bowling Green.

But as often is the case, DePaul was far from a one-man team. Helping Mikan hoist that NIT trophy was guard Edwin "Whitey" Kachan. Big for a guard at that time, Kachan stood six-foot-three and weighed 180 pounds. While Mikan was unstoppable inside, Whitey supplied spirited defense, both on the inside and on the perimeter, and was the Blue Demons floor general.

Kachan's career at DePaul started in 1943, when, as a sophomore, he helped the 1943-44 Blue Demons to the finals of the NIT. The Demons lost that game to St. John's 47-39, but one year later they would return and win the title. During the title year, Kachan averaged 8.9 points per game.

Kachan took a sixteen-month hiatus after the 1944-45 season, opting to enlist in the Army. While in the service, he remained active in basketball, playing for base teams at Keesler Field and Lowry Field.

A Chicago native from St. Phillip's High School, Kachan returned to DePaul for the 1946-47 season. With the George Mikan era ended, Kachan was welcomed back with open arms. And he picked right up where he had left off. Averaging 8.4 points per game and providing his trademark solid defense and leadership, he helped the Blue Demons to a 16-9 season.

Kachan's career didn't end with college. In 1948 he averaged 2.2 points per game in 52 games split between the Chicago Stags and the Minneapolis Lakers. On the Lakers he was again teamed with George Mikan, a team that claimed the 1949 championship of the Basketball Association of America in the final year before the BAA merged with the National Basketball League to form the National Basketball Association.

Gene Stump

Gene Stump
Forward — 1943-47

If George Mikan was the heart of the DePaul championship caliber teams of the mid 1940s, Gene Stump might have been the soul. Stump was a great player who combined scoring ability with the tenacity it takes to win games.

He also carried a fervent attitude off the court. Stump was the practical joker of the team, always doing the right thing to keep the team loose at key times.

But Stump was far from a joker on the court. In his four seasons, he helped the Blue Demons to a combined 78-21 record. He was an integral part of the two teams that played in the National Invitation Tournament, including the 1945 NIT title team.

Stump was a sophomore in that championship year. He averaged 11.1 points per game, scoring 266 points in 24 games as the Blue Demons went 21-3. This came on the heels of a freshman season that saw him score 244 points as DePaul went 22-4 and finished second in the NIT.

During his junior season Stump improved his scoring average to 12.8 a game, scoring 307 points. In 1946-47, Stump replaced George Mikan as team captain. Stump's inspired play and 10.2 points per game helped DePaul continue its success with a 16-9 record.

Stump ended his college career with 1,071 points, joining Mikan as the lone players in the 1940s to top 1,000 career points. Following college, Stump played three years of professional basketball, including two with the Boston Celtics in the NBA. His season high in points was in 1948-49 when he averaged 8.5 points per game.

Whitey Kachan pressures the ball in DePaul's 77-45 victory over Illinois Wesleyan in 1946-47. Gene Stump is the player under the basket and Ed Mikan is number 32.

things did. There was no lengthy winning streak to open this season. DePaul topped Chicago State and Kalamazoo but lost 54-39 at Minnesota in the season's third game.

A 65-45 loss at Kentucky dropped the team to 2-2 and left DePaul at .500 for the first time since Meyer took over as head coach. A pair of wins followed, but DePaul lost 61-43 to Texas at Chicago Stadium to stand 4-3 after seven games.

Wins over North Carolina and Illinois Wesleyan helped, but a 57-41 loss at Purdue left Meyer's squad 6-4. Four more wins followed, making the Blue Demons 10-4 heading into a pair of big games at the Chicago Stadium.

Both ended in defeat. Oklahoma A&M won the first contest 44-37 and Bowling Green State claimed the second 59-47. DePaul was 10-6, more losses than Meyer had suffered in any of his first four seasons.

DePaul went 6-3 the rest of the season. During that stretch DePaul gained revenge against Kentucky and beat Loyola. They also lost to Notre Dame by 35 points, as the Fighting Irish became the first team to score 80 points against DePaul. With a final record of 16-9, DePaul, for the second straight year, watched postseason basketball.

By 1947-48, George Mikan was starring in the National Basketball Association (NBA) with the Minneapolis Lakers. Gene Stump was also in the NBA, playing for the Boston Celtics. The 1945 National Invitation Tournament championship was three years removed, and only Ed Mikan, Edwin "Whitey" Kachan, Jack Phelan and Tom Niemiera remained from that team.

Ed Mikan and Kachan served as team captains in 1947-48, and the two seniors provided the bulk of the team's attack. Mikan scored 463 points and averaged 15.4 per game. Kachan poured in 353 points, an 11.7 average.

Despite losing two of their first six games, the Blue Demons returned to postseason play in 1948. Early losses at Kentucky and Minnesota made DePaul 4-2, but the Blue Demons rallied.

Victories over Loyola and Holy Cross highlighted a five-game run that saw DePaul improve to 9-2 before losing at Notre Dame. A road trip to Vincentian sister schools St. John's and Niagara proved key. DePaul took a 69-66 double overtime win over St. John's at Madison Square Garden and topped Niagara 56-53.

The St. John's game featured a big comeback. DePaul trailed by eighteen in the second half before rallying. It looked as though the run would come up short as St. John's held a 59-56 lead in the final seconds. But a traveling call resulted in a St. John's technical foul. The free throw made it 59-57 and Andy Federinko scored to tie it and force the overtime. Mikan scored a late basket and grabbed a key rebound to provide the final margin in the second overtime.

A three-game stand at Chicago Stadium was up next. DePaul won the first two, handling Michigan State and Oklahoma A&M, before losing to Kentucky.

The Oklahoma A&M contest included one of the more bizarre incidents in DePaul history.

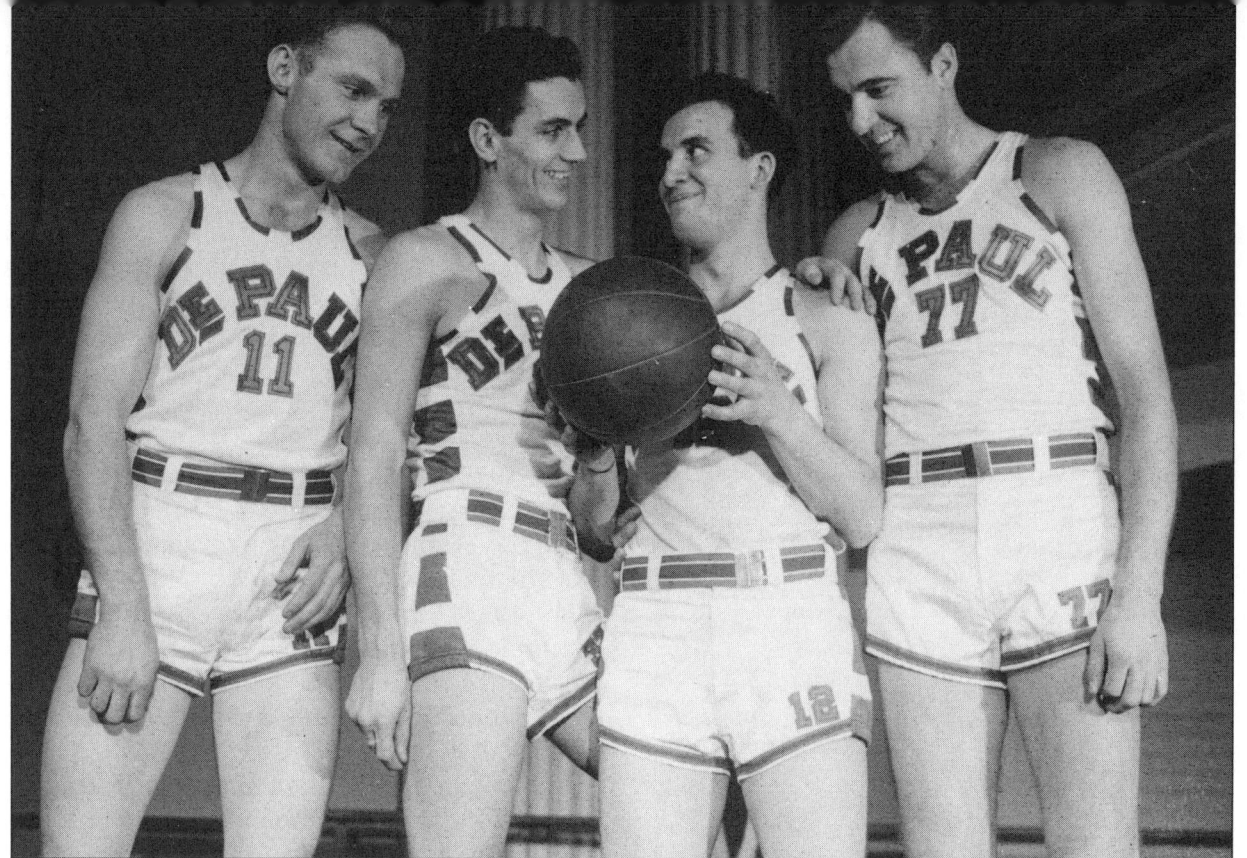

Four key players on the 1947-48 team (from left): Andy Federinko, George Leddy, Pete Coorlas, and Gordon Gillespie.

George Leddy (37) comes up short in his attempt for the ball in DePaul's 73-59 loss to New York University in the 1948 NIT. Watching the action is Charles Allen (86).

Ed Mikan
Center — 1944-48

Talk about having big shoes to fill. Ed Mikan had the misfortune of being a very good basketball player who had to follow a very great basketball player at DePaul. Because of this, Ed Mikan probably never received the credit he deserved.

The man who preceded Ed at DePaul would be voted the top basketball player in the first half century in 1950. Not only that, but the man was also Ed's older brother. So even though Ed Mikan had some very productive seasons for DePaul, his brother George is who people think of when they hear the name Mikan.

As a college player, Mikan was on DePaul teams that went 78-25. Mikan was a freshman reserve on the 1945 NIT championship team. He was a senior and team captain in 1948 when the Blue Demons again advanced to the NIT.

Mikan saw limited duty as a freshman and a sophomore as the backup to his brother. He scored just 9 points in 17 games in 1944-45 and another 32 points in 16 contests in 1945-46.

The 1946-47 season was Ed's first time to shine. With George gone off to the professional basketball ranks, Ed took center stage and averaged 15.7 points per game for the 16-9 Blue Demon squad. Mikan capped off his career at DePaul by averaging 15.4 points per game and leading the team back to the NIT with a 22-8 record.

Ed Mikan ended his career with 896 points, third behind only his brother and Gene Stump at the time. He went on to play six seasons of professional basketball, including a brief stint with the Boston Celtics in the NBA. Mikan averaged a high of 9.9 points per game as a pro rookie with the Chicago Stags.

Since coach Hank Iba's team was known for its deliberate pace, Meyer tried to outstall the Aggies in the second half. With a four-point lead and Oklahoma A&M playing a passive defense, Meyer ordered his team to hold the ball. Federinko took it to the extreme, sitting on the ball at midcourt while the Aggies stood and watched. Eventually, Meyer ordered his team to attack, and the Blue Demons held on for a 32-31 win.

Five more wins followed the loss to Kentucky, and the Blue Demons were 18-4 heading to St. Louis. The game was a matchup of Ed Mikan against St. Louis center "Easy" Ed Macauley. Macauley's Billikens survived in overtime 58-56.

Mikan and the Blue Demons responded with wins over Bradley and St. Joseph's (Ind.) before hosting St. Louis in a rematch at Chicago Stadium. DePaul won this time, 52-42. Loyola topped DePaul in the regular season finale, but the Blue Demons would be returning to the NIT.

DePaul's first NIT game since their victory in the championship game in 1945 was against North Carolina State. The Blue Demons ran their NIT winning streak to four games with a 75-64 victory. But losses to New York University and Western Kentucky led to a fourth-place finish in the tourney won by St. Louis. The Blue Demons finished the season at 22-8.

The victory total tied the school record set in 1939-40 and equaled in 1943-44. It would be sixteen years before DePaul again won more than twenty games and thirty years before a team would top the twenty-two wins.

5

Success After the Mikans

When Ray Meyer called his Blue Demons together for the 1948-49 season, he had to feel that something was missing. This was to be his seventh season as DePaul's head coach, but for the first time he was going into it without a Mikan in the middle.

For Meyer's first four years as head coach, his center and top scorer was superstar George Mikan. When George graduated in 1946, his younger brother, Ed, stepped in as the center and leading scorer.

In the fall of 1948, George and Ed Mikan were both in the NBA. Meyer was preparing for the season without the help of a player who'd ever averaged over 10 points per game for a college season.

None would average that much in 1948-49, but that didn't keep DePaul from success. A balanced attack featured five players over 5.0 per game and twelve with at least 2.0 per game.

The scoring leader was a sophomore from Chicago named Bato Govedarica. If the Mikan brothers where typical of the big men beginning to take control of basketball, Govedarica was a throwback.

At 5-foot-10, Govedarica was listed at 210 pounds. He only came to DePaul after catching Meyer's eye late in the spring in a high school all-star game in Champaign, Illinois.

With the Mikan's gone, Govedarica became an offensive force, scoring 216 points and averaging 8.5 per game. Jack Phelan, the last hold over from the 1945 NIT championship team, scored 200 points and averaged 8.0 per game. Captain Chuck Allen averaged 7.9 per game and Gordon Gillespie 7.6.

Wins over Illinois Tech and Chicago State opened the year, but the Blue Demons lost 67-36 at Kentucky in the season's third game. A 60-50 win over Illinois and a 61-57 win over Illinois Wesleyan made DePaul 4-1 tackling Minnesota at Chicago Stadium.

Charles Allen (86) and Jack Phelan (45) force Gordon Neff of Indiana to think pass. DePaul won the overtime contest 47-46 for its second win against a Big Ten foe during the 1948-49 season.

Jack Phelan (45) looks on as William Benson (12) gets his shot blocked and his face swatted. DePaul lost 67-50 to Minnesota.

Bato Govedarica
Guard — 1948-51

At 5-foot-11 and 210 pounds, Bato Govedarica did not look like the prototype for a successful college basketball guard. So, despite a stellar career at Chicago's Lane Tech High School, Govedarica was lightly recruited by colleges. It wasn't until Ray Meyer spotted him during practices for an all-star game in Champaign, Illinois, that DePaul showed any interest in Govedarica. When Bato starred in the all-star game, other school's began to call as well. But Meyer's earlier interest paid off as Govedarica opted to become a Blue Demon.

Success came quickly for Govedarica in college. His first varsity season, 1948-49, was also the first season a Meyer coached team would not feature a Mikan at center leading the team in scoring. But the sophomore Govedarica was ready to help fill the void. Supplying 8.5 points per game, Bato and the Blue Demons went 16-9 during the 1948-49 season.

DePaul slipped to 12-13 in 1949-50, but Govedarica upped his scoring contributions. He finished the season with 12.9 per game scoring average, and became only the fifth Blue Demons player to score at least 300 points in a season (joining George Mikan, Ed Mikan, Bob Neu, and Gene Stump). Govedarica's season high was 20 points, accomplished twice on the road. The first time was against St. John's at Madison Square Garden in 74-68 victory. Then three games later he again hit the twenty mark in a 74-64 win over St. Joseph's (Ind.).

The Blue Demons improved to 13-12 in 1950-51. Govedarica, a senior and team captain, averaged a career-high 14.0 points per game to close his career with 899 points. The total placed him fourth on the career scoring list behind Stump and the Mikan brothers.

Govedarica spent one season in the NBA following his DePaul career, playing 23 games for the Syracuse Nationals in 1953-54. Govedarica averaged 3.3 points per game on a team that lost to the Minneapolis Lakers and fellow DePaul alum George Mikan in the NBA finals.

Bato Govedarica shows the toughness that attracted Ray Meyer to him.

The Blue Demons came up short in that game, and lost two more in a row to Illinois and Loyola to fall to 4-4. A five-game winning streak, including victories at Oklahoma A&M and Notre Dame, pushed the record to 9-4.

The streak ended with a 57-53 loss at Niagara. The Blue Demons topped St. John's on the road, but lost at home to Kentucky and Oklahoma A&M. But again DePaul rebounded, this time with a four-game winning streak, and was 14-7 with four games to play.

The Blue Demons split those four, topping Denver and St. Norbert but losing to Notre Dame and Ohio State to finish the year with a 16-9 record.

By just showing up to coach the 1949-50 season, Ray Meyer set one school record. The campaign was his eighth as head coach, bettering the seven Jim Kelly coached from 1929 to 1936 as the longest tenure.

Despite the return of 1948-49 leading scorer Bato Govedarica, the 1949-50 season was a rough one for DePaul. The Blue Demons slipped to their first losing record in the Ray Meyer era.

Govedarica was again the leading scorer, this time posing 323 points and a 12.9 per game average. Bill Benson chipped in 11.2 per game and John Lahey 9.4. But only seven players averaged over 1.2 per game.

The season opened brightly as DePaul won its first three games, but the Blue Demons lost consecutive contests to La Salle and Indiana to slip to 3-2. A win over Loyola was followed by three more defeats. The Meyer's crew then traveled to Oklahoma to face their old nemesis, Oklahoma A&M, and came away with an impressive 41-40 win.

For the rest of the season the Blue Demons could not string together more than two straight victories. One such two-game streak came on an eastern trip that netted wins over Boston College in the Boston Garden and St. John's in Madison Square Garden.

The Blue Demons finished the season with a 73-55 loss to Bowling Green at the Stadium to fall to 12-13 and finished with the school's first losing record since the 1941-42 campaign.

St. John's Jack McMahon (21) has Bato Govedarica (41) out of position as he drives to the hoop during DePaul's 74-68 victory on Jan. 18, 1950.

Looks can be deceiving, and that was certainly the case with the 1950-51 season. On the surface, the 1950-51 campaign, with a 13-12 final record, looks little better than the 12-13 record of the 1949-50 campaign. Look closer.

In addition to getting back on the winning side of the ledger, the 1950-51 Blue Demons played competitively in virtually every game. Seven of the team's twelve losses came by a combined total of twenty points.

After opening with wins over St. Norbert and Quincy, the Blue Demons traveled to Oklahoma A&M. DePaul lost to the Aggies 60-53 in double overtime after thinking the game was won in regulation.

The score was tied with twenty-five seconds left in regulation when Bato Govedarica held for a final shot. He drove for the basket with ten seconds left and laid a shot off the backboard.

Eugene Dyker (32) and John Lahey (11) are both in position to snare this rebound. John Lahey averaged 13.1 points per game for the Blue Demons in 1950-51.

John Lahey (left) and David Matz (96) play some inside defense against St. Mary's. DePaul won this 1950 matchup 79-72 in overtime.

Captain Bato Govedarica heads for an easy layup versus St. Norbert in 1950.

John Lahey has an open shot at the hoop against Ohio State in the final home game of the 1950-51 season. Clem Pavilonis (21) and DePaul won the contest 94-67.

Ray Meyer runs some of his 1952-53 team through drills. Left to right: Bill Schyman, Ron Dreas, Russ Johnson, Ron Feiereisel, and Frank Blum.

When that shot rolled out, Clem Pavilonis tipped it in for an apparent victory.

After the gun sounded and the teams left the floor, the basket was declared no good and overtime started. DePaul was assessed a technical foul for delay of game before the overtime began, and the loss followed in a second overtime.

Other narrow losses were to Illinois, Manhattan, Lawrence Tech, Notre Dame, Kentucky, Bowling Green and Loyola. But the Blue Demons did claim their share of squeakers. DePaul won in overtime against St. Mary's (Minn.) and topped Illinois by three, Cincinnati by one and Loyola by one.

Govedarica scored 350 points for an average of 14.0 per game while captaining the team as a senior. Pavilonis averaged 13.7 and John Lahey 13.1. Sophomore Ron Feiereisel added 8.9 per game.

The team set a school record for single game points and became the first squad to top 100 in a game in a 101-70 defeat of North Central late in the season.

As a sophomore in 1950-51, Ron Feiereisel began to show the potential to be a big scorer. That potential became more evident in 1951-52.

A team captain along with Stan Hoover, Feiereisel scored 381 points, a four-year high for the Blue Demons, and averaged 14.1 per game. Gene Dyker averaged even more, at 14.8, but missed two games. Bill Schyman added 11.5 and Jim Lamkin 9.0.

These type of scorers improved DePaul's team scoring average to 74.6 per game, a school record. The Blue Demons held a 14.6 per game scoring margin, nearly as good as the George Mikan led teams of the mid-1940s. The increase in points led to an increased victory total.

DePaul opened the season with five wins, its best start since Mikan's senior year in 1945-46. DePaul was 7-1 before losing 98-60 at Kentucky and 70-61 at Illinois, but rebounded with two more wins. A 52-49 loss at Oklahoma A&M made the Blue Demons 9-4.

DePaul posted a nine-game winning streak after that, including victories over Illinois, Cincinnati and Oklahoma A&M. But the winning streak ended with losses to Notre Dame and Loyola. A victory over Fort Sheridan gave the Blue Demons a 19-6 record with two games to play.

DePaul failed twice to get its twentieth win in a pair of close games versus two teams that had already downed the Demons that season. A late Kentucky basket lifted the Wildcats to a

63-61 win at Chicago Stadium, and in the final game of the season Notre Dame took a 78-77 heartbreaker in that same facility. DePaul failed to win twenty, and once again went nowhere for postseason play.

In the first thirty-two years of DePaul basketball, only one player scored over 500 points in a single season, superstar George Mikan. He was joined by Ron Feiereisel in 1952-53 as the guard scored 503 points and averaged 18.0 per game. Jim Lamkin added 15.7 per game. Russ Johnson added 11.8 and Bill Schyman 10.6 as the Blue Demons averaged a record 75.6 points.

The first game of the season against Gonzaga set the tone for the year. Behind Russ Johnson's 29 points, DePaul won 97-90. The Blue Demons won four more, scoring over 70 points in every game, before traveling to Oklahoma A&M. But Oklahoma A&M slowed the offensive pace and won 62-51 for DePaul's first loss.

Wins over Southern Illinois and La Salle made DePaul 7-1 before a 73-64 loss to Manhattan in the second round of the Holiday Festival at Madison Square Garden. Two more wins followed, but losses at St. Louis and Bradley sandwiched a win over Lawrence Tech to make DePaul 10-4.

Ron Feiereisel
Guard — 1950-53

When Ron Feiereisel joined the DePaul varsity men's basketball team in the fall of 1950, he was coming to a team that was looking to rebound from its first losing season in seven years. When his career ended in 1953, the Blue Demons were in the NCAA tournament. Simply put, Feiereisel was a winner.

A graduate of DePaul Academy in Chicago, Feiereisel carried only 160 poundes on his six-foot-three-inch frame. But despite his size, Feiereisel was able to take the ball inside and play as a forward as well as handle the ball and shoot from the outside as a guard.

On a 1950-51 squad that would finish 13-12, Feiereisel was the only sophomore among the top players. And he quickly established himself as a big-game player. In an early season showdown with Illinois, he tallied 18 points. But it was his season-high 22 points in a 79-72 overtime victory against St. Mary's (Minn.) that people sit up and take notice. And as the season wound down, Feiereisel started fans thinking about next year. In back-to-back Chicago Stadium games, DePaul faced Bowling Green and Ohio State. In a tough fought 78-80 loss, Feiereisel kept the Blue Demons in the game with 17 points. Then, for an encore, he scored 15 points as DePaul trounced Ohio State 94-67.

Feiereisel blossomed into a star as a junior. He averaged 14.1 points per game in 1951-52, helping the Blue Demons to a 19-8 record. Once again, Feiereisel saved some of his best games for the Chicago Stadium. An Illinois squad that had beaten the Blue Demons earlier in the season 61-70 came to the Stadium trying for the sweep. But behind Feiereisel's 16 points, DePaul posted the upset, 69-65. Later in the season, Ron was voted the top player in the Chicago Stadium doubleheader series. But he saved his best performance for another large venue—Madison Square Garden. Against Manhattan, Feiereisel scored 23 points as DePaul scored a narrow 66-65 victory.

The 1952-53 season marked DePaul's return to postseason play. Behind Feiereisel and his 18.0 points per game, the Blue Demons went 18-7, good enough for an NCAA tournament bid. After a victory over Miami of Ohio, DePaul and Feiereisel ended the season with two losses for a final record of 19-9. Though disappointed over the losses, Feiereisel ended his career with 1,106 points. At the time, only George Mikan had scored more as a Blue Demon.

Feiereisel played briefly in the NBA with the Minneapolis Lakers in 1955-56. Playing in ten games, he averaged 3.0 points per game.

Russ Johnson (20) and Frank Blum (33) lose this rebound in the opening game of the 1953 season. But DePaul beat Gonzaga 97-90 as Johnson scored 29 points and Blum 21 points.

The season's best stretch followed as the Blue Demons won seven straight over the likes of Cincinnati, Oklahoma A&M (Bill Schyman, 16 points), Notre Dame and Loyola (James Lamkin, 13 points). DePaul then turned around and lost three of its last four regular season games to close the campaign 18-7.

The late season toe stubbing wasn't enough to keep the Blue Demons from postseason play.

DePaul qualified for the NCAA tournament for the first time since Ray Meyer's first year (1942-43) and was in postseason play for the first time since 1947-48. It was also Meyer's first postseason berth without a Mikan on the roster.

The Blue Demons opened NCAA play with a 74-72 over Miami (Ohio) in Fort Wayne, Indiana, behind Feiereisel's 27 points. In round two, DePaul returned home to host Indiana at the Chicago Stadium. The Hoosiers got away with an 82-80 win by converting a late technical foul to quell a Blue Demon's rally. DePaul then lost the regional consolation game 90-70 to Pennsylvania, dropping to a final record of 19-9.

With the graduation of three of the top scorers from the previous season, the offensive load in 1953-54 fell on the shoulders of junior Jim Lamkin, who along with Dan Lecos captained the team. Lamkin held up nicely, scoring 19.3 per game, the most for a Blue Demon since George Mikan averaged 23.1 in 1945-46 and the third highest average to date.

Sophomore guard Rob Sobieszczyk added 14.3 per game. Frank Blum contributed 11.6 and Ken Jaksy 11.1, but all the offense couldn't guarantee wins.

The 1953-54 Blue Demons opened 6-0 and were 7-1 after eight games, but lost nine of their last thirteen games to finish 11-10. Following a late season loss to Kentucky at Chicago Stadium, the Blue Demons owned a six-game losing streak and were in danger of a losing season. But the team topped Lawrence Tech 81-75 and then took Bradley 80-76 in overtime to close the year.

Offense was again the prevalent trend in 1954-55. Five Blue Demons averaged at least 10.0 points per game, and the team set a school record with 84.5 points per game for the season.

Ron Sobieszczyk led the way with 17.3 points per game. Bill Robinzine added 15.0 and Ken Jaksy 13.0. Captains Frank Blum and Jim Lamkin scored 12.1 and 10.3 respectively.

In the first thirty-four years of Blue Demons'

Dan Lecos heads to the hoop as two Loyola players go for the block. DePaul won the city rivalry in 1953, 68-43.

Bill Schyman (right), Russ Johnson (20), and Dan Lecos (14) battle for the ball against Indiana. DePaul lost the 1953 NCAA tournament game, 82-80.

Ron Feiereisel (21) has his shot blocked by Ed Gunderson (31) of Miami of Ohio in the first round of the 1953 NCAA tournament.

Jim Lamkin
Guard — 1951-55

When Ray Meyer went searching for a guard for his DePaul men's basketball team, two things he usually looked for were quickness and ball handling ability. Jim Lamkin has both, plus a whole lot more. At five-foot-nine and 175 pounds, Lamkin wasn't the biggest or the strongest player on the Blue Demon squad. But what he lacked in size he made up for with his forementioned quickness and dribbling skills, along with a keen shooting eye and an innate ability to score. The whole package made Lamkin one of the great DePaul stars of the 1950s.

As a freshman on the 1951-52 squad, Lamkin averaged 9.0 points per game as the Blue Demons went 19-8. The following season Lamkin increased his scoring average to 15.7, as DePaul was selected for the NCAA tournament.

Lamkin was named as a team captain for the 1953-54 season, but even his increased offensive output (19.3 points per game) could not stop DePaul from slipping to an 11-10 record.

DePaul's record improved to 16-6 in 1954-55. Lamkin, asked to score less because of an improved supporting cast, checked in with 10.3 points per game.

Lamkin ended his career with 1,306 points, pushing him into second place behind George Mikan on DePaul's all-time career scoring list.

Jim Lamkin challenges Johnny "Red" Kerr of Illinois during the 1953-54 season.

basketball, the team scored over 100 points only once. The 1954-55 squad did it five times with a high of 112 in a victory over Taylor.

DePaul swept two games from Bradley while splitting the series with Michigan State and Notre Dame. Kentucky swept the Blue Demons.

DePaul finished the campaign 16-6. Ray Meyer won his 200th career game as the Blue Demons' mentor when DePaul topped Manchester (Minn.) 103-74.

Among the top scorers, only captains Blum and Lamkin were not returning the next year. With budding stars like Sobieszczyk and Robinzine, the Blue Demons again looked headed toward success.

From the time he left Notre Dame to take the head coaching reigns at DePaul in 1942, Ray Meyer held a special place for the Fighting Irish. His Blue Demons played Notre Dame each season, and in the first twenty-three meetings held a 10-13 record.

In the last ten seasons, the two teams had played twice per year. While Notre Dame was

Ron Sobieszczyk
Guard — 1953-56

In his three seasons as a varsity basketball player at DePaul, Ron Sobieszczyk played with twenty-four other men. Of the two dozen players, Sobieszczyk shared one trait with only one other teammate. Only Ronald Dreas, a reserve guard on the 1953-54 team, and Sobieszczyk were not Chicago area natives.

When the ball went up and the game started, Sobieszczyk was as at home in a DePaul uniform as any player. A native of Sturtevant, Wisconsin, "Sobie" was an immediate factor as a sophomore on the 1953-54 Blue Demon team. A solid defender and scorer, Sobieszczyk poured in 14.3 points per game as the Blue Demons posted an 11-10 record.

Looking to bounce back from their worse season since 1949-50, DePaul looked to their backcourt of Sobie and Jim Lamkin to supply some offensive punch. Behind Sobieszczyk's 17.3 points per game and Lamkin's 10.3, DePaul improved to 16-6. Included in those sixteen victories were five wins in which the Blue Demons scored over 100 points, a record that would not be equaled until the 1965-66 season.

But possibly more impressive than Sobie's scoring average was the fact that he converted on over 50 percent of his field goal attempts. In today's college game Sobieszczyk's .504 shooting percentage would not be worthy of national recognition, but in the 1954-55 season it was good enough to place him nineteenth nationally.

The Blue Demons started the 1955-56 season with a new backcourt. Jim Lamkin was lost to graduation, and the six-foot-three Sobieszczyk was asked to move to forward. The new DePaul captain responded with 22.5 points per game, placing him twenty-ninth nationally. He also finished thirteenth in the country in free throw percentage and ninth in rebounding. The move also proved beneficial to DePaul as they went 16-8 and reached the NCAA tournament.

Sobieszczyk finished with 1,222 points and became the first Blue Demon since George Mikan to score at least 300 points in each of his varsity seasons. He ended his career with 470 free throws made, still tops in the DePaul record book. He was selected to play with the college all-star team that toured with the Harlem Globetrotters.

Sobie went on to play professional basketball for four years. A New York Knick for his first three seasons, he averaged a career-high 11.5 points per game in 1957-58. Sobieszczyk split the 1959-60 season, his last, between the Knicks and the Minneapolis Lakers. His career scoring average was 8.4 points per game.

able to sweep the season series twice (1951-52, 1953-54), DePaul was unable to win both games in one season. That changed in 1955-56.

DePaul won 77-74 at Notre Dame and then took an 80-74 decision at Chicago Stadium late in the season to sweep the season series. But there were other reasons for Meyer to smile in 1955-56.

One of the brightest spots was the offensive outburst of Ron Sobieszczyk, who averaged 22.5 points per game. Only George Mikan, who twice topped 23.0 per game, had averaged more. But Ron had some support—Ken Jaksy added 17.3 and Bill Robinzine 15.5.

The Blue Demons opened the season 3-1 and headed to Kentucky. With the game tied, DePaul was holding the ball for the final shot, but was called for an offensive foul. Kentucky hit a late shot and beat DePaul 71-69 in a tough loss.

Losses to Illinois and San Francisco, led by stars Bill Russell and K.C. Jones, followed a win over Duquesne. The Blue Demons topped Wayland Baptist, but lost to Ohio State and found themselves a .500 team, 5-5.

A 102-77 conquest of Illinois State preceded the first Notre Dame win, which was trailed by victories over Paris and Bradley, but consecutive losses at St. Louis and Illinois pushed DePaul to 9-7.

The Blue Demons then caught fire, winning seven in a row to close the regular season. Among the victims of that stretch was Kentucky.

DePaul topped the Wildcats 81-79 at Chicago Stadium in turnabout fashion. With the score tied late, Kentucky held for a final shot when it was called for an offensive foul. DePaul turned the possession into the winning basket.

The late winning streak, combined with the Kentucky victory and the Notre Dame sweep, earned the Blue Demons an NCAA Tournament berth. But the stay in the tourney was brief.

The Blue Demons dropped a 72-63 decision to Wayne State (Mich.), marking the first time in seven postseason appearances under Meyer that DePaul didn't win its first round game.

The early exit ended DePaul's season at 16-8 and closed the careers of seniors Sobieszczyk, Jaksy and Robinzine. But those familiar faces weren't the only ones leaving DePaul basketball. The 1955-56 season was the Blue Demons' last in the DePaul Auditorium. When practice opened in the fall of 1956, the team was playing on the other side of Sheffield Avenue in Alumni Hall.

6

Closing "The Barn" Door

In his forty-two years as head coach, Ray Meyer faced tough situation after tough situation, but none was tougher than moving the Blue Demons' home games from the Chicago Stadium and the DePaul Auditorium (a.k.a. "The Barn") to Alumni Hall.

In Meyer's tenure as head coach, he never lost a game in "The Barn," posting an 81-0 record. That run was especially important in the last few years the Blue Demons played there. DePaul was 11-0 in 1951-52, 10-0 in both 1952-53 and 1953-54 and 11-0 again in 1954-55. The 1955-56 team was 7-0 in "The Barn."

Success was also known in Chicago Stadium. Meyer was 78-50 in that West Side facility prior to 1956, including a 7-1 record in 1955-56.

Overall, Ray Meyer owned a 159-50 career record as the home team when he blew the whistle to open practice for the 1956-57 season, the Blue Demons' first in Alumni Hall. But the building in which that practice began was a far cry from the one Meyer expected.

Original plans for Alumni Hall called for a 10,000 seat arena. But since college basketball in Chicago was drawing considerably less than 10,000 fans per game, Alumni Hall plans were scaled down, and the building held just over 5,000 when the 1956-57 campaign tipped off against Illinois Wesleyan.

The new building was christened with an 80-62 win. That wasn't a sign of things to come.

DePaul struggled to a 3-3 start, including their first loss at Alumni Hall, heading to the Dixie Classic Tournament in Raleigh, North Carolina. A tourney opening 74-68 loss to Wake Forest made the Blue Demons 3-4, but the team evened their record the next day as it topped Iowa 73-72 in overtime.

In the Iowa game, team captain Dick Heise hit a pair of key free throws when he should

47

not have been at the line. Nick Hahn was fouled after a rebound, but Heise stepped to the line, and when the change wasn't noticed by the referees, Heise, a 79 percent career free throw shooter, proceeded to make the two baskets.

The Iowa win was to be DePaul's last visit to the .500 mark for the season. An 86-79 loss to Utah in the Dixie Classic consolation game started a seven-game losing streak. Among those defeats were three in Alumni Hall. Following an 80-76 overtime defeat by Western Kentucky, DePaul stood 4-10 overall and 3-4 in Alumni Hall.

A loss at Dayton pushed the overall mark to 4-11, but DePaul broke the streak with a 97-95 win over St. Louis. Wins over Portland, Illinois State, and Baldwin Wallace gave DePaul a four-game winning straight, all at Alumni Hall, and made the overall mark 8-11 with three games to play.

The Blue Demons returned to the losing ways in those contests, sandwiching home and road losses to Notre Dame around a defeat at Louisville. The season ended with the three-game losing streak and an 8-14 overall record, the most losses for a Blue Demons' team in Meyer's first fifteen years as head coach.

Dick Heise was one bright spot. He averaged 24.3 points per game, setting a school record and scoring one point more per game than George Mikan did in his best season. Heise also led in rebounding with 10.5 per game.

With the graduation of Dick Heise, the leading scorer and rebounder from the 1956-57 season, and a preseason knee injury to team captain Chuck Henry, the 1957-58 season was off to a bad start long before the opening game against Nebraska Wesleyan. DePaul took the opener 71-45, but struggled in the next three games in losing at Illinois, Bowling Green State, and Creighton.

A 60-55 win over an undefeated Purdue team appeared to change things as a five game home stand started. DePaul was 4-1 in that stand, topping Creighton, Duquesne and Louisville in addition to Purdue. The homecourt success made the Blue Demons 5-4 heading to Notre Dame.

A loss to the Irish dropped DePaul back to the .500 mark at 5-5, but a pair of Alumni Hall wins over Portland and Illinois State again raised hopes as the Blue Demons were 7-5 and two games over .500 for the first time since the end of the 1955-56 season and the move to Alumni Hall.

Those hopes were soon dashed. A 76-66 loss to Indiana started a spin that saw the Blue De-

Scoring ace Dick Heise (14) plays a little chin music on Dayton's Jim Palmer (31). DePaul upset Dayton 67-59 for its first win of the 1956-57 season.

mons lose seven of their last eight games. A second straight losing season ended with DePaul 8-12.

It was the first time in Meyer's tenure that the Blue Demons had consecutive losing seasons. Combined, DePaul was 16-26 overall since moving to Alumni Hall. The homecourt record was 15-10, meaning DePaul had won just one road game in seventeen tries over the two year period.

Offense was a problem in 1957-58. After averaging 74.6 per game the previous year, the Blue Demons scored just 63.6 this year. Paul Ruddy was the leading scorer at just 12.2 per game, nearly half what Heise averaged the previous season. Bill Coglianese led in rebounding with 9.5 per game.

In the late 1950s, the seeds were being sown for the civil rights movement in athletics. By the mid-1960s, it would be common for a majority of the members of the best college basketball teams to be black. DePaul was among those being integrated in the 1950s.

DePaul's first black player was Leo Blackburn, a member of the team briefly in 1944-45. As head coach Ray Meyer continued to integrate his team, he faced problems, particularly on the road.

In making hotel reservations, Meyer had to mention that a black would be in the group. When a pregame meal in St. Louis was delayed because restaurant management requested that his black team member eat outside, Meyer and the entire team left the restaurant. Similar situations occurred in other towns.

By 1958-59, Meyer was ready to take another step in the integration of college basketball. The team captain for the Blue Demons that year was McKinley Cowsen, a black man in his junior year at DePaul.

The team Cowsen captained was the one that returned DePaul to the winning ranks and postseason play. But it didn't look that way early in the year.

After topping Christian Brothers and Baldwin Wallace to open the season 2-0 for the first time since 1954-55, DePaul lost four of its next six and was 4-4 after eight games just like the previous two teams. In 1956-57 and 1957-58, the Blue Demons stood 4-4 and then went on losing streaks. The 1958-59 squad also streaked, but it was a winning one.

DePaul earned its first win over Notre Dame in five tries behind Howie Carl's 25 points and 21 by Cowsen. Wins over Valparaiso and Western Michigan made DePaul 7-4. After a loss to Indiana, wins over Western Kentucky and Marquette improved the team to 9-5 heading to Dayton. Carl scored 37 against Western Ken-

Forward McKinley Cowsen (6-4, 180) was the first black captain of the DePaul basketball team (1958-59).

Howie Carl
Guard — 1958-61

From his first season as a varsity basketball player at DePaul, Howie Carl had "star" written all over him. A scrappy 5-foot-9 guard, Carl brought a scorer's reputation with him from Von Steuben High School in Chicago. DePaul fans soon found out the reputation was well deserved.

Carl averaged a stunning 19.2 points per game in 1958-59, breaking George Mikan's sophomore school record with 461 points. The high points of Carl's season occurred in games against Western Kentucky and Marquette. Carl poured in 37 points against WKU in an 80-70 victory, and then to prove it was no fluke he scored 32 points against the Warriors in the final game of the regular season. Included in those 32 points were 23 free throws, a DePaul record that still stands. The Blue Demons finished the campaign at only 13-11, but still qualified for the NCAA tournament. And they managed to win their first game, a 57-56 squeeker over Portland, before losing the next two.

The Blue Demons returned to the NCAA tournament in 1959-60, marking the first time since the Mikan era that a DePaul team had reached postseason play two consecutive years. DePaul's final record after beating Air Force and losing to Cincinnati and Texas in the tourney was 17-7. Carl pushed his scoring average up to 19.7 and earned Little All-America honors for the second straight year as one of the top players nationally under 5-foot-10.

Carl turned into simply "All-America" as a senior. He averaged 21.0 points in 1960-61 as the Blue Demons were selected for the NIT to match the Mikan era record for consecutive postseason appearances. And once again he had a record-setting day against Marquette, this time setting an Alumni Hall scoring record on December 22, 1960, with 43 points. It was the third straight time in Carl's career that the Blue Demons beat the Warriors in Alumni Hall.

Carl finished his storied college career with 1,461 points, leaving him behind only George Mikan on the all-time scoring list. But his .853 career free throw percentage (452-498) is still the best all-time mark in DePaul history.

Carl backed his successful DePaul years with one year in the NBA. And as in high school and college, he called Chicago home, playing for the Chicago Packers in 1961-62. His one-year totals were 5.5 points per game in thirty-one appearances.

---

tucky and 31 in the Marquette victory. Only George Mikan had scored more in a game.

The win over Marquette was a thriller. A capacity crowd filled Alumni Hall on a cold and rainy night. Carl's points, along with 19 points and 15 rebounds by Cowsen, helped the Blue Demons end the Warriors fifteen-game winning streak, second longest in the country at the time.

An 88-69 loss to the Flyers was followed by wins over Western Michigan and Louisville. DePaul stood 11-6 at this point with four straight road games closing the season.

A 76-67 loss at Notre Dame started the stretch on a bad note. Things continued tough as DePaul lost 83-66 at Louisville. A 73-67 win at Canisius gave the Blue Demons hope again, but an 82-69 loss at Marquette ended the regular season with a 12-9 overall record.

One key to the success was winning at home. DePaul was 7-5 in Alumni Hall in 1956-57 and 8-5 there in 1957-58. The 1958-59 team went 9-2 at home.

The 12-9 overall mark was enough to get the Blue Demons in the NCAA tournament for the first time since 1956, but the return was far from home. DePaul was sent to Portland, Oregon, for its first round game, playing at Portland State. The Blue Demons won 57-56, advancing to the regional in Lawrence, Kansas.

Carl pops from outside.

Howie Carl ended his career second on the all-time DePaul scoring list with 1,461 points.

Carl drives to the hoop.

The success ended there as the Blue Demons were hammered 102-70 by Kansas State and lost 71-65 to Texas Christian to finish the campaign 13-11. After two losing seasons in a row, Meyer was pleased.

High scoring guard Carl averaged 19.2 per game, and was only a sophomore, giving the Blue Demons hope that the best was still to come.

Coming off a season in which it reached the NCAA tournament and returning leading scorer Howie Carl and team captain McKinley Cowsen, the 1959-60 DePaul team held high hopes. Those hopes were answered quickly.

After struggling out of the blocks for years, the Blue Demons again opened a season with a run of wins. DePaul won its first seven games, its best start since George Mikan and the 1945-46 team opened with eight straight wins.

The season opened with a 95-50 win over Illinois Wesleyan as Carl scored 20 points. Victories over Western Ontario, Bowling Green State and North Dakota made DePaul 4-0 prior to a home game with Purdue.

Carl scored 26 points and Cowsen 18 as the Blue Demons topped Purdue 87-65. The winning streak continued with victories over Ohio, Marquette and Baldwin Wallace.

A 75-74 homecourt loss to Louisville ended the winning run. A loss to Notre Dame was bracketed by victories over Western Kentucky and Valparaiso. A win over Miami (Ohio) improved DePaul to 10-2 and set up a big Alumni Hall showdown with Indiana. The Hoosiers walked away with an 82-78 win as Bill Haig's 21 points led the Blue Demons.

Three more victories, over Army, Louisville and Dayton, followed and gave the Blue Demons a 13-3 record. Losses at Notre Dame and Marquette cooled the team, but a return to Alumni Hall brought another victory. The Blue Demons topped Creighton 82-65 at home before losing to Dayton 67-66 to close the regular season 15-6 and earn a second straight NCAA berth.

Alumni Hall got its exposure to postseason play in that NCAA tourney. The Blue Demons were paired with Air Force in the opening round, and took a 69-63 win behind Carl's 24 points.

Advancing to the regionals, DePaul was sent to Manhattan, Kansas, to take on Cincinnati and All-America guard Oscar Robertson. But long before the game was played, the Blue Demons were black and blue.

After flying to Kansas City, the Blue Demons headed toward Manhattan by bus in a blinding snowstorm. The bus slid off the road and landed hard in a ditch. While major injuries were avoided, the team earned its share of bumps and bruises.

Meyer and his team was stranded overnight in a small county sheriff's office and huddled around a wood stove for heat. When a new bus finally arrived and the weather cleared, the team headed on, but was far from sharp against Cincinnati, losing 99-59. The regional consolation game was better as DePaul topped Texas 67-61 to close the year 17-7.

Carl averaged 19.7 per game to lead the team in scoring. Cowsen enjoyed his senior year with 10.2 rebounds per game to pace the squad.

When Ray Meyer took over as head coach at DePaul, he built his early teams around big men. With centers George Mikan and Ed Mikan leading the way, Meyer's first six teams were characterized by dominating play close to the basket.

After the Mikans left DePaul in 1948, the Blue Demons' style changed. In 1957, a pair of promising freshmen guards entered DePaul. Successful varsity seasons followed, and the 1960-61 year looked to be the best as guards Howie Carl and Bill Haig were now seniors.

Carl was one of the first great shooters at DePaul, firing away from all angles and capable of scoring big against any team. Haig was the forerunner of the great point guard. A solid dribbler and slashing penetrator, Haig quarterbacked the team and ran the offense.

Together, Carl and Haig averaged 32.0 points as sophomores and 32.2 points as juniors, reaching the NCAA tournament each season.

M.C. Thompson (30) has good position for the rebound against Louisville in 1961. DePaul ended the Cardinals 13-game win streak with a 78-70 victory.

They headed into their senior year looking to become the first DePaul class since George Mikan's to reach postseason three straight years.

Any doubts about the team were erased early. DePaul sprinted to an 11-0 record, its best since winning 13 straight to open the 1943-44 season (Meyer's second year).

The first eight games were at Alumni Hall. DePaul topped Baldwin Wallace, Illinois Wesleyan, North Dakota, Bowling Green State, Marquette, Miami (Ohio), Western Michigan and Western Ontario before hitting the road in January.

The Marquette game, played December 21 at Alumni Hall, turned into a Carl show. Carl tossed in 10 field goals and made 23 of 25 free throw attempts to score an Alumni Hall record 43 points in the Blue Demons' 81-78 win. Carl's point total was second only to the 53 George Mikan scored in the 1945 NIT. It would be over eighteen years before another Blue Demon topped 40 points in a game.

A two-game road swing brought two more wins. DePaul topped Dayton and Ohio before returning to Alumni Hall for a victory over Louisville, Meyer's 299th as head coach. Meyer's hope for number 300 and the dream of an unbeaten season ended at Notre Dame in the season's twelfth game. Carl was limited to 16 points as the Blue Demons lost 61-58.

Road losses at Western Michigan and Indiana kept the 300th win party on hold and left DePaul 11-3 heading into a home date with Christian Brothers. A 92-71 win gave Meyer the milestone and broke the losing run, but didn't turn the corner. Road losses at Western Kentucky and Marquette followed to make DePaul 12-5 with losses in five of its last six games.

Seven regular season games remained. The Blue Demons righted themselves to win five of those seven and end the campaign with a 17-7 record. Included in the final run was an Alumni Hall sweep of Notre Dame, Youngstown State, and Dayton to close the home year 14-0 and mark the first perfect home slate in five years in the building.

The regular season success earned the Blue Demons another postseason invitation, this time in the National Invitation Tournament. DePaul's first appearance in the prestigious NIT since the 1947-48 season was brief. The Blue Demons lost to Providence in the first round, only the second time in eight postseason berths under Meyer that DePaul lost its first round game.

The end of the season concluded the careers of Carl and Haig, but a young and talented group of players remained. After five years, Alumni Hall was becoming a real homecourt advantage. Ray Meyer's tough situation in leaving "The Barn" had been softened, and he headed toward his twentieth season as DePaul's head coach expecting continued success.

7

Guarding the Tradition

College basketball in the early 1960s was an offensive affair. Shots flew and points were scored. One of the big reasons was the influx of good scoring guards.

With the departure of graduating seniors Bill Haig and Howie Carl after the 1960-61 season, that era might have appeared to have ended at DePaul. It had not.

Although Haig and Carl were gone, DePaul still had outstanding guards. Perhaps the best was sophomore Emmette Bryant. A flashy ball handler, Bryant delighted in performing ball tricks like dribbling a pair of balls in practice and challenging players to steal one.

Bryant and the Blue Demons blasted out of the chute in 1961-62 with six consecutive victories. After opening with a 66-56 win at Minnesota, their first opening game on the road since 1943-44, the Blue Demons topped Lawrence Tech, North Dakota, Denver, and South Carolina, all at Alumni Hall.

The victories gave DePaul eighteen straight wins at home and set up a rematch with Providence, the team that had bounced DePaul from the National Invitation Tournament the previous season. The Blue Demons exacted revenge and kept both the season and home court winning streaks alive with a 68-63 decision.

The season winning streak came to a close in the next game, the opening round of Detroit's Motor City Tournament. DePaul was bumped by St. Bonaventure but rebounded to top Syracuse in the consolation game.

The Alumni Hall streak came to an end in the next game. Marquette claimed a 75-68 win to end the run at nineteen games. DePaul bounced right back to top Christian Brothers for an 8-2 record, but things were to change.

Indiana's Jimmy Rayl went for 41 points at Alumni Hall and the Blue Demons lost 98-89 to the Hoosiers. An 88-80 loss at Notre Dame

M.C. Thompson
Forward — 1960-63

M.C. Thompson is to rebounding at DePaul as Mark Aguirre is to scoring. In the early 1960s, Thompson set out to make every missed shot his personal property. And his rebounding prowess helped DePaul win 45 games and qualify twice for the NIT during his time at DePaul.

Thompson's first varsity season was the 1960-61 campaign. With guards Bill Haig and Howie Carl manning the backcourt, and Thompson the inside star, the Blue Demons went 17-8 and reached the NIT. Thompson averaged 15.0 points and a team-leading 13.3 rebounds per game. His rebounding total and per game average set school records.

Thompson broke his rebounding records the next year as he averaged 15.4 rebounds per game. The junior captain also scored 16.3 points per game. But despite Thompson's inspired play, DePaul slipped to 13-10 and missed postseason play.

Thompson returned as team captain in 1962-63, and the Blue Demons returned to the NIT. With Thompson averaging 15.6 points and 12.4 rebounds, DePaul finished at 15-8 and qualified for the NIT.

When his career ended with the 63-51 loss to Villanova in the NIT, Thompson had accumulated 1,111 career points and a school record 972 rebounds. He is still the holder of school records in rebounding average for both a single season and career. He was drafted by the New York Knicks after his graduation.

---

followed with Alumni Hall losses to Louisville and Dayton.

The Dayton defeat was a 90-88 decision in double overtime. Bryant finished with 37 points, but his season was about to end as he was declared ineligible.

Wins over Baldwin Wallace and Western Kentucky helped right the ship and gave DePaul a 10-6 record. The next game took three overtimes, but the Blue Demons topped Louisville 79-78 for their eleventh victory.

A three-game losing streak dulled the season, dropping DePaul to 11-9 before Alumni Hall wins over Western Ontario and Notre Dame. The campaign ended with a 77-61 loss at Dayton.

With a 13-10 overall mark, the Blue Demons spent postseason at home for the first time since 1958. Leaping forward M.C. Thompson led the team in both scoring and rebounding. Thompson, a junior and team captain, averaged 16.3 points and a school record 15.4 rebounds.

Whatever promise went unanswered in 1961-62 was transferred to the 1962-63 season. Forward M.C. Thompson returned for his senior year and second season as a team captain. Veterans Dick Cook and Bill Debes were seniors. A talented junior class included Emmette Bryant, eligible again, and among the sophomores were Jim Murphy and Jesse Nash.

Like so many of Ray Meyer's other teams, this one opened the season hot. Eight consecutive wins included Alumni Hall decisions over Minnesota and Marquette and the Motor City Tournament in Detroit brought victories over Western Michigan and Detroit.

Bryant scored 26 points against both Minnesota and Marquette. Thompson poured in 21 against Western Michigan, including the deciding pair with nine seconds left, as the Blue Demons claimed a 91-90 overtime decision. Cook scored 22 against Detroit as DePaul claimed the tourney title.

A two-game series against Notre Dame was next. In the first game, at Notre Dame, the Blue Demons dropped an 82-62 game as they hit only 12 of 25 free throws. The second contest, at Alumni Hall, went to DePaul 83-69 as Thompson exploded for 33 points.

A pair of road games provided some thrills.

The Blue Demons dropped a 57-56 game at Dayton and a 76-75 contest at Indiana to fall 9-3.

Wins over Bowling Green State and Louisville were followed by road losses at Providence, St. Bonaventure, and Marquette. DePaul was 11-6 and Bryant was again out of action, this time idled by hepatitis following the Baldwin Wallace game early in the season.

Despite the adversity, the Blue Demons won four of their last five games. With a 15-7 overall record, DePaul earned a berth to the NIT.

DePaul's opening round game was against Villanova. The Wildcats relied on guards Jones and Erickson for scoring punch.

Villanova's twin-gun attack proved more potent than DePaul's balanced one. Behind Jones' 28 points and Erickson's 18, Villanova won 63-51. DePaul had four players score in double figures, led by Thompson with 11 points and 10 rebounds.

Thompson paced the balanced team for the season also with 15.6 points and 12.4 rebounds, graduating with a career rebounding average of 13.7 per game.

Depth was a strength of the 1963-64 Blue Demons. Despite losing Dick Cook and M.C. Thompson to graduation, the Blue Demons returned Emmette Bryant and versatile Denny Freund as team captains for the 1963-64 season. Jim Murphy and Jesse Nash were seasoned juniors.

Among the sophomores were talented Don Swanson and Dave Mills. A 6-foot-10 center, Mills was DePaul's first long distance recruit, a native of Tuscon, Arizona.

While Ray Meyer traveled the farthest to recruit Mills, he traveled the least to recruit another talented sophomore. Tom Meyer, the coach's son, became the first of three Meyer children to play varsity basketball at DePaul. He averaged 5.5 points in 22 games during the 1963-64 season.

Murphy and Bryant combined to give DePaul an outstanding guard combination in the Bill Haig/Howie Carl tradition. Freund also played guard, and Meyer often played all three at the same time. Mills played up front along with Swanson and Nash.

Tom Meyer was the first of Ray's sons to play at DePaul.

That kind of depth paid big dividends. A 13 game winning streak established the Blue Demons as one of the nation's top teams.

DePaul was 6-0 when it traveled to Buffalo, New York, for the Queen City Tournament. Freund and Murphy scored 20 each as the Blue Demons topped Canisius 102-79. Bryant hit 13 of 15 free throws and scored 31 points in the title game as DePaul beat Xavier (Ohio) 86-80. Bryant was named tourney Most Valuable Player.

Following a win at Western Kentucky, Murphy, Mills and Bryant each topped 20 points at Notre Dame in an 86-73 DePaul victory. Alumni Hall wins over Portland, Dayton, and Indiana gave the Blue Demons a 13-0 record.

But DePaul suffered a big loss against Indiana. Bryant suffered a fractured leg early in the second half against Indiana and wouldn't return until late in the season. After missing part of his sophomore year ineligible and most of his junior year with hepatitis, Bryant had hoped his senior year would be free from injury. Like that dream, the hope for an unbeaten

The Marquette players look in awe as Dick Cook skies to the hoop in this 1964 game.

Jim Murphy attempts the shot block as Jesse Nash (24) and Emmette Bryant (4) get ready for the rebound. DePaul beat Providence, 82-64, to move to 5-0 at the start of the 1963-64 season.

Jesse Nash averaged 12.4 rebounds per game during the 1963-64 season. Here he grabs a one-hander away from two Duquesne players.

season ended with an 83-79 loss to Louisville at Alumni Hall in the next game.

A win over Notre Dame improved DePaul to 14-1, but the Blue Demons lost at Memphis State. A six-game winning streak followed, including a 70-66 victory at Louisville, making DePaul 20-2 and giving the Blue Demons their first twenty win season since the 1947-48 season.

A chance to tie the school record of 22 victories in regular season ended when the Blue Demons lost at Bowling Green State, but a win at Dayton closed the regular season with a 21-3 record. DePaul was ranked ninth nationally in the final Associated Press poll that year and could have played in either the NCAA tournament or the NIT.

The Blue Demons selected the NIT, earning a first round pairing with New York University at Madison Square Garden. Bryant was back in the lineup, but managed just seven points in the 79-66 loss.

After winning at least one postseason game in each of his first five appearances, Meyer now had lost his opening round playoff game in four of his last six appearances.

Nash led the team with 17.5 points and 12.4 rebounds per game. As a team, the Blue Demons averaged 85.7 points per game, a school record. With a 21-4 overall record, they became the first DePaul team since the 1945 NIT champions to lose fewer than five games in a season.

As the 1964-65 season opened at DePaul, a pattern was developing. As good players graduated and left the Blue Demons, other talented ones were joining the varsity club.

That was certainly true in 1964-65. Although Emmette Bryant and Denny Freund were gone, the Blue Demons remained well stocked. Veterans Jim Murphy, Jesse Nash, Dave Mills, Don Swanson, and Tom Meyer provided a nucleus that was supplemented by sophomores Mike Norris and Errol Palmer.

The 1964-65 start wasn't as fast as some other recent ones, but DePaul did go 4-0 before losing consecutive games at Indiana and Louisville. A win over Seattle made the Blue Demons 5-1 heading to the Oklahoma City Tournament.

Senior captain Jim Murphy pulls up for a jump shot versus Middle Tennessee during the 1964-65 season. Murphy helped lead DePaul to an 89-68 victory.

Playing in tournaments was a pleasure for the Blue Demons. Heading to Oklahoma City, DePaul had claimed the championship the last two inseason tournaments in which the Blue Demons had played. That run moved to three as the Blue Demons topped Florida State, Brigham Young, and Oklahoma City to improve to 8-1 on the season.

A three-game home stand brought wins over Marquette, Memphis State, and Western Ontario. A win at Dayton made the Blue Demons 12-1. A loss at Duquesne followed, but a pair of wins over Bowling Green State and Niagara at Alumni Hall gave the Blue Demons a 14-2 mark.

Success was limited the rest of the regular season. A four-game road swing opened with consecutive losses at Providence, Villanova, and Notre Dame before a win at Marquette snapped the streak. Wins over Portland and Dayton were sandwiched around an Alumni Hall loss to Notre Dame to give DePaul a 16-8 regular season record.

The team was rewarded with a berth in the NCAA tournament. Playing in the first round in Bowling Green, Kentucky, the Blue Demons

Coach Meyer with some of the 1964-65 team members (from left): Jim Murphy, Terry Flanagan, Don Swanson, Dave Mills, and Errol Palmer.

topped Eastern Kentucky 99-52 as Dave Mills had 21 points and Errol Palmer 13 rebounds.

DePaul advanced to the regionals in Lexington, Kentucky to meet Vanderbilt. Despite giving away over four inches to the Vanderbilt front line, Palmer responded with 28 points and 19 rebounds. It wasn't enough though, as the Blue Demons lost 83-78 in overtime as both Mills and Palmer fouled out. The regional consolation game was a 75-69 loss to Dayton, closing the year at 17-10.

Despite the slow closing to the year, the season was a positive. By earning an NCAA bid, the Blue Demons had made their third straight postseason appearance and their sixth such trip in a seven-year span.

Murphy, the team captain, led the scoring parade with 17.5 points per game. Palmer began his assault on the rebounding record with 11.2 per game, including a high of 25 at Notre Dame.

The Blue Demons of the mid 1940s were able to achieve greatness behind the play of Hall of Fame center George Mikan. DePaul made three straight trips to postseason play in Ray Meyer's first three years as head coach, but did not get a berth in the fourth season.

The period of DePaul basketball around 1960 was headlined by the great play of guards Bill Haig and Howie Carl. These high scoring teams earned postseason bids three straight years, but were unable to get a fourth straight invitation.

With three straight trips to postseason tourneys, the 1965-66 Blue Demons were gunning to become the first DePaul team to get that fourth straight ticket to postseason action. Senior captains Don Swanson and Tom Meyer headed the team that took aim at the record.

In typical DePaul fashion, the season opened with a winning streak, this time seven games. The Blue Demons won at Marquette as Swanson scored 19 points and beat Louisville at home behind Meyer's 25 points.

The perfect streak was on the line as the Blue Demons headed to Jacksonville, Florida, for the Gator Bowl Tournament. Another streak on the line was an eight-game winning run in inseason tournaments. The Blue Demons hadn't lost in an inseason tournament since the opening round contest of the 1961-62 Motor City Tournament in Detroit.

Local favorite Florida ended both streaks with a 72-64 win in the Gator Bowl Tournament first round, but the Blue Demons rebounded with an 80-64 decision over Alabama in the consolation game. Heading from the warmth of Florida to the cold of North Dakota, the Blue Demons lost again, this time dropping an 85-74 decision to North Dakota and coach Bill Fitch.

The losing stretch drew to three in four games as the Blue Demons lost to Dayton in Alumni Hall before running off another five-game winning streak. The Blue Demons stood 13-3 heading to St. Bonaventure.

Mills' 20 point effort wasn't enough as DePaul lost 73-69, but the Blue Demons rebounded with wins over Marquette and Bowling Green State to improve to 15-4 with six games remaining. After losing to Providence at Alumni Hall, the Blue Demons responded with victories over Duquesne and Notre Dame.

A 76-73 loss at Dayton started a spin. The Blue Demons closed the regular season with two more losses, dropping home games to Steubenville and Villanova. Despite losing its last three games, DePaul finished the regular season with an 18-7 record.

That was enough to get the Blue Demons their fourth straight trip to postseason play. DePaul accepted another trip to the NIT, but as in 1964, the Blue Demons were paired with hometown New York University at Madison Square Garden. An 88-65 loss ended the year with a four-game losing streak and an 18-8 record.

Swanson averaged 18.0 points per game in his senior year to lead the team. Palmer led the squad in rebounding with 12.5 per game, his second straight year as the top rebounder.

Palmer missed three games after breaking the wrist of his shooting hand. He came back to play with the injured hand in a cast and shot free throws left handed in a game at Notre Dame to help the team preserve a 79-71 win.

The 1966-67 season dawned at DePaul as the twenty-fifth year for head coach Ray Meyer. Meyer brought 388 career victories into the year, needing just a dozen to top the 400 mark.

In his first twenty-four years, Meyer had taken twelve teams to postseason play. He won the NIT championship in 1945, placed second in 1944, and was the fourth place finisher in the 1943 NCAA tournament.

Meyer's last four teams had reached postseason play heading into the 1966-67 season, but with the loss of Don Swanson and Tom

Despite Errol Palmer (41) missing three games because of a broken wrist, DePaul went to its fourth straight postseason tournament in 1966.

The 1966-67 DePaul team went 17-8, including Ray Meyer's 400th victory of his career. Front Row (from left): Ken Johnston, Errol Palmer, Mike Norris, Rich Shealey, Tom Kilmartin, George Poulos, Pete Ortolano. Middle Row (from left): Rich Beach, Bob Zoretich, Ray Meyer, Gessel Berry. Back Row (from left): Bob Mattingly, John Naughton, Rich Witkowski, Al Zetzsche.

George Poulos (12) hurries the ball up court as Errol Palmer (40) trails the action.

Mike Norris, the leading scorer for the Blue Demons in 1967, takes off for a layup against USC. DePaul lost for the first time during the 1966-67 game versus the Trojans, 82-79.

Meyer, the coming year figured to be a challenge. The challenge started early.

After winning at least its first four games for seven straight years, the Blue Demons tasted an early defeat in 1966-67. Wins over North Dakota and St. John's (Minn.) were followed by an 82-79 loss to Southern California at Alumni Hall.

The Blue Demons returned with a home court win over Baldwin Wallace and a victory at Villanova to take a 4-1 record to the Oklahoma City Tournament. With wins in nine of their last ten inseason tournament games, the Blue Demons looked like tourney favorites. They didn't play like it.

Stanford topped the Blue Demons in the opening round and when Massachusetts took a consolation bracket game, DePaul was playing for seventh place with a 5-3 overall record. The Blue Demons took a win from Arizona in that game and returned home 6-3.

A win over Bellarmine was followed by a road loss to Marquette. The next six games brought just three wins, making DePaul 10-7 with eight games to play.

Meyer earned his 399th career victory at Notre Dame with a 56-49 win. Win number 400 came in the next game, a 71-60 victory over St. Xavier. Mike Norris, a senior team captain, led the way with 20 points.

DePaul won three of its final five games to close the year with a 17-8 record, but it wasn't enough to keep the postseason streak alive. After earning berths four straight years and seven times in eight seasons, the Blue Demons watched the NCAA and NIT.

Mike Norris averaged 17.2 points and Errol Palmer 11.3 rebounds to lead the team. Palmer ended his career second only to M.C. Thompson in total rebounds.

After the 1966-67 season, the Blue Demons had posted a winning record nine straight years. DePaul won 148 games in that period, an average of over 16 per year, and won at least 60 percent of its contests in seven of the nine seasons.

After 1966-67, DePaul would not see postseason action again for eight seasons. It would take seven for the team to get to the 60 percent mark again. After twenty-five years as head coach, and with over 400 career victories, Ray Meyer was about to begin the toughest stretch of his career.

8

Hard Times

On college campuses throughout the country, the late 1960s were a tumultuous time. By 1967, demonstrations against the United States participation in the war in Vietnam were becoming wide spread on college campuses from coast to coast. Although many things, on the surface, looked the same, change was in the air.

That was particularly true for the DePaul basketball team. Fresh from a ninth consecutive winning season, the Blue Demons appeared a lock to continue that run of success.

The Blue Demons opened the 1967-68 season with a seven-game homestand much like previous years. DePaul sprinted to four straight wins before dropping an 82-77 decision to Loyola Marymount. Wins over Tennessee Tech and Bellarmine made the Blue Demons 6-1 and off to their typical flying start.

A loss at Marquette was followed by a win over Wisconsin-Milwaukee to make DePaul 7-2 heading into a stretch of three road games in four contests. The stretch started poorly as St. Bonaventure won 77-67 behind 25 points by star center Bob Lanier. A home court loss to Notre Dame made DePaul 7-4, but the losing streak stopped at Niagara in the next game.

Niagara's star guard Calvin Murphy exploded for 36 points, but Tom Tracy answered with 24 and Bob Zoretich 23 for the Blue Demons in the 79-72 DePaul win. A 70-65 win at Dayton, the 1967 NCAA tournament runner up came next, followed by homecourt wins over Illinois Wesleyan, Northern Illinois, and Indiana.

The hot streak left DePaul 12-4 and looking toward another postseason berth. Looks can be deceiving.

A seven-game losing streak stunned the team. After losing 97-78 at Xavier (Ohio) and 58-53 at home to Marquette, the Blue Demons played into overtime at Notre Dame before fall-

Members of the 1967-68 team that finished 13-12 (from left): Ray Meyer, Tom Hunter, Al Zetzsche, Bob Mattingly, Rich Schealey, and George Poulos.

ing 91-85. Despite the streak, things could still get better. The 12-7 Blue Demons were coming home for a four game stand in Alumni Hall.

It wasn't the answer. Villanova, Providence, Duquesne, and Dayton all escaped with wins. DePaul was 12-11 and heading on the road for the season's final two games. A losing season, the first since 1957-58, looked possible.

One of the wildest games in school history kept it from happening. The Blue Demons trailed Detroit 47-46 at the half, but rallied behind Tracy to tie the game at 89 and force overtime. Tracy kept scoring in the extra frame, again tying the game at the end and forcing a second overtime. Finally, with Tracy scoring 30 and Al Zetzsche adding 29, the Blue Demons ended the fifty-minute marathon with a 111-107 victory. Tracy hit 8 of 12 free throws, two at the end of regulation, two at the end of the first overtime, and two at the end of the second extra period to clinch the win.

Drained by the experience, the Blue Demons were hammered 89-61 by Bowling Green State in the next game, but finished the season 13-12 to preserve the winning season streak.

Zetzsche led the scoring parade for the season with 15.3 points per game. Sophomore Ken Warzynski, picking up pursuit of the rebounding records from graduated forward Errol Palmer, averaged 9.4 boards to lead the pack.

Although there weren't any seven game losing streaks, the 1968-69 season looked much like the previous year. After a hot start, the

Blue Demons stumbled a bit but finished with a winning record.

DePaul was 5-0 on a season opening home stand before heading to Philadelphia for the Quaker City Tournament. An opening round loss to St. Joseph's (Pa.) was followed by wins over Rhode Island and Penn State, giving DePaul fifth place in the tourney and a 7-1 record heading home for a pair of contests.

The Blue Demons topped Northern Illinois in the first game, but fell to Marquette 77-72. A loss at Notre Dame followed, making them 8-3 with visions of another seven game skid looming.

The visions weren't to come true. An 86-77 defeat to Xavier (Ohio), the team that started previous year's slide, helped avert disaster as losses to Dayton, Villanova, Indiana and Providence followed. DePaul was 9-7 while preparing for a three-game homestand.

The home cooking helped ease the pain. DePaul won two of three, but lost at Marquette to slip to 11-9 with five games to play.

Three of the final five were at home, and the Blue Demons swept those three including a thrilling 72-71 overtime win over St. Bonaventure. Road losses at Duquesne and Dayton balanced the final stretch and gave the Blue Demons a 14-11 record.

Al Zetzsche led in scoring for the second straight year with 17.4 points per game. Ken Warzynski led in rebounding for the second straight season as well with 11.0 per game.

The 1968-69 season also marked the second time in his career that Ray Meyer coached one of his sons. Joey Meyer was a sophomore guard on the team, averaging 13.8 points in 25 games.

Although the 1967-68 and 1968-69 season weren't the most successful ones in Ray Meyer's tenure as head coach, they were winning seasons. Heading into the 1969-70 campaign, DePaul had posted a winning record in eleven straight years, just two short of the school record thirteen straight winning campaigns set from 1928-29 to 1940-41. With veteran leaders like Tom Tracy and Ken Warzynski along with a developing playmaker at guard in Joey Meyer, the 1969-70 team seemed to have a great chance at continuing the streak.

Ken Warzynski
Center — 1967-70

At 6-foot-7 and 220 pounds, Ken Warzynski looked like a rugged inside player. But looks can often be deceiving. In his case, they weren't. For his entire varsity career at DePaul, Warzynski was the consummate warrior in the paint, going after the loose ball and scoring off the offensive glass. And, somewhat surprisingly, Warzynski was also a good perimeter shooter.

Warzynski quickly made his mark as a Blue Demon. In his sophomore year he averaged 13.9 points per game and 9.4 rebounds. But the Blue Demons suffered through a tough season, finishing just 13-12.

The Blue Demons improved somewhat in 1968-69, posting a 14-11 record. And much of that improvement can be traced to Warzynski's play. He increased his offensive output to 14.5 points per game and averaged an impressive 11.0 rebounds per game.

Warzynski continued to improve in his senior year. He averaged 19.6 points and 15.2 rebounds per game, leading the team in both categories. And on Jan 3, 1970, Warzynski set a team record by gathering in 28 rebounds versus Harvard. The Harvard game went a lot like the rest of the season. Despite the yoeman's work by Warzynski, DePaul lost the Harvard game 90-84; and the Blue Demons finished the season at 12-13.

Warzynski ended his college career with 1,203 points to make him the fifth leading scorer in DePaul history at the time. His 890 career rebounds were second all-time. Today Warzynski still holds DePaul records for rebounds in a game and in a season (379).

Joey Meyer (30), Paul Gilliam (32), Ken Lydecker (14), and Ed Goode (22) were all key contributors on the 1970-71 team.

The early season brought success. DePaul opened on the road for only the fourth time in Meyer's twenty-eight years as head coach, winning at Michigan Lutheran. The Blue Demons came home for nine in a row.

The first six were winners, making DePaul 7-0, before losing to Providence, St. Joseph's, and Harvard in consecutive games. A win at Xavier (Ohio) did little to improve things as losses to Marquette, Notre Dame, Dayton, and St. Bonaventure followed. The promising start was lost as DePaul fell to 8-7.

The Blue Demons rallied a bit with three straight wins, topping Indiana, Northern Illinois, and Missouri-St. Louis at Alumni Hall. They would win only one more time, and when Villanova walked out of Alumni Hall with a 102-90 win in the season's final game, the streak of winning seasons had ended.

Despite the 12-13 record, Warzynski had a great individual season. The 6-foot-7 center averaged 19.6 points and 15.2 rebounds per game. Warzynski closed his career as the second leading rebounder all time, trailing M.C. Thompson but just ahead of Errol Palmer.

Talk about your stacked decks. The 1970-71 season was looking tough long before the opening tip. Not only had star Ken Warzynski finished his career, but the school had quit giving athletic scholarships. Ray Meyer's twenty-ninth year as head coach would be one in which he'd play against full scholarship teams with one that consisted primarily of walk ons.

But there were some talented players. Meyer's son, Joey, was team captain and a starting guard. Harry Shields and Al Burks were young but gifted. Still, the Blue Demons just didn't have enough weapons to compete against the top college programs.

The Blue Demons were marginally successful in the early season, posting a 2-2 record in their first four games. A trip to the Kentucky Invitational ended with two losses. A home court win over Spring Hill made DePaul 3-4 heading to the All-College Tournament in Oklahoma City. Three losses followed, making DePaul 3-7 and heading home for a pair.

Wins over Illinois Wesleyan and St. Joseph's (Ind.) improved DePaul to 5-7, but a tough stretch was ahead. That stretch was a killer as the Blue Demons dropped eight straight and locked a second straight losing season.

But the end of the campaign brought some hope. DePaul won three of its last five to finish with an 8-17 record, setting a school record for most losses in a season and posting the lowest winning percentage since the 1927-28 team was 2-5.

Despite that, Joey Meyer had an outstanding senior season. Meyer averaged 19.2 points and finished his career with 1,233 points. Only George Mikan, Howie Carl and Jim Lamkin had scored more.

The 1970-71 season wasn't marked by tremendous success on the court, but perhaps the biggest win in the program's history came off the court. With scholarships banned and the team losing, the university considered dropping basketball from Division I to either Division II or Division III.

After much consideration, the decision was made to give the sport three more years to make good. Scholarships were returned and, for the first time, Meyer was given funding for a full-time assistant coach.

Meyer didn't use the money to hire one coach. He split it to hire two. One was Dr. Ken

Father and son—Joey and Ray Meyer.

Joey Meyer
Guard — 1968-71

For most, the image of Joey Meyer at DePaul is an image of a man in a suit sitting on the bench and coaching. And there is good reason for that image. Since 1971, Meyer has been on the Blue Demon's bench, first as an assistant coach and, since 1984, as head coach.

Long before Meyer donned the sport coat and grabbed a clipboard, he was a DePaul player, and a very good one. A Chicago native who attended DePaul Academy, Meyer came to the university in 1967 and moved to the varsity team for the 1968-69 season.

Meyer immediately showed himself to be a complete player. A good penetrator as well as a shooter, he averaged 13.8 points per game as a sophomore while making the fewest turnovers among the starters and leading the team in assists.

His scoring improved to 16.2 in 1969-70 while again leading the team in assists and making the fewest turnovers among the starters. Meyer's senior year was his best yet as he averaged 19.2 points and hit 80 percent from the free throw line while serving as team captain.

At the conclusion of his career Meyer had scored 1,233 points, the fourth highest total in DePaul history at the time. He also stood eighth in career free throw percentage, hitting 76 percent.

Despite Meyer's efforts, the Blue Demons struggled from 1968 to 1971. The 1968-69 squad went 14-11, and their record fell to 12-13 the following year. Meyer's senior year ended with an 8-17 mark, setting a school record for most losses in a season.

Whatever team success Meyer wasn't able to reach as a player, he more than reached as a coach. As an assistant, he was on the bench as the Blue Demons reached postseason play eight times in nine seasons. Included in that stretch was an NCAA Final Four appearance in 1979.

As a head coach, Meyer owns a 148-70 record after seven seasons and has averaged more wins per season than any other DePaul coach. And in each of those seven years, DePaul has gone on to a postseason tournament, including six trips to the NCAA tournament.

Sarubbi, DePaul's director of physical education. The other was the familiar face of Joey Meyer.

After graduating from DePaul, the younger Meyer had considered attending Northwestern University to be an assistant basketball coach and work on his master's degree in physical education. When the position was created at DePaul, he agreed to become head coach of the freshman team as well as a varsity assistant and scout.

With only three years to prove themselves, Meyer, Meyer, and Sarubbi needed immediate results. They didn't get them early in the 1971-72 season.

After opening with a win over Rocky Mountain, the Blue Demons lost three straight to Niagara, St. Bonaventure, and Providence.

Things improved after that as the team topped Parsons, Dubuque and St. Joseph's (Ind.) to go to 4-3 and set up a big road game at Dayton. Nick Hirtzig scored 20 points and Al Burks 18 as DePaul was up to the task and topped the Flyers 75-72.

A win over Wisconsin-Green Bay at Alumni Hall made DePaul 6-3 with a five game winning streak. That streak ended with a loss at Marquette, but a four game home stand followed. DePaul split that home stand but lost a pair at South Carolina and Notre Dame to fall to 8-8 with seven games remaining.

A game against Northwestern at Chicago Stadium, DePaul's first appearance in that building since the 1955-56 season, was next. Burks scored 24 points and Mike Gillespie 22 in De-Paul's 74-72 win. Hirtzig scored 18, including the deciding basket. Wins over Lewis and Duquesne made DePaul 10-8, but a three game losing streak followed. The Blue Demons were 10-11 and needed to sweep their final two games at Alumni Hall to post a winning record.

They took care of business in the first game by topping North Carolina-Charlotte 94-83. The final game pitted DePaul against Drake, and with Burks exploding for 32 points, the Blue Demons won 94-76 to finish the year 13-12. Burks averaged 20.3 points and 8.3 rebounds to lead the team in both categories.

While having a varsity winning record was nice, the thing that had the coaches smiling the most was the freshman team Joey Meyer coached. Led by talents like Greg Boyd and Bill Robinzine, the freshman team was 25-1.

Robinzine, whose father Bill played for DePaul in the 1950s, came to DePaul by chance. A 6-foot-7, 225-pound walk on, Robinzine had concentrated on music at Phillips High School in Chicago. He was an excellent trumpet player who grew to be a great basketball player.

When the Blue Demons made their major improvement in 1942-43 season under rookie head coach Ray Meyer, they did it on the back of freshman center George Mikan. But college basketball rules changed soon after, and freshmen weren't eligible to play varsity basketball. That changed in 1972-73, and DePaul immediately reaped the benefits.

While the change wasn't as severe as when Mikan and Meyer came together some thirty years earlier, the improvement in 1972-73 was apparent. Team captains Al Burks and Harry Shields were joined by veterans Nick Hirtzig, Mike Gillespie and Doug Bruno as well as talented sophomore Greg Boyd and Bill Robinzine. Added to the mix was freshman Andy Pancratz, a 6-foot-9 center.

The new look Blue Demons were hot at the start of the season. DePaul topped St. Mary's (Minn.) and Northwestern for a 2-0 start as Boyd poured in 32 points against Northwestern. A loss to Drake didn't dampen things, as the Blue Demons responded with three more victories and a 5-1 record.

Despite a 107-80 loss at Providence, DePaul remained hot with three more wins and an 8-2 record. That set up a big game at Marquette, ranked second nationally at the time and owners of a 79-game home court winning streak.

After trailing by seven in the second half, the Blue Demons rallied for a 59-58 lead in the final seconds on a free throw by Bruno. But Marquette had the answer with a follow up basket by Larry McNeill with nine seconds remaining for a 60-59 win.

The loss staggered the Blue Demons, who after a win over Westmont, dropped six in a row and stood 9-9 with seven games remaining.

Wins over Xavier (Ohio) and Villanova broke the streak, but losses to North Carolina-Charlotte and Wisconsin-Green Bay bracketed a win over Lewis to make DePaul 12-11. The final two games resulted in wins over Niagara and Toledo and gave DePaul a 14-11 record, its best record since the 1968-69 season when the Blue Demons were also 14-11.

But even more important was the ground work that was being laid. Boyd averaged 17.5 points per game, and was just a sophomore. Robinzine led with 10.1 rebounds, and was a sophomore as well. One more year remained on the three-year commitment. The improvement was obvious.

Hopes ran high before the 1973-74 season. Captain Mike Gillespie had a solid team surrounding him, including juniors Bill Robinzine and Greg Boyd. Andy Pancratz was a budding sophomore star. But pre-season optimism looked unfounded early in the season.

DePaul was just 3-3 after six games and had lost 96-61 to Tennessee and 102-93 to Utah State at the Volunteer Classic in Knoxville, Tenn. A split in the next four games kept DePaul at .500 with a 5-5 record following the Hall of Fame tournament in Springfield, Massachusetts.

The team crawled above the break even point with road wins at St. Joseph's (Ind.), Niagara, and St. Bonaventure. Robinzine scored 28 and Boyd 25 in the victory over Niagara, coached by Frank Layden. Jim Bocinsky poured in 19 before fouling out at St. Bonaventure as the

Blue Demons survived losing Pancratz and Robinzine to fouls as well in their 79-77 win.

A loss at Marquette was followed by home court wins over Marshall and Lewis to make the Blue Demons 10-6. A three-game losing streak followed, but DePaul got hot to end the year.

The Blue Demons closed the campaign with a six-game winning streak. The team ended with 16-9 record, its first time winning over 60 percent since the 1966-67 season. Robinzine led in both scoring and rebounding with 16.8 points and 10.2 rebounds per game.

Given a three year reprieve, Ray Meyer posted a 42-31 record, compared to a 34-41 mark the previous three years. With assistant coaches Sarubbi and Joey Meyer helping him and players like Robinzine, Boyd and Pancratz coming to DePaul, Ray Meyer had saved DePaul basketball from extinction. Now, it was time to flourish.

9

The Chicago Gang

The life blood of a college basketball program is recruiting. To be successful at the upper level of competition, a team has to have top flight talent.

In the early days, recruiting at DePaul was limited to Ray Meyer contacting Chicago area high school coaches, particularly those at Catholic schools. This was how most of Meyer's players had come to DePaul through the 1960s.

Meyer was limited in his ability to recruit out of town players. DePaul didn't have on campus dormitories until the early 1970s, and without a place to live, it was nearly impossible to recruit out of town players.

Also, as the DePaul program was waning in the late 1960s, college basketball as a whole was growing. As more and more teams put an emphasis on basketball, more and more coaches came to Chicago to sift through the talent pool and take the best players.

Against this background, Meyer and his assistant coaches started aggressively recruiting both locally and nationally. The local recruiting paid dividends when players like Andy Pancratz came to DePaul in 1972.

The pearl of the 1973 recruiting class for DePaul was, for a change, from out of state. Ron Norwood, a guard from East Orange, New Jersey, became the first of many players from that state to come to DePaul.

Coach Meyer stayed home in 1974 and signed a trio of Chicago area stars—Dave Corzine (Hersey), Joe Ponsetto (Provisio East), and Randy Ramsey (Thornton). It was this group that would put DePaul on the national map.

The newcomers joined a group of talented veterans. Greg Boyd, Jim Bocinsky, and Bill Robinzine were team captains and Andy Pancratz an experienced junior.

With better players in the fold, Meyer tackled a tougher schedule. UCLA, which had won the

Bill Robinzine
Forward — 1972-75

It has become a tradition at DePaul to include at least one walkon on the basketball squad each year. Chosen from a pool of candidates who try out, the walkon usually is limited to playing the final seconds of blowouts and filling the role of a practice player.

But every once in a while, a walkon comes along who can really contribute to the team's success. Such was the case with Bill Robinzine.

When Robinzine walked into Ray Meyer's office and asked for a tryout, he stood 6-foot-7 and weighed over 225 pounds. He owned international playing experience having played on a South American tour. But what Robinzine played on that tour was the trumpet.

An accomplished musician, Robinzine had limited basketball experience when he stepped into Meyer's office. But he did have some basketball lineage; he had been sent to the Blue Demons' mentor by his father, Bill, who had played at DePaul from 1953 to 1956.

Once Robinzine traded his trumpet for a pair of sneakers, things started to pick up for the Blue Demons. The 1972-73 DePaul squad posted a 14-11 record in Robinzine's first season. And Robinzine averaged 13.2 points per game and 10.1 rebounds.

During the offseason, Robinzine and fellow Blue Demon pivot Andy Pancratz participated in a benefit game in Gary, Indiana. The game was not sanctioned by the NCAA, and when their participation was reported, Robinzine and Pancratz were both hit with month long suspensions to open the 1973-74 season.

Without the two big men, DePaul struggled to a 5-5 record. But when Robinzine and Pancratz returned, the Blue Demons came on strong to finish 16-9 on the season. Robinzine was again a tough inside performer, amassing 10.2 rebounds per game and 16.8 points.

Robinzine served as a team captain in 1974-75, his senior year, and he certainly was an on court leader. He poured in points at the rate of 19.4 a game, and collected 13.5 rebounds per game. He also hit 51 percent from the field and 74 percent at the line as DePaul finished 15-10, with four of those losses coming by three points or less.

Following the season Robinzine was selected by the Kansas City Kings in the first round of the NBA draft. The tenth selection overall, Robinzine was the first Blue Demon taken in the first round. He went on to play seven years in the league, averaging 10.5 points and 6.1 rebounds a game for his career. His finest season was in 1979 when he averaged a career high 13.4 points per game, along with 7.8 rebounds for the Kings. Not bad for a trumpet player.

NCAA tournament championship nine of the previous eleven years, was added to the slate as the season opener on the road. Other road trips included visits to Washington State, Providence, Marshall, Virginia Tech, and Cincinnati.

The result of playing a team as good as UCLA right out of the chute was the Blue Demons first loss in an opener in Meyer's tenure. But DePaul bounced back with five wins in six tries for a 5-2 record heading to Providence.

The fifth win of the year, a 75-73 overtime victory over San Jose State, was the 499th career coaching victory for Meyer, in his thirty-third season as head coach. He needed to win at Providence, December 21, to get number 500 as a Christmas present.

Christmas would have to come late for Ray Meyer this year. Despite 21 points from Corzine, the Blue Demons fell 85-71 and forced the party to be delayed.

The next shot for the milestone was December 28 when Marshall came to Alumni Hall. With a victory, Meyer would become only the eleventh coach to win 500 games at the major college level. Little doubt remained after an

Greg Boyd
Guard — 1972-75

An excellent ball handler and shooter, Greg Boyd turned in a stellar varsity career in the early 1970s for DePaul. Boyd was a mainstay at guard as the Blue Demons posted three straight winning seasons from 1972 to 1975.

Boyd's finest season scoring wise came as a sophomore in 1972-73 as he averaged 17.5 points per game for the 14-11 Blue Demons. One of his finest games in a Blue Demon uniform occurred late in the season as DePaul traveled to Villanova. In front of a hostile crowd, Boyd scored 32 points as the Blue Demons defeated the Wildcats 89-80.

Boyd's scoring average dropped to 15.8 points per game as a junior but the Blue Demons improved to 16-9. It was the first time since the 1966-67 season that they finished with fewer than ten losses. And in order to accomplish the feat, DePaul won their final six games of the season.

For the opening of the 1974-75 season, Boyd was named a team co-captain. Interestingly, the opening game of the season was against UCLA. The Bruins' streak of seven consecutive NCAA titles had been broken the previous season, and they had only one returning starter from that team. But UCLA proved too much for Boyd and company as DePaul lost 79-64. The game was significant for one other reason. It marked the only time Ray Meyer coached against John Wooden.

Boyd averaged just 10.9 points per game on the season, but his all-around play helped DePaul go 15-10. Boyd joined the 1,000 club during the season and ended his career with 1,106 points.

---

early onslaught. DePaul opened with a 14-2 run and never looked back in winning 104-77. Robinzine scored 22 points.

A win over Northwestern made DePaul 7-3, but a two-game losing streak followed. DePaul rebounded from that with five straight wins and a trip to Marshall ahead with a 12-5 record.

The Thundering Herd exacted revenge for the earlier defeat with a 107-96 win. Two more losses followed, and DePaul was 12-8 with five games remaining.

The Blue Demons won three of those five to end the year with a 15-10 record and its fourth straight winning season. Meyer was ninth all time with 509 career victories. Among those was a 75-70 win over Notre Dame, DePaul's first victory over the Irish in ten tries since the 1966-67 season.

Robinzine closed his career with 19.4 points and 13.5 rebounds per game to lead the team. He was drafted in the first round by the Kansas City Kings of the National Basketball Association, becoming DePaul's initial first round pick since the draft was started in 1951.

While the DePaul program had rebounded from its tough times in the early 1970s, the Blue Demons had remained, since the George Mikan era in the 1940s, a relatively unknown team. That was to change.

With Andy Pancratz serving as team captain and the class of Dave Corzine, Joe Ponsetto, Randy Ramsey, and Ron Norwood now sophomores, the Blue Demons were well stocked. The incoming class included Curtis Watkins and Gary Garland, another of the greats from New Jersey.

The Blue Demons sprinted to a big start. DePaul was 10-2 nearing the season's mid point with wins over Memphis State, Louisville, Louisiana State, and Providence.

The rest of the season was just as good as DePaul won six of its last seven regular season games to close the year with a 19-8 record. It was enough to earn a berth to the NCAA tournament, the Blue Demon's first trip to postseason since 1965-66.

DePaul topped Virginia 69-60 in the tourney's opening round, but lost 71-66 in overtime to Virginia Military Institute in its second

Jim Bocinsky shoots an opener jumper from the corner against Notre Dame in 1975 as Toby Knight boxes out Dave Corzine in case the shot misses. DePaul beat the Irish 75-70.

game. The season ended 20-9, but bright times appeared ahead.

Ron Norwood averaged 19.3 points per game and Dave Corzine 8.8 rebounds to lead the team. Both were returning the next season, along with plenty of other talent.

Fans were also finding the Blue Demons. Capacity crowds packed Alumni Hall for the first time, and reporters from Chicago's newspapers, radio stations, and television stations appeared regularly at DePaul games. After almost thirty years off the beaten path, Ray Meyer had returned DePaul to the national basketball spotlight.

To remain in the spotlight, Gene Sullivan, DePaul's athletic director, put together a killer schedule for the 1976-77 season. The Blue Demons would face five teams that were ranked in the final 1976 AP poll—Indiana (#1), Marquette (#2) twice, UCLA (#5), Notre Dame (#7), and Maryland (#11). But with only Andy Pancrantz gone, expectations were high.

Five of the Blue Demons first seven games—UCLA, Northwestern, Wisconsin, Maryland, and Indiana—were on the road. The result was a 3-4 start. One early season highlight was Dave Corzine's 30 points in the 92-74 loss to Maryland.

Wins in four of the next six games moved the Blue Demons to 7-6 at the halfway point of the season, but they stalled. After dropping four of the next seven, DePaul was 10-10 with seven games to play.

A win over Loyola allowed DePaul to salvage a split in the city series, but it was a thrilling 77-72 win at Marquette, that highlighted the year. Dave Corzine scored 26 points and grabbed 11 rebounds in the victory, but the big difference in the game was the return form of Ron Norwood.

Limited by an ankle injury all season long, Norwood's scoring average had dropped from 19.9 the previous year to 12.3. But Norwood was his old self against Marquette, scoring 23 points and giving Butch Lee headaches on defense. Afterwards Al McGuire said, "The difference in tonight and our blowout in Chicago was Norwood. He was out (in the first game) and we took advantage. He killed us tonight. He's definitely pro material. A super player."

Ray Meyer agreed with McGuire's analysis: "With Norwood healthy, we can stay with anyone. Without him, we lacked confidence."

DePaul won three of its next four games to set up a meeting with Notre Dame in the season finale. If the Blue Demons could win, they still had an outside chance of making a post-season tournament. DePaul stayed close early, but the Irish went on an eight-point run to take an 18-10 lead with eleven minutes left in the first half. The half ended with Notre Dame on top 39-36.

An out of control Butch Lee of Marquette gets by Ron Norwood only to encounter Andy Pancrantz (33) and Joe Ponsetto (43) during the first Blue Demon-Warrior matchup of 1975-76. DePaul lost twice to Marquette that season, 72-79 and 53-64.

Ron Norwood shoots from the wing in the first round of the 1976 NCAA tournament against ACC champion Virginia. DePaul and Norwood turned back the Cavaliers 69-60 to move into the second round versus Virginia Military Institute.

Dave Corzine blocks a shot attempt by Cincinnati pivot man Robert Miller as Curtis Watkins (behind 20) and Andy Pancrantz (33) establish rebounding position. Corzine also produced on the offensive end, scoring a game-high 28 points in DePaul's 70-60 victory.

Ron Norwood
Guard — 1974-77

When DePaul moved into national prominence in the mid 1970s, one of the big reasons was the ability of a group of guards from New Jersey. Ron Norwood led the western migration and started the trend that ran for ten years and included such stars as Clyde Bradshaw, Gary Garland, and Kenny Patterson.

A prep scoring maching, Norwood attended Providence and Essex County Junior College before transferring to DePaul. He stepped into a Blue Demon uniform in time for the 1974-75 season and immediately made things happen. Playing both guard and forward, Norwood averaged 14.3 points and 5.4 rebounds that year for a 15-10 DePaul squad.

The record improved to 20-9 in 1975-76 and the Blue Demons went to the NCAA tournament. Norwood was again a big factor as he averaged 19.3 points. He also set a school record with 559 points, one better than the previous record established by George Mikan.

Norwood and DePaul served notice that 1975-76 might be their season in the season's second contest. Playing in the Sun Devil classic, DePaul beat Memphis State 100-91 as Norwood scored 35 points. Three games later they beat a Louisville squad that featured four players who would score over 1,000 points in their careers. Later in the season the Blue Demons traveled to Baton Rouge to take on LSU. Limiting the Tigers to their lowest output of the season, and behind Norwood's 29 points, DePaul won 70-67.

Norwood scored over 30 points (31) for the second time in the season against Duquesne.

In all, Norwood topped 20 points twelve times that season. But the most memorable time was probably against Virginia. Behind Norwood's 28 points DePaul won its first NCAA tournament game since 1965, defeating the Cavaliers 69-60.

The Blue Demons slumped a bit in Norwood's senior year. Slowed by injury, Norwood averaged just 11.8 points per game and DePaul slipped to a 15-12 record.

Norwood finished his career at DePaul with 1,215 points. He was selected in the fifth round of the NBA draft by the Milwaukee Bucks.

Ron Norwood.

The Blue Demons got the lead early in the second half, 43-42, on a jumper from Corzine, but Notre Dame then went on an eight-to-three run to take command. DePaul, refusing to give up, continued to scrap and after a jumper by Gary Garland and a layup by Corzine the score was tied 66-66 with 4:26 remaining. But from there it was all Notre Dame and when the final buzzer sounded the score was 76-68 in favor of the Irish. Corzine ended up with 16 points and 11 rebounds, while Ponsetto finished with 11 points, 6 rebounds, and 6 assists. But the big surprise of the game as far as the Blue Demons were concerned was the play of reserve Bill Dise—21 minutes, 13 points, 7 rebounds, and 3 assists.

Despite missing postseason play, the Blue Demons could take some solace in the win over eventual national champions Marquette and an early season victory over St. Bonaventure, which went on to win the NIT. And there was the consistent play of Dave Corzine. He averaged 19.0 points and 12.6 rebounds per game to lead the team in both categories.

Heading into the 1977-78 season, the Blue Demons again were faced with living up to expectations. Despite slipping to a 15-12 record in 1976-77, DePaul returned the nucleus of its team and featured star players Dave Corzine, Joe Ponsetto, and Randy Ramsey. Add Gary Garland and Curtis Watkins, two seasoned juniors, and talented freshman guard Clyde Bradshaw, and the potential for big things was there.

The Blue Demons started living up to that potential right from the start. DePaul was 6-0 before losing 68-67 at Louisiana State on a pair of late free throws. Seven more wins, including the championship of the Kodak Classic in Rochester, New York, made the Blue Demons 13-1 heading to Marquette for a date with the defending national champions.

The Blue Demons couldn't repeat their

Joe Ponsetto
Forward — 1974-78

While much of the publicity surrounding DePaul's 1974 recruiting class involved the arrival of star center Dave Corzine, there was a lesser publicized forward in that group who became just as big a part of the Blue Demons' success for the late 1970s.

Ponsetto didn't make as big a splash as Dave Corzine, seeing action in only 11 games as a reserve. But even in his limited role, there were signs that he would some day be a big contributor. On the 15-10 squad, Ponsetto averaged 4.5 points per game and chipped in with 2.8 rebounds.

But it was as a sophomore that Ponsetto started to blossom. He actually averaged more points than Corzine, 16.4 compared to 15.5, and grabbed 8.7 rebounds per contest. He also was a more than adequate passer, handing out 69 assists.

Ponsetto's role began to change somewhat during the 1976-77 season. With the influx of more new talent, he was not needed to score as much. He still averaged 12.7 points and 7.9 rebounds that year as DePaul finished 15-12.

The 1977-78 DePaul squad would not have reached the heights they did, 27-3 record and reaching the regional finals in the NCAA tournament, if not for Ponsetto. Corzine was the star, but Ponsetto did all the little things needed to keep DePaul winning. He was a defensive enforcer. He specialized in getting the tough, important rebounds, averaging 6.9 per game. When he was needed to score he did, at a 13.0 clip, but he was just as comfortable making the pass as he led the team in assists with 119.

Ponsetto closed his career with 1,256 points and 704 rebounds. Neither of those totals will be found on the top of the record books, but Joe Ponsetto will be thought of by DePaul fans for years to come when they remember the season that put DePaul back on the college basketball map.

Corzine blocks a shot versus VMI in DePaul's overtime loss in the second round of the NCAA tournament.

Curtis Watkins (far left), Dave Corzine, Ron Norwood (11), and Joe Ponsetto (43) all look towards the referee to see what the call is—foul or jump ball.

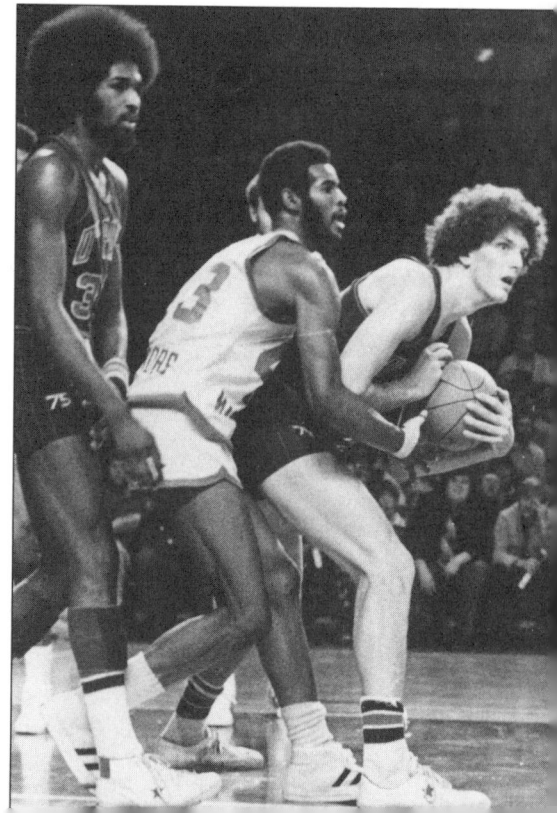

Dave Corzine shoots his familiar hook shot versus Indiana in 1976. The Blue Demons lost 50-42.

DePaul fans liked Corzine's hustle and spirited play.

Dave Corzine
Center — 1974-78

No single event signaled the renaissance of DePaul basketball in the 1970s more than the coming of Dave Corzine. At 6-foot-11 and 235 pounds, Corzine was the franchise type big man DePaul had not been able to recruit previously. Corzine's arrival from suburban Hersey High School placed DePaul squarely in the race for the top spots in the Midwest.

DePaul posted a 15-10 record in his freshman season, 1974-75. Teaming with DePaul's two returning big men, Andy Pancratz and Bill Robinzine, Corzine gave the Blue Demons a formidable frontline. He averaged 12.2 points and 8.6 rebounds, and gave DePaul fans a reason to look forward to the 1975-76 season with anticipation.

Though Robinzine had moved to the NBA, the 1976 squad still featured both Corzine and Pancratz. Corzine improved his production to 15.5 points and 8.8 rebounds. And DePaul also improved, finishing the regular season at 19-8. The record was good enough for DePaul to reach the NCAA tournament for the first time in ten years. After beating Virginia in the first round, 69-60, DePaul was slated to face Virginia Military Institute. VMI beat DePaul, but not before DePaul pushed them to overtime.

While Corzine continued to shine as a junior, the team slumped a bit. DePaul could muster only a 15-12 record despite Corzine improving in just about every offense category. His 19.0 points per game, 12.6 rebounds per game, .489 field goal shooting percentage, and .763 free throw percentage were all career highs.

If the 1976-77 season was a disappointment, the 1977-78 season was a dream one. Dave Corzine kept right on improving, averaging 21.0 points and 11.3 rebounds per game while knocking down 55.2 percent of his field goals. And DePaul also improved, finishing the season with a 27-3 record and return trip to the NCAAs. The Blue Demons reached the regional finals before losing to Notre Dame and was ranked third nationally in the final Associated Press poll. For his work, Corzine earned honorable mention All-America honors.

Corzine ended his career with 1,896 points, topping the school scoring record George Mikan had set over thirty years earlier. His 1,151 rebounds were, and still are, a school record.

The Washington Bullets made Corzine their first-round pick in the 1978 NBA draft, choosing him eighteenth overall. He returned to the city where he made his mark in 1982 when he was traded to the Chicago Bulls from the San Antonio Spurs.

---

upset of the previous season, but rebounded from that loss to win twelve straight to close the regular season with a 25-2 record. That earned DePaul a third place rating in the Associated Press poll and a spot in the NCAA tournament.

The tourney opening round game pitted DePaul against Creighton, a team the Blue Demons had defeated 85-82 in Omaha, Nebraska, earlier in the season. Garland and Ramsey rode to the rescue this time by combining for 35 points and 12 assists in an 80-78 win.

Corzine stepped up to be the hero in the next game. Facing a talented Louisville team that featured Darrell Griffith, Corzine poured in 46 points and grabbed 9 rebounds in a 90-89 double overtime win.

The victory earned DePaul a match up with arch rival Notre Dame with the winner earning a trip to the Final Four in St. Louis. The two teams had met earlier in the year in a key game. Notre Dame was ranked fourth nationally at the time of the first meeting with DePaul rated eleventh. The game was on regional television, while North Carolina faced Providence in the national game. When that contest ended, the national audience switched to the final minutes of the DePaul-Notre Dame game.

DePaul squandered a six-point lead in the final minutes and allowed Notre Dame to tie the score and force overtime. The Irish opened a 68-63 lead in the extra period, but DePaul rallied to within 68-67. Notre Dame then missed a free throw with ten seconds left. Corzine rebounded and passed to Garland, who launched a 30-footer right before the horn sounded. The shot hit the mark, giving DePaul a 69-68 win and launching the run that led the team into the NCAA tournament.

The second meeting would not be as thrilling. Corzine was limited by a finger injury suffered in practice the day before, and Notre Dame broke open a close game late to win 84-64.

DePaul ended the season with a 27-3 record. The 27 wins were a new school record for wins in a season. Dave Corzine averaged 21.0 points and 11.3 rebounds in his final season. His career numbers made him the top career scorer and rebounder in DePaul history.

With Corzine, Ramsey and Ponsetto leaving, the 1977-78 season seemed to be DePaul's best shot at reaching the NCAA Final Four. Looks can be deceiving.

10

Final Four Time

To be a success, college basketball teams are supposed to be dominated by veterans. Seniors are to score the big baskets and get the big rebounds while younger players play an auxiliary role like setting picks and boxing out. The 1978-79 DePaul team was to be quarterbacked by a sophomore guard and its top scoring threat was a freshman forward.

A five man team can't be expected to win many games. Depth is a key in college basketball. Players go as hard as possible for as long as possible, then take a break on the bench while somebody else plays. The 1978-79 DePaul team was going to play just five guys regularly.

At 6-foot-6 and over 250 pounds, the freshman didn't look like the typical college basketball player. Basketball players are lean and lanky, but this DePaul freshman was thick and solid.

Winning college head coaches are young, brash, and innovative. They're constantly coming up with new ways to win. But in 1978-79, the DePaul head coach was going to turn sixty-five years old during the season, and the year ahead was his thirty-seventh with the Blue Demons.

Heading into the 1978-79 season, DePaul did not look destined for great success. With the graduation of stars Dave Corzine and Joe Ponsetto from the 1977-78 team that reached the NCAA tournament regional finals, this squad was just too young and lacking in depth. Mark Aguirre, the team's celebrated recruit, wasn't thin enough or agile enough to dominate college games as he had high school. Ray Meyer was too old to come up with ways to win college basketball games in these modern times. All these things together were simply too much to overcome. The 1978-79 season just wouldn't be as good as last year.

Doubts about Aguirre's ability came crash-

Curtis Watkins (30) and Dennis Moore (12) from the 1978-79 DePaul squad.

The future of the DePaul basketball team in 1978: Dennis McGuire (21), Teddy Grubbs (34), Sam Manella (35), Bernard Randolph (22), and Mark Aguirre (24).

ing to earth seconds after the opening tip of the season's first game. Playing at UCLA's storied Pauley Pavilion, the Blue Demons controlled the opening tip and passed to Aguirre on the wing. Aguirre dribbled, cupped the ball in his hand and dunked over star Bruin David Greenwood.

Aguirre finished the day with a team-high 29 points and 8 rebounds. It was the first of twenty-one times that Aguirre led the team in scoring during his freshman season. While his collegiate debut was an individual success, it didn't go as well for the team. The Blue Demons lost 108-85.

Another positive that came out of the UCLA game was Jim Mitchem. Jim was forced to listen to the game from a bed because of illness. When Bill Madey started to get into early foul trouble, Jim, still weak from the flu, dressed, ran a mile and a half to Pauley Pavilion, and showed up at court side. It was this attitude that earned the players' respect and led to Mitchem winning the team's Most Improved Player award.

DePaul beat Evansville in the second game of the season, 74-55, with the recovered Jim Mitchem leading the way with 20 points and 7 rebounds. After wins over Northern Illinois and Eastern Michigan, the Blue Demons readied to celebrate Meyer's sixty-fifth birthday at Butler University. Aguirre scored 28 points and grabbed 8 rebounds to pace DePaul to an 81-62 win on December 13, 1978.

With a 4-1 record DePaul headed to Wichita to take on the Wichita State Shockers. Despite excellent performances by Aguirre (39 points) and Curtis Watkins (10 rebounds) the Blue Demons dropped a 95-92 decision.

DePaul returned home with a 4-2 record to face two Big Ten teams—Wisconsin and North-

Gary Garland
Guard — 1975-79

Sometimes it seems Gary Garland's career as a basketball player at DePaul gets lost in his music. A talented and gifted athlete, Garland also is equally talented and gifted as a musician. It comes from the family.

Garland's aunt is singer Dionne Warwick and his mother, Cissy Houston, a vocalist who worked with Warwick. His sister, Whitney Houston, became a star performer in the 1980s, and Garland himself toured with her and later launched a solo career.

But long before Garland earned stardom with his voice, he earned the adulation of DePaul fans with his basketball skills. After playing just 19 games and averaging just 3.2 points per game as a freshman in 1975-76, Garland moved into the regular rotation in 1976-77. He responded with 7.5 points per game as DePaul finished the season at 15-12.

Garland stepped into stardom his junior year. Averaging 13.6 points per game, Garland was a key contributor for a DePaul team that finished the regular season at 25-2 and gained a berth in the NCAA tournament. DePaul reached the regional finals in the tournament before falling to Notre Dame, 64-84.

But it was in the other Notre Dame game that season that Garland sealed his place as a DePaul legend. The game, played at Notre Dame, ended tied at regulation. Then, with just seconds remaining in the overtime, Garland launched a shot from twenty-two feet. The buzzer beater was good, giving DePaul a 69-68 victory and DePaul fans a new hero.

With Dave Corzine and his inside power game departed, Garland was called upon to score more during the 1978-79 season. He responded with his best season, averaging 17.0 per game. But point production was not the only area where Garland contributued to the Blue Demons. He recorded 188 assists and a school record 124 steals for the 26-6 squad. He also set a school record with 10 steals against USC in DePaul's opening round 89-78 victory in the NCAA tournament.

Garland's DePaul career ended with the Blue Demons' loss to Pennsylvania in the Final Four. He finished with 1,214 points and 385 assists. His NBA career consisted of one season with the Denver Nuggets in which he averaged 4.3 points per game in 78 appearances.

---

western. Though Wisconsin couldn't be called a powerhouse, it did pose problems for the Blue Demons. Wisconsin had a talented frontline of Joe Chrnelich, Claude Gregory, and Larry Petty as well as a talented guard in Wes Matthews. The Badgers managed to control Aguirre throughout the game, but Watkins stepped up and led the team with 21 points and 8 rebounds as DePaul won 84-78.

Seven more wins followed, vaulting DePaul to 12-2 and quelling the fears about the team's ability to win. Among the victories during this stretch were an 88-70 victory over Creighton in which Gary Garland scored 30 points, and an 80-73 victory over Loyola at Alumni Hall.

A five-game road trip was next up for Meyer's team, with the first stop being Dayton. The Flyers' relied on strong backcourt play provided by Jim Paxson and Jack Zimmerman. The Blue Demons got 24 points from Gary Garland, but it wasn't enough as Dayton won 68-64.

The Blue Demons rebounded from the Dayton loss to win at Illinois State, but then fell 82-80 at Western Michigan to slip to 13-4 with games at Oral Roberts and Loyola still ahead.

Aguirre pumped in 28 points to help the Blue Demons escape with a 75-72 win at Oral Roberts. Gary Garland scored 22 and had 10 rebounds in a 77-73 win at Loyola. The Blue Demons were 15-4 and had six of their final eight games at Alumni Hall. DePaul's two-game

Curtis Watkins
Forward — 1975-79

A steady and solid performer at DePaul, Curtis Watkins played a large role in the Blue Demons' growth and continued success in the late 1970s. In his four years, Watkins played for DePaul teams that combined for an 88-30 record and made three appearances in the NCAA tournament.

As a freshman in 1975-76, Watkins quickly showed he could contribute to a major college program. He averaged 9.2 points and an impressive 7.1 rebounds. All this for a team that finished 20-9 and reached the NCAAs. His sophomore season was a continuation of his first season in a DePaul uniform. He increased his scoring average to 10.9 and contributed another 7.0 rebounds. Unfortunately, the Blue Demons stumbled somewhat, finishing at 15-12. This would be the lone season that Watkins did not play in a postseason tournament with DePaul.

While star center Dave Corzine grabbed the headlines in 1977-78, DePaul fans knew how important Watkins was to the team. He averaged 12.6 points per game and 5.7 rebounds while often drawing the opponents toughest player on defense. But Watkins also had his big offensive days. In the third game of the season, Watkins was DePaul's big gun, scoring 31 points, in an 89-85 victory over Bradley. DePaul's regular season success continued into the NCAA tournament with two victories. After its loss to Notre Dame, DePaul had a final 27-3 record.

Watkins truly shined as a senior. Playing alongside freshman forward Mark Aguirre, Watkins had career highs with 17.0 points per game and 8.1 rebounds. And once again DePaul was selected for the NCAAs, finishing the season with a 26-6 record. In the first round of the tournament Watkins scored 27 points against Southern California in the 89-78 victory. With a chance to make the Final Four, DePaul faced another Pac 10 team—UCLA. Again DePaul won, and again Watkins was a big contributor. He scored 24 points as DePaul triumphed 95-91.

Watkins ended his career with 1,463 points, third on the all-time list behind Dave Corzine and George Mikan. His 810 rebounds also ranked him in the top five. And his 84 percent conversion rate on his free throws place him second all-time to Howie Carl. He was named honorable mention All-America after his senior year, and was selected in the fifth round of the NBA draft by the Kansas City Kings.

Curtis Watkins played in three NCAA tournaments as a DePaul Blue Demon.

winning streak grew to six as the Blue Demons defeated Centenary, Ball State, Villanova, and Valparaiso to set up an Alumni Hall showdown with Marquette.

The Warriors went nine deep, while the Blue Demons were forced to rely on five iron men. But DePaul's five proved up to the task. Watkins scored 19 points and Aguirre and Garland added 18 each in a 61-60 DePaul victory. The Blue Demons were 20-4, giving them back-to-back 20-win seasons for the first time since 1943-44 and 1944-45.

Wins over Alabama-Birmingham and Notre Dame pushed the record to 22-4 heading into

Gary Garland (24) averaged 17.0 points per game for the 1978-79 Blue Demons team.

the final regular season game, a third meeting with Loyola. The Ramblers won 101-99 to end DePaul's nine-game winning streak. But the Blue Demons were heading to the NCAA tournament with a 22-5 record.

Heading into the tournament the sixth-ranked Blue Demons had everything one could want in a team except depth and height. It all started with their sensational freshman, Mark Aguirre. All season he had astounded fans with his ability to score from anywhere on the court. Curtis Watkins added senior leadership, defense, rebounding, and scoring. Jim Mitchem, though playing out of position at center, had shown improvement throughout the year. Gary Garland and Clyde Bradshaw were proclaimed the "best pair of guards in the nation" by NBC's Al McGuire. But the bench was thin, with Bill Madey being the only player off the bench to appear in more than half of DePaul's games.

Curtis Watkins flies in for a dunk against Marquette. Watkins had 19 points and 9 rebounds against the Warriors in the second round of the 1979 NCAA tournament.

DePaul's first round opponent, USC, had a virtual home game with the game being played at UCLA's Pauley Pavilion. Senior Curtis Watkins had no desire for this game to be his last, and it showed in his play. Watkins led DePaul in both scoring and rebounding with 27 points and 9 rebounds to pace DePaul to an 89-78 victory and send the team on to the West Regional in Provo, Utah.

A rematch with Marquette was up next, and the Blue Demons were equal to the challenge. Watkins and Aguirre scored 19 each while Watkins grabbed 9 rebounds in a 62-56 DePaul victory. The Blue Demons were one win away from the Final Four.

When the 1977-78 Blue Demons made it to the regional finals, they faced Notre Dame, a team they had beat earlier in the season. The 1978-79 DePaul squad was to face a familiar foe in the regional finals. This time it was UCLA, which had beaten the Blue Demons handily in the season opening game in Los Angeles.

DePaul sprinted to an early lead in the rematch, opening a 51-34 halftime lead. But the Bruins staged a furious second half comeback that had DePaul reeling. With DePaul playing a slower pace to protect the lead, UCLA chipped away at the lead and pulled to within 93-91 in the final minute. Gary Garland's layup made it 95-91, and the Blue Demons held on for the win. Ray Meyer would make his first trip to the NCAA Final Four since his first team in 1942-43.

Garland and Curtis Watkins scored 24 points each, but Watkins was forced to leave the game late in the second half with a sprained knee. Aguirre added 20 points, Clyde Bradshaw had 13, and James Mitchem snared 9 rebounds to go with his 14 points. DePaul converted 73 percent from the field in the second half, mostly

The scoreboard tells the whole story; the Blue Demons are going to the Final Four.

on short shots and layups as a result of good ball movement.

The postgame celebration was emotional. Former Marquette coach Al McGuire was interviewing Meyer on NBC Television. Garland ran by heading to the locker room, but Meyer grabbed him and added him to the interview. Aguirre hugged Meyer, and the crowd of over 13,000 in the Marriott Center on the Brigham Young University campus roared.

All the doubts had been answered, but two more games lay ahead.

The Blue Demons next opponent was unbeaten Indiana State, led by star forward Larry Bird. Watkins' knee was still bothering him, but he knew his team needed him. He gamely played all 40 minutes, as did the entire Blue Demons starting lineup.

Bird was outstanding, hitting 11 of 12 shots in the first half and scoring 23 points as the Sycamores opened a 45-42 lead. Indiana State held a 16-8 rebound advantage at halftime, but had turned the ball over 13 times, including 5 by Bird.

Bird opened with 6 of his team's first 12 points early in the second half as the Sycamores jumped to a 57-46 lead with 16:37 to play. DePaul bounced back with a run of its own, and when Aguirre hit a 15-footer with 5:13 to play the score was tied 71-71.

Seconds later Clyde Bradshaw got a steal, fed Garland for a 12-footer, and with 4:59 left the Blue Demons had the lead 73-71.

A Bird pass to Bob Heaton led to a tying bucket with 3:27 remaining. After each team missed, the Blue Demons took a 74-73 lead as Garland hit the front end of a one-and-one with 1:37 left. But when the second shot missed, Bird rebounded the ball giving the Sycamores a chance to take the lead.

Indiana State worked the ball around until Carl Nicks found Heaton for another layup with just fifty ticks on the clock. DePaul, down 75-74, held the ball for a final shot. The shot, a 17-footer by Aguirre, missed and Leroy Staley grabbed the rebound. Garland quickly fouled Staley with just one second remaining in the game.

Staley missed the first free throw, but made the second to increase the lead to 76-74. DePaul called time to set up the game's final play. The Blue Demons last hope rested on a pass the full length of the floor. But the pass bounced to Larry Bird, time expired, and the Sycamores went on to meet Michigan State and Earvin "Magic" Johnson in one of the most storied championship games in NCAA history.

DePaul played Pennsylvania in the consolation game. Aguirre scored 34 points and grabbed 14 rebounds in the Blue Demons' 96-

Ron Kuziel gets a shot off during DePaul's 96-93 victory over Pennsylvania in the 1976 Final Four consolation game.

93 win, giving DePaul third place in the tournament.

Aguirre finished his freshman season with 767 points, a school record, nearly 150 points more than Corzine had scored the previous season. He averaged 24.0 points per game, the second best average in school history and the best ever for a freshman. He also averaged 7.6 rebounds per game, second only to Watkins' 8.1.

What could easily be called the greatest season in DePaul history ended with the Blue Demons 26-6 and ranked sixth in the Associated Press poll. Gary Garland and Curtis Watkins were graduating, but Mark Aguirre, Clyde Bradshaw, and Jim Mitchem were returning from the iron five Meyer used so well.

Making a good sequel is tough. When the first showing of something is a smashing success, it's very difficult to capture that same excitement a second time. That was the challenge facing the 1979-80 Blue Demons.

In the previous two seasons, DePaul was 53-9, reached the NCAA Final Four once, and the regional final the other year. The team had survived the graduation of the program's top career scorer and rebounder, Dave Corzine, following the 1977-78 campaign and rebounded to win a trip to the Final Four.

The Blue Demons had a good nucleus returning with senior Jim Mitchem, junior guard Clyde Bradshaw, and, of course, Mark Aguirre. To fill out the rest of the starting lineup, Meyer had to rely on four newcomers to the team— Terry Cummings, Skip Dillard, Teddy Grubbs, and Bernard Randolph.

Terry Cummings, a 6-9, 220-pound forward/center, arrived via Chicago's Carver High School. A late bloomer who did not play organized basketball until his sophomore year, Cummings averaged 25 points and 18 rebounds per game as a senior. *Midwest Basketball News* named both Cummings and Teddy Grubbs the two "most likely to scrape their knees on the rim." Coach Meyer was looking for Cummings to help fill the gap created by the loss of Curtis Watkins.

Skip Dillard was a transfer from Casper (Wyo.) Junior College, but he did have Chicago connections. He was a high school teammate of Aguirre's at Westinghouse. Dillard was known for his strength and quickness, assets that would serve him well on the offensive boards.

Teddy Grubbs was the most heralded member of the group. A high school All-American, Grubbs had averaged 25 points and 18 rebounds per game as a senior. Coach Meyer called him a tall Curtis Watkins. "He's smooth to the hole, excellent on the boards, and quick."

Bernard Randolph was known as Mr. Instant Offense. Another player from Westinghouse,

With Gary Garland and Curtis Watkins graduating, Mark Aguirre, Clyde Bradshaw, and Jim Mitchem would have to fill the void. Here Watkins (left) and Aguirre (32) apply defensive pressure on Tracy Jackson of Notre Dame.

The 1979-80 Blue Demons, though kidding around here, were quite serious about making it back to the Final Four. ON FLOOR: Dennis Moore. SECOND ROW (from left): Bernard Randolph, Skip Dillard, Clyde Bradshaw. THIRD ROW (from left): Mark Aguirre, Sam Manella, Teddy Grubbs. FOURTH ROW (from left): Dennis McGuire, James Mitchem, Terry Cummings.

he broke Aguirre's high school scoring record by scoring 50 points in one game. DePaul's coaching staff likened him to former Blue Demon Bill Dise because of his willingness to shoot from almost anywhere with accuracy and speed.

There were worries going into the 1979-80 season. DePaul's young team would play a tough schedule. Six of the opponents on the slate had appeared in the NCAA tournament the year before.

Ray Meyer opened his thirty-eighth season as head coach with 597 career victories, the most among active major college coaches. He was fresh from his 1979 induction in the Naismith Basketball Hall of Fame in Springfield, Massachusetts, and ready for big things.

The Blue Demons' first opponent was Wisconsin, a team that was coming off its best season since 1974. The Badgers had all five starters returning, including Wes Matthews (18.5 ppg and 106 assists) and Claude Gregory, who was named player of the week by *Sports Illustrated* in March of 1979. DePaul handled Wisconsin fairly easily, 90-77. Mark Aguirre led the team in scoring with 26 points, and freshman Teddy Grubbs was high man with 10 rebounds.

After a 66-60 win over a young University of Texas team, Meyer was in position to earn his 600th career victory at Northern Illinois on December 12, one day before his sixty-sixth birthday. A capacity crowd of 6,076 packed Evans Field House in DeKalb, and they saw a great show. DePaul led 29-27 at halftime, and the Blue Demons couldn't shake the Huskies in the second half. The game went into overtime, and wasn't won until Aguirre hit a pair of free throws with no time remaining to give DePaul a 57-55 victory.

Jim Mitchem gets creative against Lamar and launches a shot over his head as Aguirre (24), Dillard (44), Grubbs (34), and Bradshaw (23) look on.

The Blue Demons headed on to Los Angeles for a date at UCLA. The Bruins were not the same team that the Blue Demons had beat in the NCAAs the previous year. Larry Brown had taken over as head coach and had to replace two-time All-American David Greenwood, and guards Brad Holland and Roy Hamilton. UCLA did have Kiki Vandeweghe and his 14.2 scoring average back, along with four talented freshmen—Rod Foster, Darren Daye, Michael Holton, and Cliff Pruitt.

But the star of this contest was DePaul's Teddy Grubbs. Coming off the bench, Grubbs scored 28 points and had 15 rebounds to help lead the Blue Demons to their fourth straight victory, 99-94.

A victory over Eastern Michigan preceded the Chicagoland Classic. DePaul won the tournament by defeating Northwestern and Loyola. Cummings had an excellent game against Loyola, scoring 31 points and collecting 20 rebounds to lead the team in both categories.

After a victory over Bradley, DePaul took its 8-0 record to Missouri. The Blue Demons didn't figure to have an easy time of it against a Missouri team that included the Big Eight's highest scoring guard duo from the year before, Larry Drew and Steve Wallace, and freshman center Steve Stipanovich. But with Aguirre scoring 34 points, and Skip Dillard and Clyde Bradshaw each scoring 14, the Blue Demons cruised to a 92-79 win.

DePaul improved to 14-0 heading into a game against Louisiana State at Alumni Hall on January 20, 1980. Playing before what Meyer called the largest crowd ever in Alumni Hall, and a national TV audience on NBC, the Blue Demons earned a 78-73 win over coach Dale Brown and the Tigers. Aguirre scored 31 points and Cummings 17, along with 10 rebounds.

Nine more wins put DePaul at 24-0 with Loyola next on the schedule. This would be the teams third matchup of the season. Once again DePaul's big two were too much for the Ramblers. The Blue Demons led 49-46 at halftime, and built the final margin up to 94-87. Mark Aguirre scored 41 points on 14 of 26 shooting from the field and 13 of 17 from the line. Terry Cummings added 23 points and 17 rebounds. And though Clyde Bradshaw had only 6 points, his 14 assists and 2 steals were team highs.

The number one ranked Blue Demons now headed to Notre Dame with a 26-game winning streak, the longest in school history. At Notre Dame, Meyer and his Blue Demons were going one on one with history. The Athletic and Convocation Center was the place winning streaks and No. 1 ranked teams went to die. UCLA's record 88-game winning streak ended there in 1971. The nation's top rated team had lost there four times in head coach Digger Phelps' nine seasons with the Irish.

Notre Dame had the horses to pull off the upset. A backcourt of Rich Branning, Bill Hanzlick and John Paxson, combined with the frontcourt of All-America forward Kelly Tripucka, Tracy Jackson, and Orlando Woolridge, would give the Blue Demons all they could handle.

The game was a back and forth affair from the tip. Notre Dame led 8-2 early, but the Blue Demons rallied to lead twice and trail only 32-31 at halftime.

The nip and tuck pattern continued in the second half. DePaul opened with a run to take a 43-34 lead with 16:04 to play, but the Irish responded with an 11-0 run and a 45-43 advantage with 12:04 left. The Blue Demons opened a five-point lead, 60-55, with 6:04 to play, but the Irish responded again.

A pair of Tracy Jackson free throws tied the score at 64 with 1:08 to go. Each team committed a late turnover, and Bradshaw's bomb at the buzzer missed the mark to send the game to overtime.

The teams traded baskets in the extra period with a Rich Branning jumper with seven seconds left tying the score at 70 and forcing a second overtime.

A pair of Kelly Tripucka free throws gave Notre Dame the lead, but Grubbs and Bradshaw scored to put DePaul ahead 74-72 with 2:58 to play. Bill Hanzlik tied it at 74 with a bank shot, and when Cummings missed a free throw-line jumper with 1:55 remaining, Hanzlik snared the rebound.

A capacity crowd at Notre Dame's Athletic and Convocation Center watches the early action and waits to see if ND can upset number one DePaul in 1980.

Orlando Woolridge tries to win the jump for the Irish to start the second half with Notre Dame leading 32-31.

Mark Aguirre readies to release a one-hander in the lane as Orlando Woolridge prepares to go for the block. Woolridge hit two foul shots to give Notre Dame a 76-74 victory in the 1980 contest.

Notre Dame was looking to hold for one final shot, but Cummings fouled Orlando Woolridge with 19 seconds to play. Woolridge hit both free throws to give the Irish a 76-74 lead. After a timeout, a pair of Blue Demons shots missed and the dream of the perfect season died in a 76-74 loss.

A win over Illinois State closed the regular season with a 26-1 record. DePaul was still ranked number one nationally and headed to the NCAA tournament for the third straight time and the fourth time in five seasons. DePaul was 7-3 in those last three NCAA appearances, and expectations were high when the 1980 tourney tipped off.

The Blue Demons were paired against their old nemesis UCLA in their first game in Tempe, Arizona. The Bruins opened a 34-32 halftime lead. DePaul took a quick second half lead and the score was tied at 57 heading into the final six minutes.

UCLA made a 5-0 run, but the Blue Demons responded to tie the score at 63 with four minutes remaining. A final tie came at 67 with 1:44 left, but the Bruins hit ten straight free throws down the stretch to claim a 77-71 win.

The season ended with DePaul 26-2 and ranked No. 1 in the regular season poll. The campaign marked the team's last in Alumni Hall, and the Blue Demons left the facility with a 42-game winning streak.

Aguirre averaged a school record 26.8 points per game along with 7.6 rebounds. Cummings scored 14.2 points and grabbed 9.4 rebounds per game. And Bradshaw set a school record with 215 assists.

11

A New Home

With veteran stars Mark Aguirre, Terry Cummings, Clyde Bradshaw and Skip Dillard returning, the 1980-81 season held promise. But there was some preseason "new" to go with all that "old."

The biggest new thing was a home court. After twenty-four seasons in Alumni Hall, the Blue Demons were leaving their 5,000 seat campus home for the 17,500 seats of the Rosemont Horizon.

Before the Blue Demons could test the new home floor, they had to play defending national champion Louisville in the Tip Off Classic in Springfield, Massachusetts. Aguirre scored 24 points and snared 14 rebounds to get the season off on a winning note, an 86-80 victory over Louisville.

DePaul returned home for its first game at the Rosemont Horizon on December 1, 1980. The opponent was the Gonzaga Bulldogs. The Blue Demons cruised to an easy victory, 74-56.

Mark Aguirre was the leading scorer in the first game at the Horizon with 26 points.

Wins over Santa Clara, Northern Illinois, Texas, and North Texas State led the Blue Demons into the Chicagoland Classic. Once again the Blue Demons won the tournament, beating Loyola and Northwestern.

The 8-0 Blue Demons hosted UCLA next. The defeat in the 1980 tournament still stung, and DePaul wanted a victory. Mark Aguirre led the team in scoring, 23 points, and rebounding, 9, as DePaul took a 93-77 win over the Bruins to improve to 9-0.

Next up was the Cabrillo Classic. DePaul won its first round game against Georgetown, 72-67. In the finals, the Blue Demons met San Diego State. Clyde Bradshaw had one of his finest games of the season with 20 points and 12 rebounds to lead DePaul to a 85-69 victory.

The record stood at 13-0 when the Blue Demons hosted Old Dominion on Jan. 10, 1981.

Clyde Bradshaw helps cut down the net at the end of the 1979 season.

Clyde Bradshaw
Guard — 1977-81

To say that Clyde Bradshaw was a winner would be an understatement. In his four years as a starting guard at DePaul, Bradshaw played on Blue Demon teams that posted a 106-13 record, reached the NCAA tournament each year, went to the regional finals once, the Final Four once, and were ranked among the nation's top ten each season.

Bradshaw stepped onto the court at Alumni Hall in 1977 and immediately performed like a veteran. A slashing penetrator and quick handed defensive stopper, Bradshaw was a major part of DePaul basketball from his first day in a Blue Demons uniform.

As a freshman in 1977-78, Bradshaw played in all 30 games for the 27-3 Blue Demons. DePaul reached the NCAA tournament regional finals that year before losing to Notre Dame and was ranked third in the final Associated Press poll. Bradshaw contributed 6.1 points per game and handed out 41 assists.

The Blue Demons ended the next year ranked sixth in the AP poll and reached the Final Four, ending the season at 26-6. And Bradshaw moved into a starring role on the team. He averaged 11.0 points per game and handed out 162 assists while playing in all 32 games.

Bradshaw served as a team captain in 1979-80, and continued to establish himself as one of the top guards in the country. The junior averaged 10.5 points per game and handed out a school record 215 assists. Bradshaw's Blue Demons posted a 26-2 record and were ranked number one entering the NCAA tournament. But their season ended much earlier than expected when they suffered a second round defeat at the hands of UCLA. Bradshaw scored 13 points against the Bruins, joining Mark Aguirre, Terry Cummings, and Skip Dillard in double figures.

DePaul's success continued in Bradshaw's senior season. The Blue Demons marched through the regular season with just one defeat, a 62-62 loss to Old Dominion. And when Oregon State lost in their final regular season game of the year to Arizona State, DePaul moved into the top spot in the final regular season AP poll. But Clyde Bradshaw's final college game came quicker than expected when the Blue Demons were upset by St. Joseph's in the second round of the NCAAs, 48-49.

Bradshaw earned honorable mention All-America honors after the season. He ended his career with 1,102 points and 606 assists, then a school record. He also set the record for assists in a single game at the Rosemont Horizon when he dished out 14 in a 83-57 victory over Creighton. And It was Bradshaw's passing ability floor generalship that impressed the Atlanta Hawks enough to choose him in the second round of the NBA draft.

Ray Meyer escorts Clyde Bradshaw to the bench during the last minute of DePaul's 93-77 win over UCLA during the 1981 season.

Bradshaw pulls up for the short jumper against Georgia Tech as Mark Aguirre and Jim Mitchem (11) look for rebounding room. DePaul won the 1979 home contest 77-71.

Clyde "The Glide" Bradshaw practices his passing wizardry against Marquette.

Clyde Bradshaw shoots a fadeaway jumper against Marquette during DePaul's 62-56 victory over the Warriors in the 1979 NCAA tournament.

Aguirre wants the ball in the post. A terrific offensive player, Aguirre could score from virtually anywhere on the court.

Aguirre elevates quickly to get his jumper from the corner. Even though he played just three years, Aguirre became the first Blue Demon to score over 2,000 points.

Four Loyola players are helpless to stop Aguirre on this trip to the hoop during his freshman year.

Though he may not have had the typical physique of a great player, Mark Aguirre combined quickness and strength to become the all-time leading scorer at DePaul. Here he glides in for a layup versus Marquette during the 1979 NCAA tournament.

This interesting angle shows the patented Aguirre finger roll. Aguirre used this and just about every other move imaginable to average a career high 26.8 points during the 1979-80 season.

Mark Aguirre
Forward — 1978-81

To talk about scoring records at DePaul is to talk about Mark Aguirre. In only three years, the 6-foot-6 forward rewrote the Blue Demons' annuals in impressive fashion.

With Dave Corzine and Joe Ponsetto being seniors on the 1977-78 squad that went to the NCAA tournament, there was some question as to how the team would fare with their departure. But when Mark Aguirre announced that he would stay in Chicago and play at DePaul after his graduation from Westinghouse, all the questions were answered.

An impressive scorer, Aguirre could seemingly get his shot at any time. But he didn't look like the typical college scoring machine. Some questioned whether the somewhat rolypoly forward could excel in the college game. Two people who had no such questions were Ray Meyer and Mark Aguirre.

Aguirre didn't take long to deliver his answer. DePaul's opener was against UCLA in storied Pauley Pavilion. Aguirre took the opening tip, raced down the court, and dunked over the Bruin's All-America center David Greenwood. This was the first 2 of over 2,000 points Aguirre would score in machine gun fashion in his career.

He averaged 24.0 points per game as a freshman (just short of the single season record of 24.3 set by Dick Heise in 1956-57) and blasted the total point record with 767. He led DePaul to a 26-6 finish and a berth in the NCAA Final Four. His Blue Demons were sixth in the final AP basketball poll that season.

The next year was just as impressive. With Aguirre scoring a school record 26.8 per game, the Blue Demons rolled to a 26-2 record and another NCAA berth. This time DePaul was the No.1 ranked team in the final AP poll. But the season came to an abrupt end with a 71-77 loss to UCLA in the second round of the NCAA tournament.

As is often the case with star players, Aguirre had his temperamental times at DePaul. His work ethic was sometimes questioned, but it never seemed to effect his play in games. A player who could get his shot whenever, sometimes didn't take the shots that Coach Meyer would have liked. But through it all, Aguirre kept on scoring and DePaul kept on winning.

The 1980-81 season promised to be a great one, and it was. After an early season loss to Texas, DePaul won twenty-three straight games on the way to a 27-1 regular season record. And Aguirre continued to score. On a team with plenty of firepower, Aguirre averaged 23.0 points per game. The only thing left was the NCAA tournament.

DePaul's opening round game was against St. Joseph's (Pa.), and DePaul was a heavy favorite. But in one of the most painful losses in DePaul history, the Blue Demons lost 48-49. Though the loss was tough on everyone, it was especially so on Aguirre. He eventually opted to go hardship and enter the NBA draft and forego his senior season at DePaul.

Aguirre left DePaul with 2,182 career points, the only Blue Demon to top 2,000. He earned every major national player of the year award in 1980 and was twice picked first team All-America (1980, 1981).

The 7-4 Monarchs might not have been a household name in Chicago, but they did have talent. Coach Paul Webb had guided his team to a 26-4 record in 1979-80 and into the NCAA tournament. ODU lost in the tourney to the same team that knocked out DePaul—the UCLA Bruins. The Bobby Vaughan led team would be a tough opponent.

The Monarchs withstood a 17-point, 10-rebound performance by Terry Cummings and held on to win 63-62. The hopes of an unbeaten season had ended for DePaul.

DePaul won its final fourteen regular season games to finish the regular season at 27-1 and ranked number one in the final Associated Press college basketball poll. Aguirre was spectacular through the final half of the season, leading the team in scoring in ten of the games. His finest game came against Alabama-Birmingham when he scored 30 points and hauled down 19 rebounds. Skip Dillard also had a fine second half, leading the team in scoring three times and knocking down 30 points in DePaul's 69-58 victory over Detroit.

DePaul's first game in the NCAA tournament was at the University of Dayton Arena against St. Joseph's (Pa.). Forced to play a slow tempo, the Blue Demons only scored 48 points in the contest. And with just seconds left in the game, St. Joseph's pushed the ball up the floor and scored on a layup before time expired to claim a stunning 49-48 upset. For the second straight year DePaul had been unable to win its first game of the tournament.

After the season, Mark Aguirre announced he would enter the NBA draft and pass up his final year of eligibility. Whether the two straight early exits from the NCAA tournament had any thing to do with his decision is questionable, but there is no question that Aguirre had accomplished much in his three years at DePaul. In his final season he averaged 23.0 points and 8.6 rebounds per game. The All-American left as the school's all-time scoring leader with 2,182 and the top three single season scoring marks as well.

Star guard Clyde Bradshaw ended his career in 1980-81. He averaged 9.5 points and 6.4 assists per game. He left as the career assists leader with 606 dishes in four seasons.

With the departure of Mark Aguirre and Clyde Bradshaw, Meyer faced a new challenge heading into the 1981-82 season. How to replace his top scorer and his point guard? With Aguirre gone there would be more shots to go around, and the hope was that the three returning starters—Terry Cummings, Skip Dillard, and Teddy Grubbs—would increase their offensive production. The two possibilities to fill Bradshaw's shoes were Raymond McCoy and lightning quick freshman Kenny Patterson. Pat-

One of three incoming freshmen for the 1981-82 season, Kenny Patterson was expected to contribute immediately at the point guard position left vacant by the graduation of Clyde Bradshaw.

The 1981-82 DePaul Blue Demons went 26-2, the third straight season DePaul lost only twice. FRONT ROW (from left): Paul Goodman (manager), Skip Dillard, Tom Reinhardt (manager), Raymond McCoy, Tom Nasshan (manager). MIDDLE ROW (from left): Joe Meyer (assistant coach), Jim Molinari (assistant coach), Jerry McMillan, Jeff Allen, Tyrone Corbin, Kenny Patterson, Dr. Ken Sarubbi (assistant coach), Head Coach Ray Meyer. BACK ROW (from left): Mike McCormick (trainer), Terry Grubbs, Walter Downing, Brett Burkholder, Terry Cummings, Bernard Randolph.

terson was one of three incoming freshman—Tyrone Corbin and Walter Downing were the others.

Kenny Patterson came to DePaul with impressive credentials. A *Parade Magazine* All American, he averaged 19.7 points his senior year on a team that finished 24-2. Known for his quickness and good hands, Patterson would also benefit from having Skip Dillard in the backcourt with him.

Tyrone Corbin, a 6-6, 210-pound forward, was out of South Carolina where he led A.C. Flora High School to a 22-5 record. An insider player, Corbin had averaged 10.9 points and 11.4 rebounds as a senior. His greatest attribute was his jumping ability.

Walter Downing was the only Chicago area recruit in this class. A 6-9 center from Providence High School in New Lenox, he was known for his defense, averaging six blocks per game. Two questions existed about Downing:

1) How was his stamina? Previous knee surgery and one leg that was shorter than the other were concerns. 2) How would he handle the increased level of competition? Downing had played at a high school that was in the smaller class A level.

The new look DePaul team opened the 1981-82 season at Illinois-Chicago in a game that featured Ray Meyer against his son, Tom. A 1966 graduate of DePaul, Tom Meyer was the Flames head coach. The Blue Demons claimed a 78-53 win as Cummings established himself as the team's star with 20 points and 10 rebounds.

Four more wins followed, including a 73-67 win over a Purdue team that had finished third in the NIT the year before. Cummings again was the leader, scoring 23 points and 19 rebounds. With a record of 5-0 the Blue Demons headed to UCLA.

The Bruins were struggling a bit at just 3-2,

Teddy Grubbs makes an entry pass into freshman Walter Downing during DePaul's 73-67 win over Purdue.

Terry Cummings led the team in scoring as Skip Dillard scored 28 points and DePaul escaped with a 92-87 win. The victory was Ray Meyer's 677th as a head coach, pushing him past UCLA's John Wooden into fifth on the all-time list.

DePaul returned home to host St. Joseph's (Pa.), the team that had upset it in the previous year's NCAA tournament. The game went spookingly similar to the last for Blue Demon fans, but DePaul finally came away with a 46-44 overtime win.

Teddy Grubbs displays perfect form on his jump shot. Grubbs was an integral part of the 1981-82 Blue Demons that went 26-2.

with losses already to BYU and Rutgers. But they proved good enough against the Blue Demons, winning 87-75 despite 20 points and 12 rebounds by Cummings. The 12-point loss was DePaul's widest margin of defeat since a 108-85 defeat at UCLA in the first game of the 1978-79 season, a span of ninety-three games.

Any questions about whether DePaul could bounce back from a tough defeat were answered quickly after that first loss. The Blue Demons won twelve in a row with several impressive victories included in the string. A 75-68 home win over Derek Smith and a 6-1 Louisville squad featured a season high 37 points and 19 rebounds from Cummings. A 71-69 squeeker over Dayton. And a 79-68 win over UAB, a 13-4 team that would go on to defeat Virginia in the NCAAs.

DePaul put its 17-1 record on the line against the Syracuse Orangemen. For just the fourth time so far that season someone other than

Walter Downing goes strong to the basket versus Louisville. Beating Louisville was a big confidence builder for the 1982 DePaul squad.

Skip Dillard gave the Blue Demons a strong outside scoring threat. In 1982, he hit for 28 points as DePaul beat Syracuse 92-87.

Terry Cummings switches the ball to his left hand to get a clear shot at the basket against Louisville. Cummings scored 37 points and 19 rebounds in DePaul's 75-68 victory.

Terry Cummings
Center — 1979-82

Although his arrival at DePaul from Carver High School met with less fanfare than that of Dave Corzine and Mark Aguirre, by the end of his Blue Demon days, Terry Cummings was recognized as one of the top players in school history. In his three seasons, DePaul was 79-6 and ranked first or second in the final Associated Press poll each year.

As a freshman, Cummings averaged 14.2 points and 9.4 rebounds for the 1979-80 Blue Demons. But possibly even more impressive were his .508 field goal and .832 free throw percentages. He helped the team to a 26-2 finish and an NCAA berth, the first of three appearances Cummings would make in the tournament. The Blue Demons lost in their first game, 71-77, to UCLA despite Cummings' team-high 23 points.

Cummings averaged 13.0 points and 9.0 rebounds as a sophomore in 1980-81. He led the team in scoring three times, as DePaul posted a 27-2 record.

With the departure of Aguirre to the pros, the scoring load fell to Cummings in 1981-82. He handled it well, averaging 22.3 points, while shooting .567 from the field, along with 11.9 rebounds in a season that saw DePaul finish at 26-2 and again go to the NCAA tournament. Arguably his finest game of the season came in a December showdown with the Louisville Cardinals. Cummings exploded for 37 points, including 15-16 from the charity stripe, and 19 rebounds as DePaul won 75-68.

Like Aguirre, Cummings left after his junior year for the NBA. He was the second player taken overall, chosen by the San Diego Clippers.

Cummings finished his DePaul career with 1,398 points and 857 rebounds, both ranking among the Top 10. He also ranked in the Top 20 with 78 blocked shots and 71 steals.

Terry Cummings and Ray Meyer have a laugh together.

Cummings scores down low against UCLA. He scored a team-high 23 points versus the Bruins in the 1980 NCAA tournament.

Cummings and Aguirre made a formidable 1-2 punch during the 1979-80 and 1980-81 seasons.

Terry Cummings jumps center against Furman during the 1980-81 season. Cummings averaged 13.0 points per game in his sophomore season.

T.C. uses the basket to protect the basketball as he goes for a layup versus Syracuse in 1982. With Aguirre leaving college early, Cummings became the big gun on the 1981-82 squad.

More close games followed. The Blue Demons took a 67-66 win at Marquette and then topped Evansville 59-58 at the Rosemont Horizon to run their record to 21-1. Five more wins closed out the regular season with the Blue Demons holding a 26-1 record and ranked second in the Associated Press poll.

Another trip to the NCAA tournament was ahead. This time the Blue Demons were headed to Dallas, Texas, for a meeting with Boston College. The Blue Demons took a 34-33 halftime lead as Cummings scored 10 points and gathered 10 rebounds.

Boston College opened the second half with a 6-0 run to take a 39-34 lead, but the Blue Demons bounced back to take a 49-47 lead with 11:20 left. Boston College delivered a 10-0 run to take a 58-49 lead with 9:49 to play and was never seriously challenged again.

For the third straight season, the Blue Demons lost their first game in the NCAA tournament after entering postseason action with just one loss and ranked first or second nationally.

Cummings averaged 22.3 points and 11.9 rebounds to lead the team in both categories. Skip Dillard closed out his career by averaging 13.4 points per game and 2.5 rebounds. When Cummings declared for the NBA draft as an undergraduate, DePaul was faced with replacing 46 percent of its points, 37 percent of its rebounds, 29 percent of its assists, 35 percent of its steals, and 36 percent of its block shots. But the most telling numbers of what the Blue Demons would be up against in 1982-83 were that in only two games during the 1981-82 season did someone other than Cummings or Dillard lead the team in scoring, and only four times did someone other than the departing duo lead the team in rebounding.

After forty seasons as head coach, Ray Meyer owned a 676-339 record. He was 132-15 in his last five seasons and owned thirty-five winning seasons in forty years. But without a star like Dave Corzine, Mark Aguirre or Terry Cummings, he was faced with the prospect of "rebuilding" at age sixty-eight.

Given that only one veteran player on the 1982-83 Blue Demons had ever averaged over

Terry Cummings (32) lets Raymond McCoy (11) know he's not happy with the latest turn of events. Cummings was the leader of the 1981-82 team both statistically (22.3 ppg, 11.9 rpg) and emotionally.

10 points per game in college, it probably wasn't reasonable to expect DePaul to win over 20 games and again get a bid to the NCAA tournament. Dates with UCLA, Louisville, Georgetown, and St. John's didn't help ease the situation any.

It wasn't, however, as if the cupboard was bare. Senior Bernard Randolph returned with his 14.7 scoring average. Ray Meyer called him, "Instant offense! He's a great shooter and the best player on the team without the ball." Joining Randolph on the frontline would be Walter Downing, who led the team in blocked shots, and Tyrone Corbin. Returning in the backcourt were Kenny Patterson, who led the team in assists, and third guard Jerry McMillan, the team's best defensive guard.

Bernard Randolph was the only returning player on the 1982-83 squad that had averaged over 10.0 points per game (14.7) in college.

Joining the returning cast were five recruits from all over the country. Marty Embry came from Michigan, Kevin Holmes and Tony Jackson from California, Lemone Lampley from Chicago, and Greg Mullee from Florida. Of the five, the most immediate help figured to come from Embry, Holmes, and Jackson.

Marty Embry, a 6-8, 225-pound forward, had led his high school team to two state championships. As a senior he averaged 11.3 points and 14.3 rebounds a game. Of Embry, Meyer said, "He's a big, rugged player. We like his kind of rebounding."

Another strong rebounder was Kevin Holmes. He averaged 18 points and 15 rebounds as a senior, and hauled down a school record 27 rebounds in one game as a junior. He was expected to give Meyer some flexibility on the front line.

The other California recruit, Tony Jackson, was expected to contend for Dillard's off-guard spot. The California Player of the Year and a *Street and Smith* All-American, Jackson averaged 19.0 points and 11 rebounds per game. With what looked like a good rebounding team on paper, DePaul looked for Jackson to use his open court skills.

Despite the challenges, the Blue Demons opened with wins over Davidson (79-39) and Arizona State (73-72 in OT) to win the Crush Classic. As expected, Randolph was the leading scorer for the two games with 21 and 19

Jerry McMillan, the best defensive guard on the 1982-83 team, had his moments on the offensive end.

Randolph was the go-to guy for DePaul in the first three games of the season. Here he pulls up for a jumper during DePaul's 73-70 overtime loss to UCLA.

points, while Corbin led the team in rebounding in both games with 12 and 9.

A second straight overtime game resulted in DePaul's first loss as the Blue Demons fell to UCLA, 73-70. A win over 2-0 South Florida was followed by a loss at Illinois State, which put the Blue Demons at 4-2, equaling their loss total from each of the previous three seasons.

A 63-42 victory over Western Michigan was a coming-out party of sorts for two players. Jerry McMillan led the team in scoring for the first time in his career with 18 points, while Wayne Embry led the team in rebounding (7) for the first time.

After a victory over Northern Illinois, the Blue Demons had what many fans considered an easy game against Fairleigh Dickinson. The fans were right. DePaul won 105-64. The leading scorer and rebounder for DePaul was Embry with 19 points, an impressive 9 for 11 shooting, and 8 rebounds, both career highs. Kevin Holmes added a career high 14 points, while collecting 8 rebounds.

DePaul put its three-game win streak on the line against Purdue at Mackey Arena. The Boilermakers, 6-1, had a victory over Louisville to their credit and a potential All-American at center in Russell Cross. The Blue Demons seemed to have things well in hand with a 14-point lead in the second half, but Purdue clawed its way back to squeek by with a 2-point victory, 65-63.

After Christmas DePaul started a three-game homestand. It was quickly apparent that the Blue Demons did not have the killer instinct of previous years. DePaul barely escaped the first with a victory, beating Creighton by 2 points. The second game came after an almost two-week vacation, but the Blue Demons seemed to have things in order. Behind a season-high 28 points from Bernard Randolph and 12 assists from Kenny Patterson, DePaul beat Pepperdine 78-73.

In the final game of the homestand, the Blue Demons finally couldn't overcome their problems. Gonzaga University had never beaten DePaul. The series record stood at 5-0, and DePaul fans fully expected it to go to 6-0. It did not. Gonzaga, playing a deliberate game, won 49-48.

After a loss to Loyola, 82-76, DePaul faced Louisville on national television. At stake for DePaul was the longest losing streak since the 1976-77 squad dropped four in a row. Louisville was 12-2 on the season, with both losses coming against teams DePaul had lost to—UCLA and Purdue.

On paper the Louisville-DePaul contest looked to be a close affair, and that is how it turned out. Neither team could break open the game and take command. Kevin Holmes played a great game, collecting a career-high 11 rebounds, but it was Tyrone Corbin who repeatedly kept DePaul close. Every time the Blue Demons needed a score or a key rebound, Corbin came to the rescue. He finished the game with a team-high 19 points to go with 8 rebounds.

Coach Meyer had to find a way to snap his players out of their doldrums. And things wouldn't get any easier with Dayton next on their slate. Though Dayton had lost four of its last five games, Don Donoher always had the Flyers ready for DePaul. Meyer, looking for some kind of spark, fiddled with his lineup and inserted three freshmen—Embry, Holmes, and Jackson. Whether it was the lineup change or not, Depaul came out on top for the first time in four games, 56-52.

DePaul's January 26 game against Princeton matched two veteran coaches against each

Sophomore Tyrone Corbin averaged 10.6 points per game during the 1982-83 season.

The Blue Demons utilized their height advantage over Princeton in a 51-41 triumph in 1983.

other—Ray Meyer and Pete Carril. Playing Princeton also meant DePaul would be playing another opponent who liked to keep the tempo slow. But this time the Blue Demons didn't seem to mind. Most of that was because Jerry McMillan had his shooting eye. McMillan hit 10 of 15 from the field for 23 points as DePaul triumphed 51-41.

The Blue Demons once again found themselves on national television, and once again gave the viewing public a show. As in the Louisville game, Tyrone Corbin took to the TV lights and scored 17 points and 18 rebounds against Alabama-Birmingham. But despite Corbin's play, DePaul did not ice the game until McMillan stole a pass with 3 seconds left to seal the 56-54 victory.

The winning streak stretched to five games with victories over St. Joseph's and Detroit.

Tony Jackson skies for the jumper against Northwestern in the NIT. Jackson's 16 points in a 14-minute stretch did in Nebraska, 68-58, in the fourth round.

Kenny Patterson celebrates after his 30-footer at the buzzer beat Northwestern, 65-63, in the second round of the 1983 NIT.

Tyrone Corbin continued his all-around steady play during the 1985 NIT. Here he readies to launch a jumper versus Mississippi in the third round.

Freshman Kevin Holmes goes for the dunk against Minnesota in the first round of the 1983 NIT. DePaul won the game 76-73.

The Detroit game was significant for the fact that a little used player, Raymond McCoy, got a chance to shine. With Kenny Patterson in foul trouble, McCoy was called on to play extended minutes and he responded with 7 assists in the 78-53 victory.

Georgetown was next up for DePaul in yet another televised game. The Hoyas, featuring Patrick Ewing, proved to be a bit too tough. Tony Jackson and Brett Burkholder were two unlikely stars in this game for the Blue Demons. Though Jackson had been improving all season long, against Georgetown he was a man possessed. Consistently driving the lane and challenging Ewing, the 6-5 Jackson scored 22 points and was named the Player of the Game. Burkholder also held his own against Ewing, pulling down 8 rebounds.

A 1-point win at Evansville was followed by a 1-point, double overtime loss at Ohio University and a 12-point loss to St. John's at Madison Square Garden. With a 14-9 record, the Blue Demons knew they would probably have to win all five of their remaining games to make the NCAA tournament.

The first hurdle was Notre Dame. Over 17,000 fans packed the Rosemont Horizon, and they got their money's worth. Like many in the series, the game could have gone either way. But this time it went DePaul's way with the help of Kenny Patterson's 16-footer at the buzzer.

When DePaul lost to South Carolina, 52-51, its chances of making the NCAAs became slim to none. Back-to-back victories over Marquette and Pan American set up DePaul's rematch with Dayton. This time the game was at Dayton, and this time the Blue Demons lost, 80-71. The loss closed out a 17-11 regular season, not enough to earn a trip to the NCAA tournament.

The Blue Demons were content to spend the middle of March at home, because that is where they would open the NIT against Minnesota. A 76-73 victory put DePaul in the second round matchup against Northwestern. The Wildcats played with more drive than the Blue Demons and, with 3:34 left in the game, held a 9-point lead. DePaul then went on a furious rally prompted by its aggressive defense. With just seconds left, DePaul tied the score and had possession of the ball. DePaul set up several offensive options, but with just seconds left Kenny Patterson was forced to fire a 30-footer. The ball found the bottom of the basket and DePaul was still alive in the tournament.

A 75-67 victory over Mississippi sent DePaul on its way to Madison Square Garden for the semifinals of the tournament and a match with the Nebraska Cornhuskers. The game was virtually even except for the play of Tony Jackson. In a 14-minute stretch, Jackson scored 16 of his 17 points for the game. That was the difference as DePaul won 68-58.

The Blue Demons felt confident about their chances against Fresno State. The Bulldogs were known for their defense, but DePaul would be tough to defend because everyone could score. During the regular season six players had led the team in scoring, and so far in the tournament Jackson, Corbin, and Randolph had all taken turns leading the way in scoring. But this strength turned out to be somewhat of a weakness against Fresno State. DePaul didn't have the go to guy like it had so many years before with George Mikan, and thus lacked someone to take over the game when a lift was needed. The final score was 69-60 in favor of Fresno State.

The 1983 team was led in scoring by Bernard Randolph. The senior averaged 13.7 points per game and was the second leading rebounder on the team with 4.1. Tyrone Corbin, the hustling sophomore, added 10.6 points per game and led the team in rebounding with 7.9 a game.

Kenny Patterson pressures Alvin Franklin of Houston after he crosses the timeline in DePaul's 65-58 victory.

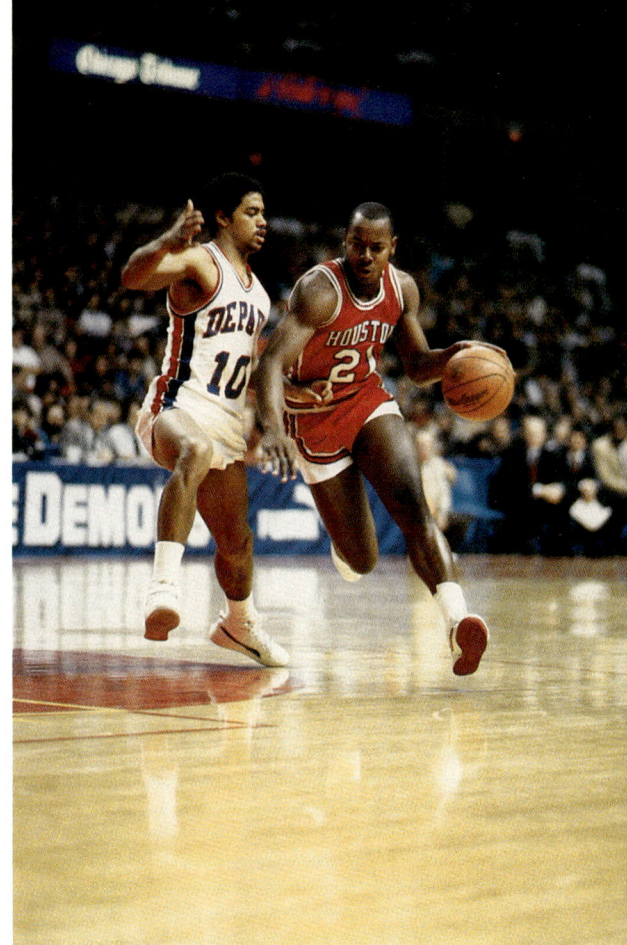

Tyrone Corbin weaves through the defense and looks for the open man.

Kenny P scores 2 of his 18 points versus Pan American in 1985.

Terry Cummings soars for the slam.

Cummings stakes his claim down on the blocks against Louisville.

David Booth turns to shoot a short jumper against Houston at the Rosemont Horizon. DePaul won the 1991 contest, 76-62.

DePaul has developed a strong rivalry with Georgetown over the last ten years. Here David Booth challenges Mark Tillmon during DePaul's 74-64 defeat in 1990.

Rod Strickland has to use evasive measures to get this shot off against Vinnie Del Negro of N.C. St. The Blue Demons won the game 84-62 as Strickland chipped in with 18 points.

Strickland takes a short jumper during the opening game of the 1986-87 season versus Northern Illinois. With ex-DePaul assistant Jim Molinari taking the head job at NIU, Blue Demon-Huskies clashes have taken on more importance.

Known for his gritty, inspired play, captain Brett Burkholder goes back up strong with an offensive rebound during DePaul's 69-45 whipping of NIU in 1982.

Finding himself in the Land of the Giants, B.J. Tyler thinks better of challenging Alonzo Mourning and looks for a cutter in this 1991 Georgetown-DePaul matchup.

Comegys finds Ed Young (30), Damon Goodman (23), and Roosevelt Chapman (22) of Dayton flatfooted as he soars to the hoop.

Stanley Brundy gets a piece of Duane Ferrell's shot. Though Ferrell scored 31 points, DePaul beat Georgia Tech 84-67 for its ninth win in a row during the 1986-87 season.

LaBradford Smith (23) and the other Louisville Cardinals can only watch as Melvon Foster readies to score. Foster scored 8 points and dished out a career high 10 assists in DePaul's 66-62 victory.

COACHES

COACHING

Comegys rises above the crowd to snare a rebound against Louisville.

Kevin Edwards squares up to the basket in his final regular season game for the Blue Demons. DePaul won 77-65 as Edwards scored 17 points.

DePaul runs through its pregame drills.

When Felton Spencer is forced to help out on defense, Kevin Edwards is able to hit the open man.

Jerry McMillan's contributions to the Blue Demons went beyond just scoring. Though his highest scoring average was only 8.9, his all-around skills made him invaluable.

Chuck Murphy pulls up for the "J" against Alabama-Birmingham as Bearden (3) and Wilkerson (24) watch.

This scene was all too familiar by the end of the only DePaul-Davidson game ever played. DePaul won the opener of the 1982 Crush Classic by the score of 79-39.

Crawford Richmond (22), Wayne Sappleton (35), and Darius Clemons (41) of Loyola watch Aguirre float in for the one hander.

Stephen Howard pulls up for the jump pass in DePaul's 1990 victory over UAB. Howard had his typical game finishing with 15 points, 13 rebounds, and 2 assists as the Blue Demons won 74-68.

Bernard Randolph lays in two against Creighton during the 1982-83 season. DePaul beat Creighton all four years Randolph was a Blue Demon.

Tony Jackson made things happen. Whether it was a twisting, spinning layup or a jump pass to a cutter on the wing, he was ready to supply the offensive spark the Blue Demons needed.

T. Greene lets one fly.

Notre Dame and DePaul's rivalry has consisted of 83 games over the years. Here Stanley Brundy elevates over Donald Royal for the jumper.

Houston tries to solve DePaul's zone during its loss on Jan. 12, 1991.

Wayne Embry admires Kevin Holmes' shooting technique.

The 1983-84 DePaul Blue Demons celebrate a big 63-61 win over the Georgetown Hoyas.

12

A Fond Farewell

The 1983-84 season was to be the end of an era. After forty-two years as head coach, Ray Meyer was stepping down as head man.

Meyer entered the year with 697 career victories, an apparent lock to become the fifth major college coach with at least 700 victories. But little else was assured as Meyer's final season began. After coaching stars like George Mikan and Gene Stump early in his career, and Dave Corzine, Mark Aguirre, and Terry Cummings in the latter stages, Meyer entered his final season with a team full of questions.

The returning team was deep, but lacked the star that can carry a team when things get tough. Four of the five top scorers from the 1982-83 squad returned, but none of them had averaged more than 11 points per game and only one of them was a senior.

Jerry McMillan, a senior, was the fifth leading scorer on the club in 1982-83 with 6.7 a game. He would start in the backcourt with Kenny Patterson (10.3 ppg). The frontline would be manned by junior Tyrone Corbin and sophomores Kevin Holmes and Marty Embry. That left Tony Jackson, Lemone Lampley, Raymond McCoy, and two freshmen as the bench.

Ray Meyer's last recruiting class, while small, was impressive. The center piece of the class was the most-chronicled, sought-after Philadelphia high school player since Gene Banks—Dallas Comegys. Out of Roman Catholic High School, Comegys was an explosive leaper who could score and block shots. One writer described him as having arms that stretch two exits on the Philadelphia turnpike and a shot as smooth as a crystal coffee table. Recruited by every college program in the nation, he chose DePaul because he had always dreamed of being a Blue Demon and playing for Ray Meyer.

The second freshman, though less heralded, was quite talented, too. Lawrence West, a 6-7,

1983-84 DePaul Blue Demons—Ray Meyer's Final Team

Coach Ray Meyer's forty-second, and final, team. FRONT ROW (from left): Tom Nasshan (manager), Bob Carzoli (manager), Kevin Holmes, Dallas Comegys, Lemone Lampley, Lawrence West, Marty Embry, Mike Thompson (manager), Dornell Johnson (manager). BACK ROW (from left): Kenny McReynolds (assistant coach), Joey Meyer (assistant coach), Tony Jackson, Jerry McMillan, Kenny Patterson, Raymond McCoy, Tyrone Corbin, Ray Meyer (head coach), Jim Molinari (assistant coach).

195-pound forward out of San Diego, was considered the best small forward prospect in California. Another leaper, West was capable of putting the ball on the floor and taking it to the basket.

With farewell ceremonies scheduled at every stop, Meyer and his team started on the final season at Northern Illinois. Tony Jackson scored 20 points and Kevin Holmes had a career-high 19 points to pace the Blue Demons to a 73-58 win. A home victory over Ohio University gave Meyer career win 699, setting up lllinois State to be the 700th victim.

It quickly became apparent that the 2-0 Redbirds wanted nothing to do with being a part of history. Making nothing easy for the Blue Demons, Illinois State hung close throughout the game. But in the end the depth of DePaul was too much. Dallas Comegys led the way off the bench with 21 points and 7 rebounds. Not only had Comegys realized his dream of playing for Ray Meyer, but he was the leading scorer and rebounder in Meyer's 700th victory.

As the last few seconds ticked off the clock, the Rosemont Horizon was up for grabs. All the memories of the great teams and players that Meyer had coached came flooding forth. The 13,057 fans in attendance were screaming their appreciation for the man everyone simply refered to as Coach.

When the celebration had finally died down, Ray Meyer started to worry about a letdown for his team. Sandwiched between the excitement of the ISU game and an important matchup with Georgetown was a game against Western Michigan. After victory number 700, Meyer wanted no part of loss number 352.

There was no letdown. DePaul won its fourth game of the season 84-60. The bench got to see a lot of action in the game, and Lemone Lampley tied for high rebound honors with 6, while Lawrence West grabbed a career high 4.

Georgetown entered the December 10 matchup at 5-0, but the competition had been less than stiff. But if anyone was concerned that the lack of early season competition would hurt the Hoyas, they need not worry.

The game was a beautifully coached game between two of the best—Meyer and John

The DePaul players were able to get in a little sightseeing while in Japan for the Suntory Ball. Here Jerry McMillan (far left), Tony Jackson, Kevin Holmes, and Ty Corbin sit in front of the Heian Shrine in Kyoto.

Thompson. Neither team could get a foothold or build up momentum, but as the game stayed close the young Blue Demons team gained confidence. With Marty Embry working hard to control Patrick Ewing, and Tony Jackson picking up where he left off the year before against Georgetown, the Blue Demons were in a position to win the game. Jackson and Kenny Patterson led the team in scoring with 15 points. With Embry doing a job on Ewing, Corbin and Comegys were able to grab 8 rebounds a piece. And the Blue Demons took a big step towards a successful season with a 63-61 victory.

Meyer took his troupe to Japan for its next two games. The Demons barely escaped with a victory in the first game against Alabama. Jackson sealed the victory with two free throws with 15 seconds remaining and DePaul won 77-76. The sweep was completed with a 50-47 win over Texas Tech.

The season was starting to turn into a Cinderella story as DePaul won three more in a row including a 68-61 win over Purdue. Next up was a West Coast swing and Marty Embry was the star. The confidence he had gained battling Patrick Ewing and Benoit Benjamin early in the season showed itself in victories over Pepperdine and St. Mary's. Against Pepperdine he scored 17 points and 13 rebounds. Then four days later he added 10 rebounds and

Tyrone Corbin took enough time off from guarding Patrick Ewing to collect 8 rebounds in DePaul's two-point victory.

Jerry McMillan thinks better of shooting and drops off a pass to a teammate during DePaul's 63-61 victory over Georgetown.

Freshman Lawrence West shoots over Patrick Ewing after the whistle sounds.

Assistant coaches Joey Meyer and Jim Molinari are all smiles as they congratulate Ray Meyer after DePaul defeated Georgetown, 63-61.

When two talented teams play a tough, physical, close game, sometimes tempers flare. Here the referees try to separate several players from both teams, including Patrick Ewing and Wayne Embry.

10 points, including the game-winning basket on a tip-in.

DePaul strung together four more wins during the rest of January to run its record to 16-0. The Alabama-Birmingham game during this stretch helped solidify Tyrone Corbin's standing as a star. The leading scorer in six of the last seven games, Corbin set a Rosemont Horizon record against UAB by hitting 83 percent of his shots (10 of 12). His totals for the day, 25 points, 9 rebounds, and 7 assists, showed his superior all-around skills.

The first game in February brought the talented St. John's squad to town. Led by Chris Mullin, with a supporting cast of Bill Wennington, Mark Jackson and Willie Glass, the Blue Demons expected a battle.

As in the last game against a Big East team, the game was close and everyone seemed to contribute for DePaul. Kevin Holmes led the team with 11 points, Tyrone Corbin had 13 rebounds, Dallas Comegys was a force inside with 7 blocked shots, and Marty Embry gave Bill Wennington everything he wanted. But as he had done twice as a sophomore, it was Kenny Patterson who made the final difference. Kenny P played a strong all-around game, but it was his 10-foot jumper with three seconds left in overtime that kept the Blue Demons' record perfect at 17-0.

DePaul headed to St. Joseph's (Pa.) for its next contest. The same team that ruined the 1979-80 season by beating the Blue Demons in the NCAA tournament spoiled the perfect part of this year as well. DePaul could never get on track and St. Joe's won 58-45.

DePaul rebounded to beat Notre Dame and Loyola. In the Loyola game, Comegys became the first Blue Demon since Terry Cummings to score 30 points in a game when he tallied 32 in the 93-77 win.

Next up were back-to-back games with Dayton. DePaul lost the first one at Dayton 72-71, but bounced back to win with the second 79-59.

In a televised game against the 21-6 Louisville Cardinals, the country saw a preview on just how good Dallas Comegys was going to be. The Blue Demons won 73-63 as Comegys

Marty Embry slams home two points during DePaul's 96-65 victory over Evansville. The turning point of Embry's season was a two-game West Coast trip when he averaged 13.5 points and 11.5 rebounds per game.

scored 19 points, collected 14 rebounds, and blocked 6 shots.

The Blue Demons were not really tested in their next four games. One thing that did bode well for the Blue Demons was the play of Lemone Lampley during this stretch. He set career highs in points (13 against Evansville), rebounds (11 against Detroit), and blocked shots (6 against Pan American).

DePaul was 25-2 heading into Ray Meyer's final regular season game. Coaching stars John Wooden and Al McGuire were part of the pregame festivities as Meyer prepared his Blue Demons for their final test, a Rosemont Horizon game with Marquette. A season of ceremonies ended with Meyer addressing the crowd, saying simply "let's get on with the ball game."

The Blue Demons followed his word, grabbing a 34-21 halftime lead. The second half was an even affair, and when the game ended

DePaul had a 64-49 victory. The leading scorer in the March 10 game was Kevin Holmes with 17 points, while Wayne Embry grabbed 9 rebounds for the team high.

The 26-2 Blue Demons ended the season ranked fourth in the Associated Press poll. Meyer would start his final NCAA tournament in Lincoln, Nebraska, against the same team that he recorded his 700th victory against—Illinois State. DePaul again beat the Redbirds, this time by the score of 75-61, behind Corbin's 20 points and 9 rebounds.

The regional semifinals were the next week in the St. Louis Arena. With 20,143 people on hand, a Missouri state record for a college basketball game, the Blue Demons battled Wake Forest in the second game of the evening session.

The Blue Demons, not wanting the season or Coach's career to end, built a 39-35 halftime lead. In the second half they stretched the lead to an 8-point advantage, 67-57, with 3:08 remaining in the game. But then Wake Forest started its comeback. When Delaney Rudd hit a pair of free throws with under a minute left, the Deacons were within two, 67-65.

Kenny Patterson lost the ball on a fast break with 26 seconds left, giving the ball back to Wake Forest. But with 11 seconds left Mark Cline missed a 19-footer and Dallas Comegys seemed to have the rebound, but had trouble controlling it and Wake Forest gained possession. Rudd got the ball on the right side and at the buzzer sank a 20-footer to force overtime.

DePaul had played two overtime games during the season and won both, 59-57. With 19 seconds left and the game tied, Patterson was fouled. Patterson was only a 57 percent free throw shooter on the season, but DePaul fans had grown accustomed to the junior hitting pressure shots to win games. This time he missed. Mark Cline grabbed the rebound and Wake Forest decided to hold for the last shot. With four seconds left the Demon Deacons made their move. Senior guard Danny Young started his drive to the hoop and with just two seconds left hit the layup. The game was over. The Demon Deacons had advanced 73-71. And the storied career of Ray Meyer had come to an end after 1,078 games (724-354)

Junior Tyrone Corbin was the leading scorer and rebounder on Meyer's last team, averaging 14.1 points and 7.4 rebounds. Dallas Comegys, who was the leading scorer in the Wake Forest game with 17 points, had averaged 11.2 points per game and 6.4 rebounds as well as leading the team in blocked shots with 79. Kenny Patterson had led the team in both assists (189) and steals (68).

Meyer ended his career as the fifth winningest coach in college basketball history. He headed the program from the time college basketball was just beginning to catch on nationally until the time it was among the top spectator events in the country.

When Meyer inherited the Blue Demons in 1942, he was the program's third coach in four seasons. He stabilized the DePaul basketball program and helped raise it to the pinnacle of college basketball.

He would leave large shoes to fill.

III

The Joey Meyer Era

13

The Second Coach Meyer

By April 1984, when he took over as head coach, Joey Meyer was not a stranger to DePaul University basketball fans, players or opponents. The son of legendary head coach Ray Meyer, Joey Meyer first came to the university in 1967 as a college freshman.

The younger Meyer was a star player for the Blue Demons, finishing his varsity career with 1,233 points. He was team captain in 1970-71 on the DePaul team that went 8-17 and set the school record for losses in a season.

After graduation, Meyer stayed at DePaul and became one of the country's most successful assistant coaches. He recruited the players and helped coach the teams that during the late 1970s and early 1980s made the DePaul program one of the best.

During his thirteen years as an assistant, Meyer was part of DePaul teams that went 272-92 (.747) and qualified for postseason play eight times. Including seven trips to the NCAA tournament and an appearance in the 1979 NCAA Final Four.

The man taking over as head coach in April 1984, though a Meyer, was not a carbon copy of Ray Meyer. For all the things Joey Meyer had learned from his father, he also learned to be his own man. The team would be his and the program would go forward molded in his image.

Joey Meyer had a good returning team to mold. With eight of the top nine scorers returning, Meyer had basically the same team that had compiled a 27-3 record and the No. 4 ranking in the final AP and UPI polls.

The trademarks of the 1984-85 edition of the Blue Demons was expected to be a pressing man-to-man defense and an offense that relied on the transition basket and a well-balanced attack.

The 1983-84 team had finished second in the nation in field goal percentage allowed

(.414). Dallas Comegys (79), Lemone Lampley (28), and Marty Embry (23) possessed excellent shot-blocking ability, and those three combined with Tyrone Corbin and Kevin Holmes had helped DePaul to a 38.2-32.7 rebounding advantage per game. Add Kenny Patterson and Tony Jackson's aggressive backcourt style, and the Blue Demons were expected to be an intimidating opponent.

On offense the key would be the frontline. Joey Meyer planned to run a stack offense featuring a small forward and two power players. A sure bet to start was co-captain Corbin. An All-America candidate, Corbin was called "a coach's dream" by Joey. The 6-6 senior averaged 14.1 points per game and 7.4 rebounds the previous year, and was at his best in big ballgames—MVP honors in six nationally televised contests in 1984.

The two power spots would be filled by juniors Embry, Holmes and Lampley, and sophomore Comegys. Of the four, Comegys seemed the most likely to start. The second leading scorer and rebounder on the team, Dallas had come off the bench in all 28 of the games in which he had appeared. If Comegys could improve on his consistency and stamina, the budding star would see more time.

Holmes and Embry had both started every game in 1984, and neither showed any signs of giving up their spot easily. Holmes held the advantage in scoring (10.1 to 5.1 ppg), while Embry's rebounding numbers (5.8 to 5.4 rpg) were better. The final two pieces were Lampley and Lawrence West. Both players saw limited action in Ray Meyer's final season, but Joey was expected to throw them both into the fray.

Graduation had robbed DePaul of one of its starting guards, but returning was preseason *Playboy* All-American choice Kenny Patterson. Kenny P. had all the skills a point guard should have to excell. The coaches felt the senior point guard could improve his scoring while not sacrificing his playmaking.

The second guard spot looked to belong to Tony Jackson. A good scorer, Jackson had only to develop a little more consistency on offense and defense.

Joey Meyer's Blue Demons opened up the

Tyrone Corbin watches Kenny Patterson lay one in on a fast break. Corbin and Patterson, both seniors, were expected to play important roles on the 1984-85 team.

1984-85 season against the Northern Illinois Huskies at home. It was a lucky thing the first game was at home, or the Blue Demons may have started the season at 0-1. NIU gave DePaul everything they could handle before the Blue Demons squeaked by 59-58.

The next visitors to the Rosemont were the UCLA Bruins. UCLA, under new head coach Walt Hazzard, was coming off an 8-point loss to Santa Clara, and DePaul handed them loss number two, 80-61. Dallas Comegys was the leading scorer with 19 points, while Embry snagged 11 rebounds. The Blue Demons out shot the Bruins 54 percent to 40 percent.

The Blue Demons handled their next four opponents handily, including a 77-37 drubbing of Chico State. Wayne Embry was the big gun in that game leading the team in both scoring

Tony Jackson fires up an outside jumper in the 1984-85 season opener against Northern Illinois. DePaul barely won the game, 59-58.

Kenny Patterson strains to put more arc on this shot to avoid having it blocked aginst UCLA. DePaul beat the Bruins in the second game of the 1984-85 season, 80-61.

Marty Embry shoots a jump hook during the Blue Demons 77-37 victory over Chico State. Embry led the team in both scoring and rebounding during the game.

Lawrence West grabs an offensive rebound against UCLA. West was hoping to see more playing time in the 1984-85 season.

(14) and rebounding (11). Over the four-game stretch DePaul shot 52 percent from the field.

The 6-0 Blue Demons next ventured into the Capital Centre to play Big East powerhouse Georgetown. The Hoyas were defending National Champions and favored to repeat. With a lineup that included Patrick Ewing, Bill Martin, Michael Jackson, and David Wingate, it was easy to see why. John Thompson's team handed Joey Meyer his first loss. And there would be no moral victory here. The final score was 77-57 as the Ewing-led Hoyas forced DePaul into a 33 percent shooting performance.

DePaul went on to Kalamazoo, Michigan, next to play Western Michigan. Though the Broncos had four returning starters, they had just lost to Michigan by 24 points. But the adage "on any given night" held up as Western Michigan clipped DePaul 65-64.

After defeating Northwestern by six, the Blue Demons took on Creighton and its all-star center Benoit Benjamin. On this day the De-

Kenny Patterson
Guard — 1981-85

Kenny Patterson was the consummate iron man among DePaul guards. For the better part of four years, DePaul fans expected to see Patterson on the floor for the opening tipoff.

Patterson cracked the starting lineup in the seventh game of his freshman season and was never bumped out. He eventually started 114 consecutive games and played in all 120 over his four-year career.

Patterson burst onto the DePaul basketball scene during the 1981-82 season. The highly-recruited guard out of New Jersey moved into the starting lineup in the seventh game of the season. Returning home on December 22, 1981, following a road loss to UCLA, the freshman got the starting call against Maine. That day Patterson led the Blue Demons to a 90-67 victory, and on the season DePaul went 26-2 and were ranked second nationally in the final Associated Press poll. Patterson averaged a modest 7.3 points per game, but he was the team leader in assists, with 92, and steals, with 56.

DePaul slumped a bit in 1982-83, but Patterson continued to improve. He averaged 10.3 points per game, handed out 187 assists, recorded 77 steals, and played a school record 1,205 minutes. DePaul, ending the regular season at 17-11, had to settle for the NIT that year. But with something to prove, they opened the tournament against Minnesota. A 76-73 victory set up a meeting against another Big Ten team, the Northwestern Wildcats. The game came down to the final seconds when Patterson nailed a buzzer beating jumper to lift DePaul to a 65-63 win at the Rosemont. Three games later DePaul lost to Fresno State in the NIT championship game.

Patterson and the Blue Demons stepped back into the NCAA tournament in 1983-84. Playing their final season under head coach Ray Meyer, the Blue Demons went 27-3 and were fourth in the final AP poll. Patterson averaged 8.3 points while handing out 187 assists, and amassing 68 steals.

Joey Meyer expected to have a point guard he could depend on, and Kenny P. did not disappoint. As a senior Patterson had his best year, averaging 10.9 points per game with 201 assists and 79 steals — all career highs. DePaul posted a 19-10 record and were selected for the NCAA tournament, losing to Syracuse, 70-65. Patterson finished his career with 1,111 points. He set school records with 669 assists, 280 steals, and 4,039 minutes played. He earned honorable mention All-America honors in his senior year, and was drafted by the Indiana Pacers in the third round of the 1985 draft.

Patterson passes to a teammate on the wing. Kenny P set a new assists record with 669 during his career.

Kenny Patterson's quickness and defensive pressure led to many fastbreak layups for both himself and his teammates during his DePaul career.

Kenny Patterson challenges a Northwestern guard during DePaul's 65-63 victory over the Wildcats in a 1983 NIT game.

mons were hitting on all cylinders as they beat Creighton 87-58. Kevin Holmes hit for a career-high 23 points on 11 of 15 shooting, while Ty Corbin added a team-high 10 rebounds.

After a third straight home victory, DePaul traveled to Birmingham, Alabama, to play UAB. A combination of poor shooting and 16 turnovers proved too much for the Blue Demons to handle as they lost their third straight on the road despite Corbin's season-high 25 points.

A two-game homestand resulted in back-to-back wins and two consecutive strong performances by Wayne Embry. In a nationally telecast game with Houston, Embry had 17 points and helped boost DePaul to a 45 to 30 rebounding edge with 11 rebounds. Two days later, he collected 13 points and 12 rebounds against Old Dominion.

Dallas Comegys dunks during the first Notre Dame game of the 1984-85 season. Comegys averaged 11.7 points per game for the season, including a season-high 24 points against Dayton.

DePaul headed to Notre Dame to try and break a three-game road losing streak. Behind Corbin's 18 points and Embry's 9 rebounds, DePaul had its first road win since December 12, beating Notre Dame 71-56.

A home win over Eastern Washington was followed by the first DePaul-Dayton matchup of the season. The Blue Demons played their usual tight defense, a little too tight for the officials liking. DePaul was whistled for 25 fouls to Dayton's 15, and shot only 12 free throws to Dayton's 28. DePaul was right in it until the end, with Dallas Comegys hitting 11 of 12 shots for a season-high 24 points. But DePaul fell for the fourth time of the season (all on the road) on a last second basket.

A win at Princeton was followed by a disappointing loss to Louisville. The Cardinals had lost five of their previous six games, including a 21-point loss the game before. Again, the homecourt advantage was too much for DePaul to overcome as Louisville scored 12 more points from the line than DePaul to win 77-74.

A return to the Rosemont did nothing to shake the Blue Demons out of their doldrums. Dayton completed the season sweep by winning game two 67-63. The loss put DePaul at 14-6 with eight games to play. Six victories would give DePaul twenty for the eighth straight year, and probably assure a spot in the NCAA tournament.

After a victory over Pepperdine, DePaul went on the road for two games. Perhaps guilty of looking ahead towards their matchup with 21-1 St. John's, the Blue Demons shot just 33 percent and lost to Loyola 78-71. The St. John's Redman made it two losses in a row for DePaul with a 93-80 victory. DePaul was now faced with the possiblity of having to win all of its remaining five games to receive an NCAA tournament bid.

With their backs to the wall, Joey Meyer's club won four straight. Seniors Kenny Patterson and Tyrone Corbin played superbly during the streak. Patterson led the team in scoring twice, including a season-high 21 against LaSalle, while Corbin scored 21 and grabbed 18 rebounds against Marquette.

The final game of the season was game two

in the Marquette series. As if the game wouldn't be tough enough for DePaul, the 17-10 Warriors felt they may need a victory against DePaul to receive a postseason invitation. Both teams shot well over 50 percent from the field, but the difference in this game was turnovers. DePaul turned the ball over 21 times compared to just 12 by Marquette, and Marquette won the game 68-64.

Losing to Marquette did not keep the 19-9 Blue Demons out of the NCAA tournament. DePaul's first round opponent would be Syracuse. The 21-8 Orangemen were led by Rafael Addison, Dwayne "Pearl" Washington, and freshman Rony Seikaly. Washington was the Big East assist leader, averaging 5.7 per game, and had averaged 15.4 points per game during the season.

Joey Meyer's first NCAA tournament victory would have to wait at least another year. The Blue Demons fell behind in the game early and were never able to get on track. Meyer's first season as head coach ended with a 70-65 loss, ending the twenty win season run at a school record seven.

Tyrone Corbin scored 17 points in his final game at DePaul. For the season he averaged 15.8 points per game and 8.1 rebounds, both team highs. Dallas Comegys added 11.7 points while starting only 11 games. Kenny Patterson bettered Clyde Bradshaw's career assists record with 201 in his senior season to push his career

Tyrone Corbin
Forward — 1981-85

It is hard to find a DePaul player who was more consistent during his college career than Tyrone Corbin. Corbin earned a reputation as a hard nosed, blue collar type player who gave 100 percent all the time.

In four years with the Blue Demons, Corbin led the team in scoring twice and in rebounding three times. He was part of three teams that went to the NCAA tournament and took another to the championship game of the NIT.

As a freshman in 1981-82, Corbin was a reserve on the Blue Demon's 26-2 team that finished the season ranked second nationally in the Associated Press poll. In his role he averaged 5.1 points and 6.1 rebounds for the NCAA qualifier.

Corbin stepped closer to the spotlight during the 1982-83 season. As a starting forward, he contributed 10.6 points and 7.9 rebounds as the Blue Demons went 21-12. The disappointment of not making the NCAA tournament that year was softened by the fact that the Blue Demons reached the NIT title game, losing to Fresno State. For his efforts in the tournament, Corbin was rewarded with a spot on the NIT all-star team.

As a team captain in 1983-84, Corbin was part of a team of overachievers that made up Ray Meyer's final team as head coach. After forty-two years as the head man at DePaul, Meyer went out in a blaze of glory. The upstarts managed a 27-3 record and were ranked fourth in the final AP poll. DePaul reached the regional semifinals of the NCAA tourney before losing to Wake Forest. On the season Corbin averaged 14.1 points and 7.4 rebounds and was named honorable mention All-America.

Corbin's finest season came in 1984-85. With Joey Meyer now the head coach, Corbin again served as a team captain. He led the squad with 15.8 points and 8.1 rebounds and earned honorable mention All-America for the second straight year.

Corbin scored 1,378 points and grabbed 893 rebounds while at DePaul. His point total placed him among the Top 10 and his rebound total was third behind Dave Corzine and M.C. Thompson.

Drafted in the second round of the NBA draft by the San Antonio Spurs, Corbin has also played with the Phoenix Suns and the Minnesota Timberwolves.

Tyrone Corbin beats everyone down court and gets an easy 2 points. Corbin averaged almost 16 points per game his senior season, many coming on plays like this.

Ty enjoys a rest during a break in the action. Corbin's love for the game and hustle prompted Joey Meyer to call him "a coach's dream."

An aggressive rebounder, Corbin often ignited the Blue Demons' running game with a defensive rebound and finished the play on the offensive end as the trailer.

total to 669. He also led the team in steals with 79, and averaged 10.9 points per game on the season.

While Joey Meyer's first season as head coach didn't end with a great run through the postseason, it was a winning one. His second one would be a greater challenge.

"I'm primarily interested in seeing the team progress on a game-by-game basis," says Meyer. "The wins and postseason bids will fall in place if we play at a consistent level. I want to see us get off to a good start in the season opener and then maintain it in the second game. We're gonna play 'em one at a time this season."

The Blue Demons would have to play one game at a time during the 1985-86 season without two of its leaders from the previous season, Tyrone Corbin and Kenny Patterson. And if that prospect didn't overjoy Meyer and DePaul fans, the Blue Demons would also face sixteen teams that had played in postseason tournaments the year before.

Coach Meyer would have to rely a lot on his four seniors—Marty Embry, Lemone Lampley, Kevin Holmes, and Tony Jackson. Co-captains Embry and Lampley would man the pivot. Embry had upped both his scoring and rebounding averages during the 1985 season. Lampley had again been second on the team in blocked shots, and had worked hard on the weights during the offseason.

Tony Jackson was expected to see time at both small forward and guard. A smart defensive player and a fine passer, Jackson was considered one of the finest athletes on the team and the toughest cover besides Comegys.

Many experts believed Kevin Holmes held the key to the Blue Demons' success. Holmes had a lackluster junior year, but there was no reason to believe that he couldn't bounce back. A great jumper, Holmes had to contribute in the scoring column and on the boards for DePaul to make a move nationally.

If Holmes could man the power forward spot, Meyer would be free to use Dallas Comegys at the small forward spot more in 1985-86. With his height, quickness and jumping abil-

Tony Jackson's jumping ability and quickness gave Joey Meyer the option of using him at off guard or small forward.

ity, Comegys would cause fits for other small forwards.

With Kenny Patterson gone, Joey Meyer had to find a point guard. The most likely candidate was Rod Strickland. A prep All-American, Strickland had all the tools to make an immediate impact. A capable scorer, he could hit the open jumper, drive the lane, and go baseline. But he was not just a scorer. An extraordinary ball handler and passer, Strickland made his teammates better by getting them the ball where they could do something with it offensively.

The other two incoming freshmen, while not receiving the buildup that Rod Strickland was, were both very talented. Terence Greene, a

6-4, 190-pound off guard, was known for his aggressiveness. Greene could have played football at a major college, but he decided to attend DePaul and concentrate on basketball. Blue Demon coaches were glad he did.

Stanley Brundy, the second freshman, reminded people of Tyrone Corbin because he loved to play the game and gave his all. Brundy was an excellent leaper and the type of player who would do the little things necessary to win.

The Blue Demons opened the season on the road at Northern Illinois. As they had done of late, the Huskies played the Blue Demons tough. DePaul managed a 34-28 lead at halftime, but NIU kept whittling away at the lead in the second half. DePaul eventually won, 63-61, but not before they made it interesting with 19 turnovers. Comegys was the leading scorer with what would turn out to be a season-high 28 points.

The second game of the season was a laugher, and the 93-48 win over St. Francis (N.Y.) allowed some of the subs to get valuable playing time. One player that took advantage of the easy opponent was Comegys. Not only did he score 18 points, but he had season-highs with 13 rebounds and 6 assists. Freshman Stanley Brundy also had a season-high 11 points and 6 rebounds.

Games four and five of the season, against Western Michigan and Houston, were significant because Lemone Lampley showed what he was capable of doing on a basketball court. Lampley averaged 20.5 points for the two games and even handed out 3 assists against Houston. DePaul won both games to set up a meeting with Northwestern.

The Northwestern Wildcats played the Blue Demons very tough in the first half, and held a 1-point advantage, 32-31. It was the first time that season DePaul had trailed at the halfway mark. The second half was no easier for DePaul. Though for the most part outplaying Northwestern, DePaul could not pull away because of absymal foul shooting (22-39 for the game). In the end DePaul prevailed 70-67 behind Kevin Holmes' 18 points.

The 6-0 Blue Demons were set to welcome

Senior Lemone Lampley led the team in both scoring and rebounding in back-to-back games against Western Michigan and Houston early in the 1985-86 season.

John Thompson's Georgetown Hoyas to the Rosemont. Georgetown had lost Patrick Ewing to graduation, but it was hardly a team without weapons. Reggie Williams and David Wingate had stepped to the forefront, with 6-9 freshman Jonathon Edwards supplying some firepower from the center spot.

Not having a dominate center allowed the Hoyas to open things up on offense and get everyone involved. The approach worked well against DePaul, as Georgetown ran to a 41-34 halftime lead. The second half was a continuation of the first half. DePaul played no better, and by the time the final second ticked off the game clock, Georgetown had stretched its lead to 85-70. The leading scorer for DePaul, for the first time in his career, was Rod Strickland with 20 points.

Losses at Purdue and against David Robinson and Navy in the opening round of the Cotton States Classic followed to put the Blue Demons at 6-3. In the Navy game, DePaul blocked 7 shots to Navy's and Mr. Robinson's 6. The big man for DePaul was Comegys with a season-high 6 blocks. The Navy game marked the first time in the 1985-86 season that DePaul had lost after leading at halftime (40-30). In the second game of the Classic, DePaul beat Texas 63-62 behind Dallas Comegys' 16 points and Tony Jackson's season-high 8 rebounds.

Returning home for a seven-game homestand, Joey Meyer hoped to build a long winning streak off the Texas win. DePaul opened with wins over Dayton (66-52) and Pepperdine (70-57). Rod Strickland was high scorer in both games and Dallas Comegys (6 steals) helped lead a suffocating DePaul defense against Pepperdine that totaled a season-high 19 steals.

Heading into its January 11 matchup with Notre Dame, DePaul looked to have turned things around. After the game, the Blue Demons looked like anything but a team on the rise. The problems with DePaul's free throw shooting continued (12 of 21), and carried over to its shooting from the floor. The Blue Demons hit on just 21 of 56 shots from the field for a season-low 37.5 percent.

Coach Kevin Mackey and Cleveland State were the next visitors to the Rosemont Horizon and they made themselves right at home. Holding a slight 33-30 win after the first half, State was all over DePaul in the second half and came away with a 90-75 victory. The only high point for DePaul was the 24 points Rod Strickland scored, the most so far in his short career. The low points included just 26 total rebounds and only 7 made free throws on 14 attempts, both season lows. The Blue Demons did establish one season high, they had 26 turnovers.

Coach Meyer made a lineup change before the Blue Demons' matchup with twelfth ranked Alabama-Birmingham. Stanley Brundy received his first career start. The move seemed to help. DePaul ran to a 33-22 halftime lead and won the game 70-61. Brundy scored 7 points, grabbed 5 rebounds, and had a season-high 3 assists. Coach Meyer said after the game,

"Stanley gave us a big lift." Also supplying "lifts" were Embry with team-highs in points (17) and rebounds (22), and Comegys with 6 blocked shots.

The Blue Demons cruised to victories in their next two games. The first victim was Loyola. DePaul ran off in the first half and took a 51-20 lead. On the game the Demons, behind Embry's 16 and Holmes' 12, had 62 rebounds in the 90-55 victory. Northern Iowa faired even worse, losing 96-53 to DePaul. Though the leading scorer for the Blue Demons was Holmes with 16, the player of the game was Terence Greene. The freshman had 14 points and 14 assists as DePaul posted a season-high 29 assists.

The Blue Demons started the month of February with a loss to Dayton. Ater a 73-41 victory over Evansville, DePaul dropped four in a row starting at Marquette. The Warriors game was a disappointment because the Blue Demons had fought back from 6-point halftime deficit to force the game into overtime. The next three losses, versus Old Dominion, Louisville and Creighton, were not pretty. DePaul was beat by a cumulative 45 points in the three games. In none of the three games did DePaul shoot over 50 percent from the field, and in only one game did it shoot over 50 percent from the free throw line.

Coach Meyer and his team now had a 13-10 record with just five games remaining on the schedule. With ten losses already, the feeling was that DePaul had to win all five games to receive an NCAA tournament bid. A 48-44 win over Indiana State started things off well, and brought St. John's, led by Walter Berry and Mark Jackson, to town for a nationally televised game.

DePaul rose to the occasion against a St. John's team that would finish the year with 31 wins. Moving the ball well, and shooting well, the Blue Demons jumped to a 38-31 halftime lead. The Redmen had several spurts in the second half, but DePaul was not giving up this game. Behind Dallas Comegys' 21 points and Rod Strickland's 17, the Blue Demons held on for a 81-72 win.

The impressive win was followed by two

losses on the road. Notre Dame beat the Blue Demons for the second time that season, 70-59, and then DePaul lost a heartbreaker against UCLA. The Blue Demons didn't play their best game of the season, but they kept fighting back. They erased UCLA's 6-point halftime lead, despite not shooting well for the game. Kevin Holmes had 19 points and 11 rebounds, Strickland had 16 points, and Andy Laux chipped in with 4 points and 5 rebounds off the bench, but the Blue Demons lost 65-63.

The final game of the season was at home against Marquette. In the first half the Blue Demons looked like a team that had just lost two straight games and wanted to make it three. Marquette went to the locker room with a 43-42 lead, and the Blue Demons went to the locker room with a very disappointed coach.

Rod Strickland and Tony Jackson congratulate each other during the second half of the Marquette game. DePaul won the final game of the 1985-86 regular season 98-87 as Strickland scored 27 and Jackson 22 points.

The Blue Demons came out for the second half looking like an NCAA tournament team. They out scored the Warriors 53 to 44 in the second half and had themselves a 95-87 victory. There was plenty of praise to go around, but three players stood out—two seniors and a freshman. Marty Embry led the team in rebounding with 10 and chipped in with 2 assists. Tony Jackson scored a season-high 22 points and hit on 8 for 8 from the free throw line. Rod Strickland kept up his great play in the latter part of the season with 27 points and 6 rebounds.

DePaul's only postseason hope seemed to be the NIT. But Joey Meyer and company hoped their difficult schedule and some good performances in losses against good teams would make a difference. The Blue Demon's just had to wait and see if the selection committee would choose a strong independent school with a 16-12 record.

The committee did choose DePaul, and the Blue Demons were determined to show they belonged in the tournament. Traveling to Greensboro, North Carolina, the Blue Demons would face Virginia in the first round of the East Regional.

The Blue Demons jumped to an early lead and held a 34-26 advantage at halftime. Virginia rallied in the second half and tied the game at 49 with 8:32 to play. DePaul bounced back with a 6-point run and was headed en route to a sparkling 72-68 upset of the Cavaliers. As is often the case in postseason play, the seniors stepped to the forefront. Lemone Lampley led the team with 15 points and Embry grabbed 11 rebounds to lead in that category.

The second round brought the Blue Demons up against Oklahoma. DePaul again started quickly, and had built a 38-33 lead by intermission. Oklahoma twice cut the lead to one in the second half, including 64-63 with 3:58 remaining, but the Blue Demons hit the shots down the stretch and came away with a 74-69 victory and a trip to the regional finals in East Rutherford, New Jersey.

The magic ran out for the Blue Demons in New Jersey. Facing the Duke Blue Devils, the

Blue Demons just ran into a better team. DePaul only trailed 37-32 at halftime, but Meyer's team could never get the lead and eventually lost 74-67. Duke proved how good it was by making it all the way to the tournament finals before losing to Louisville and Never Nervous Pervis Ellison.

The final ledger read only 18-13, but a strong performance in the tournament made fans optimistic for next year. Rod Strickland averaged 14.1 points and 5.1 assists, becoming the first freshman since Mark Aguirre to lead the team in scoring. He also set freshmen records for most assists (159) and steals (69). Dallas Comegys was second in scoring with 13.8 points per game and second in rebounding with 5.6 per game.

Another positive from the tournament was that Joey Meyer answered all questions about his ability to coach. It is never easy to succeed a legend, and it can be even harder when that legend is your father. When Meyer did not lead the Blue Demons to the 20-win level in his first two seasons with the team, people began asking questions. But by winning two NCAA tournament games, the most since 1979 when the team went to the Final Four, Joey Meyer proved once and for all that he belonged on the DePaul bench as head man.

With the graduation of Kevin Holmes, Tony Jackson, Lemone Lampley, and Wayne Embry, the Blue Demons were losing their number three, four, five, and six scorers. They were also losing over half of their rebounds, the number

Joey Meyer, pictured here with assistant coach Jim Molinari, quieted all of his critics by coaching DePaul to two NCAA tournament victories in 1986.

two man in blocked shots, and the number two and three man in steals. These four players would be missed.

14

A Perfect Fit

There are times in athletics that all the parts just fall into place and something special happens as a result. With guards Rod Strickland and Terence Greene now veteran sophomores, head coach Joey Meyer knew he had some talented and consistent players in the backcourt. Meyer said about Greene: "A year of experience and maturity will help and we look for him to make a big contribution." And on Strickland Meyer said: "At the end of last year, Rod was playing as well as any point guard around."

But there were some questions to be answered. Could senior center Dallas Comegys live up to his potential to be a star? Could juniors Andy Laux and Kevin Golden become valuable role players? Was athletic sophomore Stanley Brundy ready to play regularly? How would the Blue Demons respond to the three-point shot being used in college basketball for the first time this season? And how much help would the new recruits be to this year's team?

The key recruit was Kevin Edwards from Lakeland (Ohio) C.C. The second-team junior college All-American was considered an outstanding shooter and leaper with great quickness and strength. He had averaged 27.5 points and 7.5 rebounds while leading his team to a 27-5 record and the Ohio junior college championship. "Kevin has a good chance to contribute in his first year at DePaul because of his junior college experience," said Coach Meyer.

The rest of the newcomers were big men. James Hamby, 7-0, 230 pounds, was out of Elgin High School and had redshirted in 1985-86 to work on his basketball skills and strength. He only averaged 12.7 points per game as a high school senior, but blocked 116 shots. Kevin Holland, 6-7, 215 pounds, was being favorably compared to Kevin Holmes. An excel-

The 1986-87 DePaul Blue Demons opened at home versus Northern Illinois. Rod Strickland (10) scored 9 points and his new backcourt partner, Kevin Edwards, added 7 points as DePaul won 78-51.

lent rebounder, Holland was called "the best rebounder in southern California" by his high school coach. Charles Sowell, 6-9, 230 pounds, was rated among the top 100 high school players in the nation. A shot blocker and rebounder, Sowell could earn some playing time in his freshman season. And the fifth newcomer was a senior walk-on who had previously played two years at Drake, James O'Shaughnessy.

When Meyer decided to go with a smaller lineup, with Green at forward and Edwards in the backcourt, on opening day, things started to click. Edwards seemed to be the missing ingredient. Comegys grew to be a star. Strickland and Greene both began to score. Golden and Laux began to fill their roles. And Brundy became a rebounding force.

The opening game was against Northern Illinois at the Rosemont Horizon. It didn't take DePaul fans long to fall in love with the 1986-87 edition of the Blue Demons. DePaul shot off to a 34-23 halftime lead and won going away, 78-51. Rod Strickland dished out 9 assists to go along with his 9 points. And several of the preseason questions were starting to be answered. Comegys scored 23 points and had 13 rebounds. Golden started at one forward spot and scored 4 points to go with 5 rebounds. Laux had 4 points and 3 assists off the bench. And Brundy, though not starting, supplied 6 points and 7 rebounds.

Terence Greene, playing at the small forward spot, scored 17 points on 6 for 7 shooting from the field. And the man who made the Greene position switch possible, Kevin Edwards, had 7 points, 5 rebounds, and 2 assists. He also hit the Blue Demons first three-point goal.

DePaul defeated North Carolina-Wilmington next to set up a meeting with the 1-1 Illinois State Redbirds. The Blue Demons won by eight after leading by ten at halftime. But the reassuring thing was they did it without their center. Comegys only scored 2 points on 1 of 9 shooting, but other players picked up the slack. Strickland scored 24 points, Edwards added 10, Greene 9, and Andy Laux 8 points on 3 for 3 shooting including 2 three-pointers.

An easy victory over Western Michigan

moved DePaul to 4-0 and set up the teams first real test of the season. The Blue Demons took on the national champion Louisville Cardinals in Freedom Hall.

The Blue Demons opened an early lead and held a 37-30 advantage at the break. Though Pervis Ellison and Herbert Crook got their points as expected, the Blue Demons held everyone else pretty much in check. On the Blue Demons side, Kevin Edwards had his first big game. After averaging just under 9 points a game and shooting only 15 of 36 in the first four games, Edwards scored 20 points on 7 of 13 shooting. Other players in double figures were Comegys (23), Greene (12), and Golden (10) as DePaul won 75-68.

DePaul wasn't seriously tested in its next six games, against Creighton, Old Dominion, Northwestern, Pepperdine, Dayton, and Furman. Comegys led the team in scoring in three of the games, Strickland in one, Edwards in one, and Greene, Comegys, and Brundy were co-leaders in the Pepperdine game with 17 points a piece. Brundy also had 10 rebounds in the Pepperdine game, while Strickland had his first double-figure assists total of the season against Old Dominion with 10.

The 11-0 Blue Demons welcomed the 8-2 Fighting Irish to the Rosemont Horizon next. Notre Dame's two losses had come in the first two games of the season. Led by Donald Royal, David Rivers and Mark Stevenson, the Irish would be a good test for DePaul.

The game was a hard fought defensive affair. DePaul held a 29-25 lead at half. In the second half Notre Dame held tough, in part because of poor foul shooting by DePaul, but DePaul managed to win 59-54. One of the keys in the game was the Strickland-Rivers matchup. River shot only 2 of 13 from the field for 10 points, 6 points under his season average. The big gun for Notre Dame was Royal with 21 points, but he fouled out of the game late in the second half. Strickland led the way for DePaul with 17 points, while Greene added 16 points. Stanley Brundy continued his excellent play off the bench with 8 points and a team-leading 7 rebounds.

DePaul beat Loyola 84-65 in its next game behind the scoring of Comegys and Edwards. The duo both scored over 20 points, the third time they had done so in the same game. Kevin Golden also had an impressive outing with 6 points and 12 rebounds.

Three more victories made the Blue Demons 16-0 and ranked third nationally. When the two teams ahead of them lost, DePaul found itself playing at Georgetown as the nation's last unbeaten team. A win over the Hoyas would make the Blue Demons the nation's top ranked team.

This was the third straight year that the Blue Demons had met Georgetown with a perfect record. The two previous years the Hoyas had ended the winning streaks. The 1987 Georgetown Hoyas were 13-2 and led by senior Reggie Williams and freshman Mark Tillmon.

Dallas Comegys shoots the jumper versus Loyola. His 23 points led DePaul in its 84-65 win in 1987.

Georgetown sprinted to a 41-30 halftime advantage behind the play of Williams, Tillmon, and Perry McDonald. With 14:37 remaining, the Hoyas had a 51-40 lead. And then DePaul made its move. Back-to-back Stanley Brundy baskets completed the Blue Demons comeback, and with 2:44 remaining the Blue Demons had run up a 9-point lead, 70-61.

The Hoyas were not dead, however, and they mounted a comeback of their own. In the next two minutes the Hoyas went on an 8-1 run to pull within 71-69. With 28 seconds remaining, Williams buried a three-pointer for a 72-71 lead for Georgetown. After DePaul failed to score they fouled Williams, who was perfect on the day so far from the line. He calmly hit the two free throws and the last unbeaten team in the country fell 74-71.

DePaul had four players in double figures, led by Comegys with 19 points and Strickland with 18. Georgetown got 23 points from Williams, including the all-important last 5, and 19 points from Tillmon, 10 points over his season average. But the difference in this game was rebounding. DePaul had outshot Georgetown 59 percent to 46 percent, but the Hoyas had taken 21 more shots thanks to 11 more rebounds than the Blue Demons grabbed.

The Blue Demons won back-to-back games against Weber State and LaSalle before North Carolina State came to town. The Wolfpack were 12-7 and had lost three games in a row. DePaul held Charles Shackleford to just 6 points and Vinnie Del Negro to 8 points in winning 84-62. The leading scorer for N.C. State was Walker Lambiotee, who would later transfer to Northwestern. The Blue Demons had five players in double figures and five players with 7 or more rebounds, for a rebounding advantage of 51 to 32.

DePaul won its next five games in easy fashion. One highlight during this stretch was the continued good play of Stanley Brundy. He scored in double figures in four of the games, averaging 13.2 points per game. In DePaul's 83-71 victory over Alabama-Birmingham, Brundy scored 20 points and grabbed 16 rebounds, both career highs.

The Blue Demons finished the regular season with Georgia Tech, Notre Dame, and Marquette. Georgia Tech was 16-11 as it made its way into the Rosemont Horizon. The Yellow Jackets were led by two forwards, Duane Ferrell and Tony Hammonds. Both players were averaging around 17 points per game.

The game turned into the Comegys-Ferrell show. Comegys scored 33 points and Ferrell 31 points to lead their respective teams. Comegys grabbed 10 rebounds and Ferrell nabbed 11 to, again, lead their respective teams. The difference in this game was that Comegys had more help from his teammates. Strickland added 28 points, 8 rebounds, and 9 assists as DePaul won 84-67.

The addition of Kevin Edwards allowed Terence Greene to move to forward for the 1986-87 season. Here Edwards shoots a one-hander against N.C. State. DePaul beat the Wolfpack 84-62 as Edwards scored 10 points and grabbed 9 rebounds.

DePaul next dropped in at Notre Dame. If Notre Dame was to win this time around, Donald Royal would have to receive more help from his teammates. The game was tied at twenty-nine at halftime, and continued to be close in the early going of the second half until Notre Dame broke loose. With Brundy in foul trouble, the frontline of Royal, Mark Stevenson, and Gary Voce were able to get a foothold. Behind Royal's 32 points and 14 rebounds and Stevenson's 15 points, Notre Dame coasted to a 73-62 victory.

After a win over Marquette closed the regular season at 26-2, DePaul waited to see where it would start the NCAA tournament. The where turned out to be the Rosemont Horizon against Louisiana Tech.

Louisiana Tech, though not well known, had some talent on its team, but DePaul proved to have more. DePaul stretched a 37-28 halftime lead to 76-62 final score. Dallas Comegys led the way with 29 points on 12 of 14 shooting from the field. Not so impressive was his 5 for 12 shooting from the line. Rod Strickland added 25 points and Kevin Edwards was the third player in double figures with 12.

The victory over La. Tech earned DePaul a chance at St. John's. The 21-8 Redmen had squeeked by Wichita State, 57-55, in their first round game. St. John's and DePaul had some opponents in common. Louie Carnesecca's team had defeated Georgia Tech by nine points and split its series with Georgetown. St. John's relied on three players for most of its scoring—Mark Jackson, Willie Glass, and Shelton Jones.

DePaul played about as well as a fan could

Dallas Comegys
Center — 1983-87

In his forty-two years as head coach of the Blue Demons, Ray Meyer generally limited his recruiting trips to the Chicago area. In his later years, while his assistant coaches would travel all over the country to recruit, Meyer generally stayed at home. When it came time to recruit Dallas Comegys, a prize center from Philadelphia's Roman Catholic High School, Meyer hit the road, and Comegys was a Blue Demon.

Comegys showed his flash as a freshman in 1983-84. Despite coming off the bench, he was second on the team with 11.2 points and 6.4 rebounds per game. His contributions can not be overlooked when determining how the Blue Demons, in Meyer's final season, finished 27-3, ranked fourth in the Associated Press (AP) poll, and played in the NCAA tournament.

Comegys' sophomore year was somewhat of a disappointment. Though he averaged 11.7 points and 4.5 rebounds, and was again second on the team in scoring, there wasn't the improvement DePaul fans hoped for. And it didn't help that the Blue Demons slipped to 19-10 and lost immediately in the NCAAs.

As a junior, and starting regularly for the first time, Comegys improved to 13.8 points and 5.6 rebounds in 1985-86. He was again second in scoring and rebounding on an 18-13 team that reached the NCAA regional semifinals.

Comegys was to be second to no one as a senior in 1986-87. Playing the best ball of his college career, he led the team with 17.5 points and 7.5 rebounds per game while blocking a school record 108 shots. And against the Dayton Flyers he blocked 10 shots as DePaul won 88-65.

Comegys lifted the Blue Demons to a 28-3 record, setting a school record for wins. DePaul was fourth in the final AP poll and again went to the NCAA regional semifinals. Comegys earned third team All-America honors.

Comegys was taken in the first round of the National Basketball Association draft by the Atlanta Hawks, the twenty-first player selected. He ended his DePaul career with 1,555 points. Only Mark Aguirre, Dave Corzine, and George Mikan scored more. He also set a school record with 297 blocked shots and was among the Top 10 with 714 rebounds.

Patrick Ewing steps out to try to block Comegys' shot in the 1984 Georgetown-DePaul matchup. The Blue Demons upset the Hoyas to remain undefeated.

Dallas Comegys protects the basket against Georgia Tech in 1986 as Kevin Golden and Terence Greene look on. Comegys scored 33 points in DePaul's 84-67 victory.

Comegys and Kenny Patterson do a little celebrating after a DePaul score against Notre Dame in 1984-85. DePaul won the game 95-83 to move to 5-0 on the season.

Dallas Comegys displays perfect follow-through on his jump shot against LaSalle. The Blue Demons won the 1985 game, 87-50.

The DePaul bench reacts to a little showtime from Dallas.

want in the first half and cruised to a 42-30 lead. But the Redmen, behind their big three, staged a comeback. They finally tied the score—and then took the lead. With just 19 seconds left in the game the Redmen held a 69-65 lead.

With 12 seconds left, Comegys scored on an offensive rebound and was fouled. Still trailing by two points, Comegys intentionally missed the free throw. Kevin Edwards grabbed the rebound and found Strickland for the tying layup to force overtime.

DePaul dominated the extra period, outscoring the Redmen 14-6 for an 83-75 win. Kevin Edwards was high scorer for the game with 26 points. The duel of the point guards was about even. Strickland scored 16 points with 5 assists and 3 rebounds, while Mark Jackson had 23 points, on 8 more shots, with 7 assists and 2 rebounds.

DePaul now moved to Cincinnati to play Dale Brown's Fighting Tigers. Louisiana State was led by Nikita Wilson (15.6 ppg and 7.0 rpg) and Anthony Wilson (16.6 ppg). LSU had defeated Georgia Tech by six in the first round and Temple by ten in the second round to earn a shot at DePaul.

LSU took a 38-34 halftime lead behind the two Wilsons. The second half was as tight as the first, but DePaul could never get the upper hand. Behind Nikita Wilson's 24 points, LSU ended DePaul's season with a 63-58 victory. Dallas Comegys ended his career at DePaul by leading the team in scoring with 14 points. For the tournament he averaged over 19 points per game and 9 rebounds.

With a 28-3 record, the Blue Demons set a school record for victories while finishing the regular season ranked fourth nationally in the Associated Press poll. Meyer earned national Coach of the Year honors from Chevrolet and CBS Sports. Comegys averaged 17.5 points and 7.5 rebounds while earning All-America honors. He also had 108 blocked shots. Strickland added 16.3 points and 6.5 assists per game. And junior college transfer Kevin Edwards averaged 14.4 points per game and totaled a team-high 65 steals.

People associated with the DePaul basketball program began referring to the 1987-88 season as A.D.—After Dallas. The 6-9 center/forward had taken his game to the pros, and Joey Meyer was faced with replacing the talented player.

There was no shortage of candidates. Two of the four newcomers could play the middle and two veterans were looking to increase their playing time.

The newcomers, Bill Heppner and Curtis Jackson had impressivecredentials. Freshman Bill Heppner was a McDonald's All-America selection after averaging 20.6 points, 13.0 rebounds, 3.3 blocks, and 2.0 assists as a senior. The Chicago Sun-Times called him one of the top five high school players in the area. Prop 48 sophomore Curtis Jackson was from Brockton, Massachusetts. As a senior in high school he averaged 14 points, 10 rebounds, and 5 blocked shots a game. At 6-10 and 230 pounds, he had the size to play center at the college level.

Both the veterans, sophomores Charles Sowell (6-10, 230) and James Hamby (7-1, 225), had size also, but had played limited minutes as freshmen. Sowell was a strong rebounder who ran the court well. Coach Meyer said, "Sowell has good size and fine touch. He has the tools." Hamby had only played 36 minutes in 1986-87, but did show some progress. He would have to continue to improve to get more minutes.

DePaul returned the rest of its starting unit, and it was these four players that had Meyer and the fans optimistic. The backcourt of Rod Strickland and Kevin Edwards were receiving preseason praise, and Meyer rated them among the nation's best. "I don't know all the guard combinations in the country, but I'm extremely pleased with ours. I don't know for sure, but I would think they're one of the best." The two guards combined for 30.7 points per game in 1986-87, and were 1-2 in steals on the team.

Backing up the pair were long-range bombers Andy Laux and Brad Niemann. Laux had made 34 of the 69 three-pointers that DePaul had in 1986-87. Niemann, a freshman out of Glenview, Illinois, had made 76 consecutive free throws as a prep senior. He was also expected to be a three-point threat off the bench.

Starting forwards Terence Greene and Kevin Golden returned along with the top two subs, Stanley Brundy and Kevin Holland. Joining this group was Chris Henderson, who missed last season because of Prop 48.

"Terence Greene, although playing small forward, is really a guard. He gives us some flexibility with his ball handling and shooting skills, said Coach Meyer. Greene averaged 10.5 points per game as a sophomore and was second on the team in assists.

Brundy had averaged more minutes than Golden in 1986-87, but Golden had started every game. With the strides Brundy had made in his first two years, he had to be considered for the starting job. Joey Meyer knew well of Brundy's strengths. "He has a tremendous nose for the ball and was a big factor in several of our wins last year because of that nose for the ball. He seemed to be able to come up with the big block or the big rebound." Allowing Meyer flexibility was the fact that Golden was the type of player that could start or come off the bench and perform well.

Holland and Henderson seemed certain to come off the bench. Of the two, Holland looked to be the most prepared to contribute right away. Coach Meyer praised his hard work during the summer and his versatility.

Everything looked in place for another assault on the national championship, even without Comegys. But when star guard Rod Strickland was declared ineligible for the first term, the early season got tougher.

The Blue Demons showed how important Strickland was to their success very early in the season—the first game. For the first time in four years, DePaul opened against a team other than Northern Illinois. Pepperdine, however, was not a stranger to DePaul. The Waves lost to DePaul 92-75 in 1987. Coach Jim Harrick, now at UCLA, had four returning starters from that 12-18 team, including Levy Middlebrooks and Craig Davis.

DePaul won the battle in the first half, taking a 37-32 lead. Without Strickland to help supply the knockout punch in the second half, the Waves fought back. In the final seconds Terence Greene was fouled and missed a free

Kevin Golden, known more for his defense and rebounding, slams down 2 points against Dayton. Golden started all 31 games in 1987 and began the 1988 season in the starting lineup.

throw that would have put DePaul ahead. The game went into overtime and Pepperdine outscored DePaul 14-6 in the extra period to win 84-76.

Not all the Blue Demons problems could be traced to the missing Strickland. It was not Strickland that allowed Pepperdine to out rebound DePaul 56 to 48. Nor was it Rod who missed 16 of 35 free throws.

DePaul played its second overtime game in a row as Niagara, behind 30 points by Mark Henry, looked to win its opener. This time the Blue Demons came out on top by the slimmest of margins, 88-87. Greene, for the second game in a row, led the team in scoring. For the first two games of the season, he was averaging 29 points.

Things looked a little better after DePaul defeated Illinois State in the third game of the season. The Blue Demons forced 21 turnovers and out scored the Redbirds by sixteen in the second half to win 76-55. For the third game in a row Stanley Brundy led the team in rebounding, while Kevin Edwards topped the scorers with 21 points.

Strickland returned for the next game against Western Michigan and led DePaul to a 94-64 win. Looking like he was never gone, Rod led the team in scoring with 21 points off the bench on 7 of 10 shooting. Kevin Holland also had a good game off the bench with a team-leading 8 rebounds.

Coach Meyer inserted Strickland into the starting lineup in the next game against Notre Dame. As in the games between the two last season, the point guard matchup would be interesting. This year, though, David Rivers was being asked to score more for the Fighting Irish than in previous years.

Behind the play of David Rivers and Mark Stevenson, Notre Dame took a 36-30 halftime lead. With six minutes to play its lead was up to 57-49, and with just under two minutes left DePaul was still trailing by six. But a Stanley Brundy tip-in made the score 63-59 with 1:38 on the clock. Seconds later Terence Greene converted his own steal into a layup for a 63-61 score.

When DePaul got the ball back Kevin Edwards scored off a Strickland assist to tie the score at 63. Then with just three seconds left, Brundy fouled sophomore Keith Robinson. Robinson had scored 14 points in the game, but he missed both free throws and the game went to overtime.

DePaul had the upper hand during the extra period, and took a 3-point lead in the final seconds on an Edwards 18-footer. Strickland added a free throw and the Blue Demons won 73-69.

Strickland and Rivers were the high scorers for their teams. Rivers had 26 points to go with 4 rebounds and 4 assists. Strickland hit for 22 points and added 5 rebounds and 9 assists.

Easy wins at Weber State and Washington

Kevin Edwards
Guard — 1986-88

To talk about Cinderella stories is to talk about Kevin Edwards. A lightly regarded player out of St. Joseph High School in Cleveland, Edwards was cut from an NCAA Division III team and played junior college basketball before coming to DePaul and stepping into the national spotlight.

A tremendous work ethic, as evidenced by the hours of practice he put in, lifted Edwards from a marginal player to a professional star. And the biggest steps were taken at DePaul.

Though Edwards had averaged 24.1 points and 7.5 rebounds per game at Lakeland Community College, it was somewhat of a surprise when he stepped into the starting lineup for DePaul in his first season. But the 6-3 Edwards fit in well with Rod Strickland, Dallas Comegys, and the other Blue Demons. He averaged 14.4 points, on .536 shooting from the field and .808 from the line, and 5.0 rebounds per game on the 28-3 squad.

Edwards' work ethic continued to pay off during the 1987-88 season. He increased his scoring average to 18.3, his rebounding average to 5.3, while handing out 117 assists and recording 68 steals. The Blue Demons finished the season at 22-8 and advanced to the NCAA tournament for the fifth straight season.

Edwards finished his career at DePaul with the highest career three-point field goal percentage (.446) and a career scoring average of 16.3.

The Miami Heat made Edwards the twentieth selection in the 1988 NBA draft. Picking up where he left off at DePaul, Edwards averaged 13.8 points per game in his rookie season and was named to the NBA All-Rookie Second Team.

Kevin Edwards scored 17 points during DePaul's 73-69 overtime victory over Notre Dame during the 1987-88 season, including the tying basket during regulation.

Kevin Edwards crashes the boards against Northwestern during the 1986-87 season. Though only 6-3, Edwards was the third leading rebounder both years he played at DePaul.

Edwards (20) was second to Rod Strickland in scoring during the 1987-88 season with 18.3 points per game.

Edwards' quickness and jumping ability allowed him to block 19 shots in 1988.

gave DePaul a six-game winning streak and a 6-1 record going into Welsh-Ryan Arena to play Northwestern.

The Wildcats had control of this game almost from the start. Grabbing a 40-32 halftime lead, Northwestern would not allow DePaul back in the game. Good defensive rebounding, and 25 for 30 shooting from the line helped Northwestern to a 78-64 victory over the Blue Demons.

A home game against Texas-San Antonio and a road contest against Hartford were next for DePaul. The Blue Demons won both games

Rod Strickland slips inside for 2 of his 9 points versus Georgetown. The Hoyas beat DePaul 74-64.

Terence Greene (13) slips inside for an offensive rebound and basket against Texas-San Antonio during the 1987-88 season. Greene scored 11 points in the contest giving him double figures in scoring for the first nine games of the season.

with Edwards and Strickland the top two scorers in each game. The Hartford game marked the first start of the year for Kevin Holland, in place of Brundy, and he responded with 11 points and 8 rebounds in DePaul's 68-61 triumph.

John Thompson and 10-1 Georgetown visited the Rosemont next. The Hoyas continued their recent mastery of the Blue Demons, winning 74-64. Brundy returned to the starting lineup to score 16 points and collect 9 rebounds, second to Edwards in both categories.

The Blue Demons would entertain Dayton next without Rod Strickland. Idled by a disciplinary suspension, Strickland would be replaced in the starting lineup by Andy Laux. Dayton had lost six straight games, but the Blue Demons knew full well that Dayton-DePaul games were always tough.

Dayton did not look like a team that hadn't won in three weeks. The Flyers took a 36-29 lead at half and would not allow DePaul back into the game. For the game Dayton shot 31 of 49 from the field behind 8 for 11 shooting performances by Negele Knight (23 points) and Anthony Corbitt (20 points). Terence Greene was high man with 24 points for DePaul.

Strickland returned to the lineup at Notre Dame, scoring 28 points in the Blue Demons 79-72 win. Edwards chipped in with 20 points on 9 of 12 shooting. The backcourt continued to provide the spark in three more victories as the Blue Demons improved to 12-4.

The Blue Demons next traveled to Raleigh, North Carolina, to face North Carolina State. DePaul sprinted to a 24-15 lead, but Jim Valvano's team rallied back to within 31-29 at half. The difference for the Wolfpack during the comeback was their frontline. Charles Shackleford, Chucky Brown, and Brian Howard stood 6-10, 6-8, 6-7, respectively. Though Brundy had a good game for DePaul, leading rebounder in the game, both he and Kevin Holland fouled out of the game. N.C. State's starting frontline outscored DePaul's 40-18 and out rebounded it 24-17.

A nip and tuck affair went to the Wolfpack after freshman guard Chris Corchiani hit two free throws late in the game. DePaul then missed in the final seconds and N.C. State had the victory. A dunk at the buzzer provided the final margin, 71-66.

DePaul beat Indiana State 64-56 before arriving at another ACC school's home. This time the opponent was Georgia Tech, and again DePaul got out to an early lead. But Georgia Tech chipped away at the lead and went into the locker room at half with a 1- point lead after Craig Neal hit a three-pointer from near midcourt as time expired.

DePaul was nursing a 1-point lead when Kevin Holland was fouled and sent to the line with three seconds left. Holland hit the first shot for a 70-68 lead, but missed the second shot. The Yellow Jackets rebounded the miss and called time out.

Georgia Tech had several options for the last shot. Brian Oliver was 8 for 11 from the field

Kevin Edwards heads skyward for 2 of his 20 points against Notre Dame. DePaul shot 60 percent from the field in the 1988 victory.

It is best to get out of Stanley Brundy's way when he has a clear leap to the basket. Here Brundy scores 2 of his 13 points against N.C. State.

win 65-63. The loss put DePaul at 14-7 with seven games remaining.

DePaul won all seven games, including an impressive 77-58 win over Louisville. Also impressive was the play of Stanley Brundy during the last four games of the season. It started against Miami of Florida when he scored 31 points and 16 rebounds against a frontline that included Tito Horford. Brundy then scored 30 points against Dayton, and followed that up with a 26-point, 11- rebound game against Louisville and Pervis Ellison. In the regular season finale, Brundy scored 15 points and had 9 rebounds in a 77-65 victory over Marquette. During the stretch Brundy averaged 25.5 points

including 2 for 2 from three-point land. Duane Ferrell was the leading scorer with 21 points and had hit his only three-point attempt of the day. Dennis Scott had attempted over half of Tech's three-pointers in the game but was only 2 for 8. And, of course, there was the first half buzzer beater, Craig Neal.

It was Dennis Scott who received the inbounds pass near midcourt. He dribbled twice to his left and let a 30-footer go that swished at the horn to lift Georgia Tech to a 71-70 victory.

DePaul returned home and topped 15-3 Bradley and its All-America guard Hersey Hawkins, 86-80. Hawkins scored 25 points, but the high man for the game was Rod Strickland with 29 points.

Evansville supplied DePaul with another last second loss with a tip-in at the buzzer to

Senior Andy Laux gets his shot off before Hersey Hawkins of Bradley can get to him. Laux supplied outside shooting and careful ball handling to the 1987-88 Blue Demon team.

and 11.5 rebounds per game, compared to his season averages of 14.7 and 8.7. His .671 shooting percentage was similar to his season mark of .658, but .842 free throw percentage was remarkable considering he shot only .520 on the year.

The Blue Demons, with a 21-7 record, reached the NCAA tournament for the fifth straight year. Their first opponent in the tournament would be Wichita State. Stanley Brundy continued his great play with 26 points and 9 rebounds as DePaul downed the Shockers 83-62.

Next up was Kansas State. State employed a tough zone defense to limit DePaul's inside play and force DePaul into outside shots. The zone worked. Brundy and Holland only managed five shots a piece, and Strickland, Greene, and Edwards could not get their shots to fall with any regularity. On the day DePaul shot 22 of 59, including 8 of 21 from beyond the three-point line. Kansas State hit on 22 of its 43

Rod Strickland
Guard — 1985-88

Any discussion of DePaul's greatest guards has to include Rod Strickland. A three-year starter, Strickland was a complete player for DePaul. He could score, he could pass, and he could play defense. He was very quick, very fast, and completely ambidextrious. At times it appeared he could do anything with the ball he wanted.

As a freshman in 1985-86, Strickland was the leading scorer on a team that was spotted with talented veterans. He averaged 14.1 points per game and also dished out 159 assists while recording 69 steals. With his help the Blue Demons qualified for the NCAA tournament with a 16-12 record. Though their record was not sparkling, DePaul quickly proved they belonged in the tournament with a 72-68 victory over Virginia. Then after a victory over Oklahoma, their Cinderella season ended as they lost to Duke 67-74.

Strickland's play improved in 1986-87 and he played a major role in a record setting season. The Blue Demons went 28-3 on the season, setting a school mark for victories in a season, and were ranked fifth nationally in the final AP poll. In the first two rounds of the NCAA tournament DePaul defeated Louisiana Tech, 76-62, and St. John's, 83-75, in overtime. That set up a meeting with the LSU Fighting Tigers, featuring Nikita and Anthony Wilson (no relation). The Wilson Gang proved too much as DePaul lost 63-58.

On the season, Strickland averaged 16.3 points per game with a .582 field goal shooting percentage. He also led the team with 196 assists and chipped in with 60 steals while earning honorable mention All-America honors.

Strickland showed he had even more scoring punch as a junior in 1987-88 when he finished with a 20.0 scoring average. He also posted career highs in assists (202) and steals (75), and set a Rosemont Horizon record with 8 steals in a 93-82 victory against Texas-San Antonio. Rod was named honorable mention All-America for the second straight year, and DePaul (22-8) played in the NCAA tournament for the third time during his career.

Strickland decided to forego his senior season and applied for the NBA draft as an undergraduate. He was selected in the first round as the nineteenth pick overall by the New York Knicks. He was traded to the San Antonio Spurs during his second season, teaming him with former DePaul great Terry Cummings.

Strickland left DePaul with 1,448 points, just 13 short of Howie Carl's school record for points by a guard. His 557 assists were third all-time behind Kenny Patterson and Clyde Bradshaw, who both played four years. And he was second to only Kenny Patterson with 204 career steals.

Rod Strickland averaged 20.0 points per game during his final year at DePaul, while handing out 7.8 assists.

Strickland drills 1 of his 9 field goals during the overtime victory against Notre Dame in 1988. Rod led the team in scoring with 22, and assisted on the tying basket in regulation.

No one can catch Strickland as he goes in for an uncontested layup versus Creighton during the 1986-87 season. The combination of Dallas Comegys inside and Rod Strickland outside led DePaul to a 28-3 record.

Rod Strickland splits Del Negro and Giomi North Carolina State to score on a left-hand layup. Strickland led the Blue Demons with points as DePaul won 84-62.

shots, including 10 of 13 from three-point land. The result was a 66-58 loss for the Blue Demons and an end to their 1987-88 season.

The two leading scorers for the Blue Demons were Rod Strickland, 20.0 points per game, and Kevin Edwards, 18.3 points per game. Strickland and Edwards were also 1-2 in assists and steals, while Edwards was third in rebounding. The number one rebounder and number three scorer was Stanley Brundy. His back-to-back 30-point games were the first for a Blue Demon since Mark Aguirre accomplished it. Much of the success and consistency of the Blue Demons in the latter part of the season can be traced to Brundy and Kevin Holland.

Playing their final games in a DePaul uniform in 1987-88 were Kevin Edwards, Andy Laux, Kevin Golden—and Rod Strickland. The first three names were expected because they had no more eligibility left, but it was somewhat of a surprise when Strickland announced for the the NBA draft. When the DePaul guard duo was drafted back-to-back in the 1988 draft, it marked the end of one of the most potent backcourts in DePaul history.

15

Fast Forwards to the Future

With the loss of star guards Rod Strickland and Kevin Edwards, Joey Meyer was facing a new experience as the 1988-89 season began. From the beginning of his tenure as an assistant coach in 1971-72, Meyer had always had a good point guard to run the team.

It was different this time. Veterans Stanley Brundy and Terence Greene primarily played forward as did highly touted freshmen David Booth, Stephen Howard, and Curtis Price. Though these players had talent, there was no point guard or bonafide superstar among the bunch.

"Every year your team has a personality," said Joey Meyer. "We're going to have to develop a chemistry. We have to play well together. We don't have a superstar like we've had with Dallas Comegys, Rod Strickland, or Kevin Edwards the last couple of years. We have to develop a unity to win. We have some talent, but not the super talent. We have to blend it together."

The blending together would start with the seniors—Terence Greene and Stanley Brundy. "When you build a team, you look at your seniors first," said Meyer. "It's very important that they provide leadership for the younger players."

"Stanley Brundy was coming on strong late last year. He was second in the country in shooting, and started to rebound. I hope that can carry into this year. We need Terence Greene to settle down and play his game. He has the talent to have a big senior year."

DePaul played most of 1987-88 without a center in the lineup, using forwards Brundy, Kevin Holland, and Kevin Golden as twin posts. In 1988-89, Meyer was looking for a contribution from a big man. The candidates were basically the same as the year before—James

Terence Greene (13), one of two returning seniors, was expected to be a key contributor on the 1988-89 squad. Here Greene unleashes a shot from the perimeter against Notre Dame.

Hamby, Curtis Jackson, Charles Sowell, Bill Heppner.

The most likely player to step forward was Hamby. A junior, he had become a solid reserve late in the season playing 80 minutes in the last 9 games of the year. "James got some playing time last year at the end and did some things for us," Meyer said. "He can block shots, but he needs to be a dominant factor on the defensive boards to go along with that."

The new addition to the center race was freshman center/forward Stephen Howard. The 6-9 Howard was an all-stater from Dallas, Texas, who was a pre-season honorable mention All-America in *Street & Smith's Basketball* before his senior year in high school. As a senior he averaged 24.6 points and 16.2 rebounds per game.

Three starters returned at the forward spots. Senior Stanley Brundy was the top returning scorer, forty-ninth on the career scoring list with 733 points, with an average of 14.7 points per game. He also led the 1987-88 squad with 8.7 rebounds per game.

Junior Kevin Holland, 6-7, 210 pounds, had started 12 games last year. He averaged 5.6 points and 5.7 rebounds. Said Coach Meyer, "Last Year, Holland did exactly what we needed him to do rebounding and playing defense. Now, we need him to move forward offensively."

Depending on how other players developed, Terence Greene would play forward or guard. He averaged 11.3 points per game last season and had played in every game the last three seasons. Greene was expected to add leadership to the team as well as an improved outside shot.

Incoming freshmen David Booth, Curtis Price, and the above-mentioned Howard also could see playing time. Booth and Price were both rated in the top 100 high school players by talent scout Bob Gibbons. Of the two, Booth's basketball skills were probably farther along, especially on offense. But Price had all the athletic skills to develop into a great player.

If you took away Brundy, Greene and Holland, the remaining players had provided only 6 percent of the total offense in 1987-88. The inexperience was most notable at guard. If Greene was needed at forward, Meyer was left with sophomore Brad Niemann and three newcomers. Melvon Foster, a Prop 48 sophomore seemed to have a slight edge over junior college transfer Gilbert Miller and freshman Chuckie Murphy, a non-scholarship player.

DePaul suffered its first loss of the season before the first game when Bill Heppner went down with a knee injury. Also ailing was Kevin Holland, suffering from a back injury. He later would be redshirted. It now looked like Greene would have to remain at forward at least until one of the younger players proved himself.

Melvon Foster got the nod at point guard for the season opener against Nevada-Las Vegas in the Maui Classic. The rest of the starting lineup was Niemann at the other guard spot,

Greene and Brundy at forward, and freshman Stephen Howard playing the pivot.

The UNLV Runnin' Rebels had lost seven players from their 1987-88 squad that had gone 28-6. But no one was taking pity on Jerry Tarkanian because he had only one starter returning. The Tark would blend his holdovers with a group of talented junior college transfers.

UNLV beat DePaul behind Greg Anthony's 28 points and George Ackles' 12 points and 9 rebounds. Melvon Foster, in his first game as a Blue Demon, led the team in scoring with 21 points. He hit 9 of 11 shots and also dished out 6 assists. Three other newcomers had their moments, too. Howard scored 10 points and had 4 rebounds, while Booth and Price pitched in with 6 points apiece.

DePaul's second round opponent figured to be as tough as the first. Ohio State returned four starters including two players that had double figure scoring averages the year before. Ohio State pulled out to a 35-31 halftime lead behind Jay Burson and Perry Carter. DePaul hung tough in the second half behind David Booth and Terence Greene. With the score tied late in the game, Burson hit a short jumper to take a 72-70 lead, and the victory. The loss dropped DePaul to 0-2 for the first time in its history. Booth and Greene each scored 20 points to lead the Blue Demons in scoring.

Victories over Chaminade and Maine moved the Blue Demons to 2-2. In the Chaminade game, Brad Niemann hit 7 of 10 three-pointers to lead the team with 25 points.

DePaul next made the short trip to Normal, Illinois, to play Illinois State. ISU had five starters returning off an 18-13 team, and Horton Field House was always a tough place to gain a victory. The game was a classic Redbird-Blue Demons duel. ISU had a 4-point halftime advantage, 35-31, but the Blue Demons kept hammering at them behind seniors Greene and Brundy. And when DePaul was down by two with just seconds on the clock, it was Greene who launched a buzzer beating three-pointer to win the game. The shot capped a 25-point performance by Greene to go with Brundy's 24 points and 8 rebounds.

Meyer's team returned home to the Rosemont and lost a stunner to Washington. DePaul had led at the half, 39-29, but Washington got back in the game behind the three-point shooting of Mike Hayward.

The Blue Demons defeated Niagara and American in their next two games. Brundy had strong performances in both games, 23 points and 10 rebounds against Niagara and 33 points and 9 rebounds against American. Brundy wasn't the only player to put up good numbers against American as DePaul scored 120 points to win by 35 points. DePaul shot 42 of 64 from the field as Howard didn't miss (5-5, 10 points) and Melvon Foster hit 8 of 10 off the bench.

The Georgetown Hoyas were waiting for the Blue Demons next at the Capital Centre. The 5-0 Hoyas would present all kinds of problems for DePaul. Not only did they have Charles Smith, Mark Tillmon, and Jaren Jackson returning (42 points between them in Georgetown's victory last year), but they had added freshman sensation Alonzo Mourning. It was the 1-2 punch of Smith and Mourning that did DePaul in this game. Smith scored 37 points, while Mourning added 19, as Georgetown prevailed 74-64. DePaul had 26 turnovers in the game and shot only 16 free throws, 2 less than Mourning alone.

The Old Style Classic would be DePaul's last action before Christmas. After beating North Carolina A&T in the first round, DePaul was matched up against Paul Westhead's high-scoring Loyola Marymount team. For a fan who liked offense, the game was a dream come true. Combined the two teams took 156 shots and scored 226 points. The Lions were led by Hank Gathers with 32 points and Jeff Fryer with 30. For DePaul the story was Stanley Brundy. To say he took to the up-and-down style of play would be an understatement. Brundy exploded for 47 points and 20 rebounds before fouling out. The point total was second only to George Mikan's 53 points and DePaul won the game 115-111.

DePaul next played in the USF&G Sugar Bowl tournament against Mississippi State. DePaul took almost as many shots in this game as in the Loyola Marymount game, but with far different results. While hitting 45 of 72 shots against the Lions, DePaul connected on only 25 of 65 against the Bulldogs. The most important one of the twenty-five was another buzzer beater by Greene to give DePaul a 62-60 win.

DePaul's shooting woes continued in the title game against Seton Hall. The Pirates swarming defense forced DePaul into 21 of 48 shooting and 28 turnovers as Seton Hall won the tournament final 83-60.

Things didn't get any easier for Joey Meyer's club. North Carolina visited the Rosemont and ran off to a 52-36 halftime lead on its way to a 20-point victory. Two days later the Blue Demons were in Kentucky to take on the Louisville Cardinals. DePaul was down only six at halftime, but behind Pervis Ellison the Cardi-

Curtis Price scores on a tip in as David Booth (30) and Melvon Foster (20) look on. Price contributed 8 points, 4 rebounds, and 4 assists to the Blue Demons victory over Loyola Marymount.

nals went on a late run that buried the Blue Demons and resulted in their third straight loss.

DePaul's record stood at 8-7 at the halfway point of the season. The optimists pointed out that the Blue Demons had played six games against teams ranked in the top twenty. The pessimists argued that DePaul had been unable to beat even one of those six teams. Most fans, though, seemed to be guardly optimistic. The team was young and improvement was expected. And playing ranked teams now should help in the long run.

The reasoning seemed sound as the Blue Demons won two straight at home, defeating Eastern Illinois, 89-75, and Loyola Marymount, again, 122-108. Stanley Brundy was again the big gun for DePaul against Marymount with 41 points and 23 rebounds.

DePaul then traveled to Milwaukee to take on Marquette in the first game of a four-game road trip. DePaul was beaten badly in the second half of the game, being out scored 40-28. The result was a 72-64 loss.

The Blue Demons returned to Chicago for a

Freshman Stephen Howard gets into the lane for a short jumper versus Loyola Marymount. Howard scored 8 points and 5 rebounds in DePaul's 115-111 victory.

Terence Greene pushes the ball up court in DePaul's second meeting with Loyola Marymount in 1989. Greene scored 20 points and dished out 11 assists during the up tempo game that DePaul won 122-108.

road game against Loyola. DePaul had the lead at intermission, 35-31, but in the second half Loyola, using basically five men, played inspired basketball. It was only fitting that Keith Gailes (24 points, 13 assists, 3-3 on three-pointers) hit the winning free throw with no time on the clock.

With a 10-9 record and a two-game losing streak, the DePaul Blue Demons entered Carver Arena in Peoria to play Bradley, owner of a fourteen-game homecourt winning streak. The two seniors, Greene and Brundy, knew something had to happen quickly or their final season at DePaul would be a lost one. DePaul beat Peoria 85-82 behind Brundy's 28 points and Greene's 17. Brundy was also the leading rebounder (9) and Greene the leading assist man (6). The last game on the road trip was at South Florida. DePaul fell behind 31-25 at half and it seemed the up and down season was continuing. But the Blue Demons regrouped and came out strong in the second half. Behind Brundy and Stephen Howard, the Blue Demons outscored the Bulls 42-28 in the second half for a 67-59 win.

Joey Meyer's 100th career victory came against Duquesne and put DePaul over the .500 mark for the month of January. Meyer made several lineup changes before DePaul's next game against North Carolina State. Howard was moved back to starting center and Curtis Price took David Booth's spot at forward. The changes seemed to work as Howard scored 19 points and had 8 rebounds, while Booth scored 10 points off the bench, to help DePaul beat N.C. State 81-74.

Two more victories gave DePaul a six-game winning streak as St. John's visited the Rosemont Horizon. St. John's roared to a 38-23 lead by halftime, and looked like it would make this one a laugher. Behind Brundy and Greene, the Blue Demons made a comeback, but it fell short and DePaul lost 67-64.

DePaul won three of its next four to head into the final game of the regular season against Notre Dame at 19-11. The Irish had been the Blue Demons one loss in that four-game stretch, but this time the game would be played at the Rosemont. Brundy and Greene stepped to the forefront in their final home game—Brundy scored 20 and Greene 21. But it was Howard, a freshman, that sealed the 73-70 victory with a pair of free throws with ten seconds left in the game.

A sixth straight NCAA berth landed the Blue Demons in Boise, Idaho, against Memphis State. For the fourth year in a row, DePaul won its first game in the tournament. Stanley Brundy scored 20 points and had 15 rebounds, while Greene added 14 points and Booth 17, as DePaul won 66-63.

The win placed DePaul against the team it had begun the season with back in Hawaii—UNLV. DePaul played the Rebs much tougher in the first half than in their previous meeting and had the score tied at halftime. But UNLV broke the game wide open in the second half and cruised to an 85-70 win.

As they had for most of the season, Stanley Brundy and Terence Greene stepped forward in the final game of the season to lead the team. Brundy led in rebounds with 15 while scoring 10 points. Greene led the team in scoring, with 29, and assists, with 6, and was tied for second in rebounds with 7. On the season Brundy (19.5) and Greene (14.9) were 1-2 in scoring and steals (67 to 53). Brundy also led the team

David Booth goes baseline for the dunk during DePaul's 73-70 victory over Notre Dame in 1989. Booth scored 6 points and added 5 rebounds in his final regular season game as a freshman.

in rebounding (10.2) and blocks (47). Greene was tops in assists with 5.1 per game and third in rebounds with 4.7.

"When you lose your best inside scorer and your best outside scorer, your leading rebounder, and your two leading scorers, you have some holes to fill," said Joey Meyer heading into the 1989-90 season. For the second straight year Meyer would have to replace his top two players. The returnees had some talent but were short on experience.

DePaul's three seniors were all centers, but the player who saw the most starts at center the previous year was only a sophomore. James Hamby, Curtis Jackson, and Charles Sowell (the seniors) had averaged only a combined 3.9 points and 3.6 rebounds per game over the entire 33-game schedule. But each player had his

Stanley Brundy
Forward — 1985-89

Of the hundreds to play basketball at DePaul through the years, perhaps no one improved as much from their freshman year to their senior season as Stanley Brundy.

A lightly regarded forward from basketball power Crenshaw High School in Los Angeles, Brundy was talented but raw as a freshman. He started four times as a freshman in 1985-86, but played in only 18 games, averaging 2.5 points and 2.0 rebounds.

Brundy moved into a more vital role in 1986-87. The top reserve forward, Brundy averaged 8.0 points and 6.5 rebounds on DePaul's 28-3 team that reached the NCAA regional finals.

Brundy cracked the regular starting lineup for the first time as a junior. He improved his scoring ability as the year progressed, scoring 33 at Miami (Fla.) and 31 at Dayton in consecutive late season victories. Brundy's final stats for the year were 14.7 points and a team leading 8.7 boards per game as DePaul was 22-8 and again NCAA tournament participants. Brundy also set the single season field goal percentage record, shooting .658 from the floor.

With the departure of stars Rod Strickland and Kevin Edwards, conventional thought was that Brundy would have a tough time matching his junior year totals. But Brundy used his quickness and leaping ability to its fullest in 1988-89.

The 6-foot-7 Brundy finished his senior year with 19.5 points and 10.2 rebounds per game, joining Bill Robinzine, Dave Corzine and Terry Cummings as the only Blue Demons to average in double figures in both since 1970.

Brundy had three record-setting games early in the 1988-89 season. First, in an 120-85 victory over American, Brundy set a Rosemont Horizon record by shooting .875 (14-16) from the field. Three games later, in the Old Style Classic, Brundy scored 47 points, a Horizon record, while making 21 field goals, a team record, in a 115-111 victory over Loyola Marymount. Less than a month later DePaul faced Loyola Marymount again, and this time Brundy grabbed 23 rebounds, another Rosemont Horizon record.

Brundy scored 642 points as a senior. Only Mark Aguirre scored more in a season. He snared 336 rebounds as well, the sixth best single season mark, as DePaul finished at 21-12.

Brundy left with 1,375 career points and 835 career rebounds, placing him in the Top 10 in both categories. He was selected in the second round of the National Basketball Association draft by the New Jersey Nets.

own strengths that Coach Meyer could utilize in different situations. Stephen Howard, the sophomore, started 22 games and was second on the team in rebounding. A good high post player, Howard needed to improve his scoring down on the blocks.

Three players returned at the forward position with starting experience—David Booth, Curtis Price, and Kevin Holland. Booth had shown during his freshman year that he could be a bigtime scorer (23 points vs. Notre Dame). The only thing holding him back was his strength and defense. Price played both inside and outside for Meyer. A solid defender and rebounder, Price's offensive skills needed some work. Holland had bulked up during his time off for his back injury and looked ready to mix it up underneath. How much the time off would hurt him was yet to be determined.

At guard DePaul had three players who had started in 1988-89. Chuckie Murphy was a starter at season's end, and with improved defense he could remain there for 1990. Melvon Foster's big problem was consistency. He had all the weapons, now all he needed to do was rein them in a bit. Brad Niemann was the team's three-point threat. Meyer hoped Niemann's back problems were a thing of the past.

The freshmen class consisted of a forward and two guards. All three players were ranked among the top fifty high school seniors. Deryl Cunningham was a 6-7 forward with good all-around skills. B.J. Tyler, a 6-1 guard, had led his high school team to two Texas state titles. Terry Davis had good size for a guard and was known for his shooting ability. It looked like he might have the best chance of contributing right away considering the personnel situation.

Heading into the 1989-90 season, the Blue Demons were on a roll. DePaul had averaged nearly 24 wins per season the previous three years and had reached the NCAA tournament six straight times. It was now time to see if this team could keep up the momentum.

DePaul opened the season at home against Ohio State in the Dodge Preseason NIT. The starting lineup was Hamby at center, Holland and Booth at the forward spots, and Melvon Foster and B.J. Tyler at the guards. The 1989-90 team shot out of the gate and built a 45-22 halftime lead behind Booth, Holland, Tyler, and Howard. The Blue Demons sustained the lead in the second half and Meyer was able to empty his bench. Howard ended as the high scorer with 15 points, and Booth added 11 points along with 11 rebounds.

The second game of the tournament brought North Carolina State to town and the result was the same. N.C. State put up a much better battle, but, behind Booth's 23 points and 10 rebounds, Howard's 18 points and 10 rebounds, and Holland's 16 points and 13 rebounds, the Blue Demons won 70-63. The win earned DePaul a trip to the tournament semifinals at Madison Square Garden in New York City.

Playing against St. John's, regular occupants of the Garden, the Blue Demons led throughout most of the game. DePaul was up 40-32 in the second half when St. John's went on an 8-0 run to tie the game. The Blue Demons answered the challenge and pulled ahead to lead 52-49 in the final minute. A pair of free throws moved St. John's to within one, 52-51. DePaul, attempting to run the clock out, was called for traveling with just six seconds remaining in the game. St. John's inbounded the ball to Greg "Boo" Harvey who dribbled the length of the floor and rang up his fifteenth and sixteenth points of the night on a jumper at the buzzer to win the game 53-52.

Whether it was the disappointing loss or the overall skill of DePaul's next opponent, the Blue Demons got hammered in the consolation game. Nevada-Las Vegas took third place in the tournament with an 88-53 victory. Considering that the Runnin' Rebels went on to win the national championship, their skill might have had something to do with it. Larry Johnson led all scorers for the game with 32 points and DePaul committed 31 turnovers.

The Blue Demons rebounded from the UNLV loss with a victory over Hartford at home. Then the wheels fell off. LaSalle came to the Rosemont and, behind 26 points from Lionel Simmons and 20 points by Doug Overton, defeated the Blue Demons soundly, 83-62.

The loss was the first of five in a row. Houston, Western Illinois, North Carolina, and Dayton defeated DePaul in succession, dropping Coach Meyer's club to 3-7. During the first ten games of the season, DePaul failed to shoot 50 percent from the floor in any game. The Blue Demons had made just 38 percent of its shots during the losing streak.

Before the next game against Marquette, Joey Meyer made another lineup change. He had been trying different combinations for most of the season, and this time he went with Holland and Booth at the forward positions, with Howard at center, and a backcourt of Foster and freshman Terry Davis.

The move seemed to work as DePaul jumped to a 30-22 halftime lead. The second half was played virtually even, and DePaul had broken its losing streak with a 71-62 victory. Everyone in the starting five contributed to the win, with four of the five scoring in double figures. This was the lineup that Meyer would stick with for most of the season.

The Marquette game started DePaul on a five-game winning streak. The Blue Demons shot over 50 percent in three of their next four games led by Holland (12 for 18), Booth (27 for 53), and Howard (22 for 36). Booth, Howard, and Davis scored in double figures in all four of the games.

DePaul put its winning streak on the line against Georgetown on January 13 in the Rosemont. Charles Smith had completed his eligibility, but the Hoyas still had Alonzo Mourning, Mark Tillmon, and an assortment of other great athletes. In the first half it looked like the Blue Demons might make it six in a row, taking a 35-32 lead into the locker room. But the second half was all Georgetown. The combination of Mourning and Tillmon proved too much as Mourning scored 26 points and grabbed 14 rebounds, while fouling out both Hamby and Howard. Tillmon added 21 points, and Georgetown left town with a 74-64 victory.

A win over Niagara preceded the second game of the season with Marquette. This time Marquette ripped the Blue Demons 77-55 at the Bradley Center in Milwaukee. The Blue Demons rebounded with a 5-point victory over Detroit to improve to 10-9 with Louisville on the horizon.

The Louisville Cardinals were a different team from the one that defeated the Blue Demons 81-67 during the 1989 season. Gone were Pervis Ellison and Kenny Payne who had combined for 35 points during last year's meeting. DePaul no longer had Brundy and his 20 points from the year before, but it did have David Booth, who had scored 20 himself. In the 1989-90 matchup, Booth was the difference. He totaled 37 points, on 15 of 23 shooting from the field, 7 rebounds, and 3 steals. Everytime Louisville got close it was Booth hitting a key basket. For his effort he was named *Sports Illustrated* National Player of the Week. Melvon Foster had his second straight strong perform-

Stephen Howard (21) hits a short jumper as Terry Davis (25) and James Hamby (44) cover the boards in DePaul's 64-56 victory over Hartford during the 1989-90 season. Howard had a game-high 14 rebounds to go with his 19 points.

B.J. Tyler looks for an outlet after penetrating among the tall timber of Georgetown. The Hoyas won the 1990 matchup, 74-64.

ance running the team as he dished out 10 assists. And Kevin Holland and Stephen Howard both grabbed 10 rebounds.

The Blue Demons then fell into an alternating pattern for three weeks, winning their midweek games but losing on the weekends. A win against Miami (Fla.), followed by a loss to UCLA, followed by a win against Fordham, followed by a loss to N.C. State, followed by another win over Miami (Fla.), followed by a very tough loss to Alabama-Birmingham at home. In the UAB game, DePaul led throughout the game before falling behind down the stretch and dropping a 74-68 decision.

With the loss, DePaul dropped to 14-12 with six games remaining. The first of the six games was at Notre Dame and things looked bleak from the start. DePaul trailed 29-11 at one point in the first half before pulling to within ten, 34-24, at the break. The Irish stretched the lead to 41-30 before DePaul started to make its move.

The comeback was completed when Booth hit a basket, was fouled, and dropped in the free throw for a three-point play to put the Blue Demons up by one with twelve seconds left. Notre Dame had one more chance, and with five seconds left Elmer Bennett missed a shot but was fouled. Bennett stepped to the line and calmly knocked down both shots to move the Irish ahead 62-61.

Without a timeout, the Blue Demons immediately inbounded the ball. Sophomore guard Chuckie Murphy let fly a desperation three-pointer that was wide left, but Stephen Howard grabbed the rebound and dunked it at the buzzer for a stunning 63-62 win.

Despite the emotional win, DePaul could not shake the alternating win-lose approach and lost to St. John's, 77-74. Next on the schedule was Bradley, a team having a tough year. DePaul won 59-48 as Terry Davis hit on 10 of 13 shots (8 of 9 in the first half) for a career-high 22 points. The victory put DePaul at 16-13 with three games left.

Texas handed the Blue Demons their fourteenth defeat, the most by a DePaul team since

DePaul celebrates its 66-62 victory over Louisville in 1990. David Booth was player of the game with 37 points.

Kevin Holland pulls up on the break for a short jumper versus Texas. DePaul lost the 1990 contest, 89-79, even though Holland scored 12 points and nabbed 11 rebounds.

Creighton. Rather than play at the Rosemont Horizon, DePaul opted to play at Alumni Hall. Behind a balanced scoring attack, DePaul took a 40-37 halftime lead. The Blue Demons extended the lead throughout the second half and ended up with a 89-72 win. Stephen Howard was the high scorer for DePaul with 23 points including 11 for 11 from the line. Kevin Holland pitched in with a career-high 17 points.

Alumni Hall was to be the site of DePaul's second round matchup against Cincinnati. DePaul took a 28-25 halftime lead behind steady play from the frontline. The second half was a back and forth affair, with no team being able to open a lead. With then seconds left the game was tied and DePaul had the ball looking for the victory. That is when lightning struck for the 1970-71 season, by the score of 89-79. DePaul bounced back to beat Northern Illinois 69-51. That left DePaul with one more regular season game.

Notre Dame was looking for revenge for the heartbreaking loss a few weeks earlier, while DePaul felt a win over the Irish could propel it to the NCAA tournament. The Blue Demons again fell behind early, trailing the Irish 27-22 at halftime. A quick second half rally evened things up and then put DePaul ahead to stay. When time expired, DePaul had won 64-59.

With an 18-14 record and a pair of wins over Notre Dame, the Blue Demons hoped for a berth in the NCAA tournament. But when the field was announced, DePaul was nowhere to be found. Worse, a team the Blue Demons had twice defeated, Notre Dame, had been included.

The Blue Demons accepted a bid to the NIT and were awarded a home game against

With both teams fighting for an NCAA tournament bid, the DePaul-Notre Dame contest was at times tense. DePaul won the game 64-59, but still did not receive a bid.

Chuck Murphy tries to wrap up a Notre Dame player for a held ball. Murphy came off the bench to score 9 points, all on three-pointers, and dish out 6 assists.

the second time in the season. With five seconds left, Chuck Murphy took a tough jumper from the right of the key. The shot missed, but Stephen Howard won the fight for the rebound and hit a short jumper with just one second on the clock. Once again DePaul had won in the last seconds of a game.

DePaul traveled to Kiel Auditorium for its next game against St. Louis University. After hitting over 50 percent of their shots in the first two games of the NIT, the Blue Demons went cold. Their final shooting numbers were just 19 of 64 from the field including just 1 of 16 from three-point land. St. Louis defeated DePaul, 54-47.

On the season David Booth was the team's high scorer with a 16.9 average. His 592 points scored were the second most scored by a sophomore in the history of DePaul. Stephen Howard was second in scoring (14.4 ppg), while leading the team in rebounding with an 8.1 average.

Despite not reaching the NCAA tournament for the first time in his career, Meyer may have done his best coaching job during the 1990 season. After opening 3-7, he abandoned his run and press style of play for a slower deliberate pace. His team played better defense and became a good free throw shooting and rebounding team.

Although it hit only 43 percent from the field, this team scored enough points to win twenty games for the fourth straight season. With a 20-15 record, the Blue Demons learned enough about winning to make the future look bright.

The 1990-91 season would be different for Joey Meyer. For the first time since his rookie season, DePaul would have its leading scorer and rebounder returning. Not only that, but DePaul would have all five starters back.

"This is a unique situation for us," Meyer said. "This is having the players back and having to ask them to improve. You know where their potential lies and you know what it will take for them to reach it."

The Blue Demons were losing some talent. Gone were the three backup centers that supplied bulk and defense against some of the bigger teams—Hamby, Sowell, and Jackson.

"We have almost everybody back, but you can't lose sight of the fact we lost fifteen ball games," Meyer said. "The players have to work hard. There is not an automatic improvement. Just coming back does not mean you are coming back better."

The frontline of DePaul looked to be the strength of the 1990-91 squad. The top two scorers the previous year were forward David Booth and center Stephen Howard. Kevin Holland also returned as did Curtis Price. Price had been forced to redshirt in 1989-90 because of wrist surgery. The backups would come from a group that included Bill Heppner and two freshmen—Jeff Stern and Michael Ravizee.

The guard situation was strong, but needed improvement in several key areas. Senior Melvon Foster, sophomore Terry Davis, and junior Chuck Murphy all had good games in the past. Better perimeter shooting, ball handling, and consistency were what Meyer wanted the guards to concentrate on for the upcoming season. It was hoped that Brad Niemann could return to help with the perimeter shooting problem, but his back still made him a question mark. Newcomer Joe Daughrity, from Oxnard (Calif.) Community College, was a six foot point guard who was expected to see some action.

After struggling out of the chute the last few seasons, the 1990-91 Blue Demons wanted to start the season with a winning streak. That goal was achieved as DePaul won its first four games for the first time since 1986-87.

DePaul's first opponent was Hartford. Returning three starters from a team that had finished 17-11 in 1989-90, the Hawks would make a good opening game opponent. The Blue Demons starting lineup consisted of Howard and Booth at forward, Foster and Davis in the backcourt, and freshman Jeff Stern at center. DePaul came out strong and on its way to a 36-28 halftime lead. The second half was a higher scoring affair, and a bit closer. But DePaul held on to win 84-73. David Booth led the way with 22 points, while Stephen Howard scored 15 points and grabbed a team-high 12 rebounds. Melvon Foster had a strong game with 10 points, 4 assists, 5 rebounds, and 4 steals. And Brad Niemann scored 15 points off the bench on 3 of 6 shooting from beyond the three-point line.

The next three victories over Florida International, Pepperdine, and Illinois State were fairly easy. Chuck Murphy scored 21 and 20 points off the bench against Fla. International and Illinois State, respectively, while Howard averaged 21.5 points for the three games.

DePaul next faced the Louisville Cardinals in Freedom Hall. Louisville had three starters back from its 27-8, 1989-90 squad and figured to give the Blue Demons a battle. Denny Crum's team did not disappoint.

Howard and Booth kept the Blue Demons in the game in the first half, but Louisville turned up the heat in the second half. Up only four at half, the Cardinals out scored the Blue Demons 58-43 in the second half to win 94-75. Louisville had 13 steals and forced 24 DePaul turnovers. Brad Niemann hit on 4 of 8 three-point

David Booth goes up for a jumper with half the Louisville team draped over him. Booth has averaged 27.3 points per game against Louisville in his first three seasons.

shots, but the rest of the team missed all 7 shots it took.

Things didn't figure to get any better against DePaul's next opponent, UCLA, and they didn't. Despite the insertion of Kevin Holland into the starting lineup and 40 points from David Booth, the Bruins won a tight one, 92-90. The difference in this game was rebounding. DePaul had more steals (11 to 7), fewer turnovers (11 to 18) and more free throws (20 to 15), but UCLA grabbed 45 rebounds to DePaul's 28.

The third annual Old Style Classic field was one of the strongest yet, with DePaul, Wisconsin-Green Bay, Oklahoma State, and Southern Illinois all appearing in the NIT the previous year. DePaul's opening round opponent would be Wisconsin-Green Bay. The Fighting Phoenix handed DePaul its third-

Stephen Howard
Center — 1988-91

When looking for the perfect example of a true student athlete, many college basketball observers point to DePaul's Stephen Howard. In addition to being an outstanding basketball player, Howard is a top student as well.

The son of a pair of Dallas, Texas, educators, Howard made his mark at DePaul both on and off the court. As a student, he carried a 3.4 grade point average through his junior year and was pointing toward law school after graduation.

On the basketball floor, Howard was among the best inside/outside big men in school history. The 6-foot-9, 225-pound Howard averaged 7.5 points, including 16 double-figure games, and 4.9 rebounds as a freshman in 1988-89, helping DePaul to a 21-12 record and an NCAA tournament appearance. His rebounding totals were seventh all-time for a freshman.

He improved to 14.4 points and a team leading 8.1 rebounds in his sophomore season. He scored 26 points, including a game winning dunk at the buzzer, in a 63-62 victory over Notre Dame late in the season. DePaul went 20-15 and reached the quarterfinals of the National Invitation Tournament (NIT). Howard was named an NIT All-Star following the tournament, after averaging 16.7 points per game, including the game winner over Cincinnati in the second round with one second left, and 7.7 rebounds.

As a junior, Howard continued to improve, averaging 15.3 points and 6.3 rebounds as DePaul went 20-9 and returned to the NCAA tournament. Howard was named first team Academic All-America and earned the prestigious Anson Mount Scholar Athlete Award from *Playboy* magazine. With one year remaining in his college career, he stood twentieth in career scoring with 1,195 points. He also was sixteenth in career rebounds.

---

straight defeat, 57-56. When Oklahoma State beat DePaul 72-70, the Blue Demons were a .500 team heading in the wrong direction. Most disappointing was the fact that the Blue Demons had three straight losses at home by two points or less. If DePaul couldn't win the close ones at home, what would happen on the road?

Next up was North Carolina in the first round of the Red Lobster Classic in Orlando, Florida. After battling early, the Blue Demons succumbed to the talented Tar Heels 90-75. It took overtime to finally notch one in the win column. Central Florida's Ken Leeks, a 6-9, 235 pound center/forward was having his way with the Blue Demons to the tune of 25 points, 15 rebounds, and 2 blocked shots. But behind Stephen Howard's 26 points and David Booth's 20, the Blue Demons won 81-78.

The winning streak grew to four as the Blue Demons topped Dayton, Marquette, and Houston. Stephen Howard scored 20 or more points in each of the three games, while Booth averaged 18.0 points and 10.7 rebounds per game during the stretch.

Joey Meyer and team traveled to DeKalb, Illinois, to take on an old friend in Jim Molinari, an assistant at DePaul for eleven years under both the Meyers, and the Northern Illinois Huskies. The Huskies were a senior led team that was experiencing great success. The Huskies jumped all over the Blue Demons early and led at halftime 39-28. The record-setting crowd of 6,261 fans at Evans Field House were looking for a continuation of the trouncing in the second half but were a bit disappointed. DePaul staged a furious second half rally ignited by good defense. But NIU held together at the end and put to rest a 70-61 victory. Donnel Thomas led all players in scoring and rebounding with 20 points and 17 rebounds. Booth was high man for DePaul with 18 points, while Melvon Foster pitched in with 7 points and 4 steals.

Melvon Foster (20) is in position for a pass or a rebound versus St. John's in 1991. Foster averaged 6.9 points per game on the season.

A loss at Texas dropped DePaul to 8-7. Terry Davis scored 28 points off the bench on 11 of 14 shooting (4 of 5 from three-point land), but he wasn't enough to offset the inside-outside attack of Locksley Collie (22 points) and Joey Wright (26 points on 6 three-pointers).

The Blue Demons thankfully returned home and they got hot. Coach Meyer juggled the starting lineup, sitting Stephen Howard down and promoting Terry Davis to a starting forward spot. Back-to-back victories over Drake and Duquesne put DePaul at 10-7 going into a road contest against Marquette.

DePaul led at halftime, 30-24, before coming out in the second half and attacking with its defense. Sparked by a 22-0 run early in the second half, DePaul took an 84-56 decision. Terry Davis, Joe Daughrity, and Curtis Price had 2 steals a piece, while Jeff Stern added 2 blocked shots. It was the sixth straight game that Stern had at least 2 blocked shots.

The winning streak looked to be in jeopardy as the Blue Demons took on Georgetown and its twin towers at the Capital Centre. The Hoyas opened a 20-8 lead midway through the first half, but then DePaul went on its own run. A 16-10 run made the halftime score 30-24 in favor of Georgetown, but DePaul outscored the Hoyas 24-7 to start the second half and never looked back. The 72-63 win was Coach Meyer's first win at the Capital Centre in his seven years as head coach.

The four-game winning streak grew to eight as the Blue Demons defeated Detroit, Bradley, Loyola, and Niagara. Starters Davis and Booth both averaged in double figures over the four-game stretch as did Howard off the bench.

DePaul took a 16-7 record to Notre Dame and let one slip away. Behind Daimon Sweet's 26 points and Elmer Bennett's 21, Notre Dame won in overtime 80-77.

The Blue Demons won the final four regular season games by double digit margins. Miami (Fla.), St. John's, Miami (Fla.) again, and Notre Dame all fell victim to DePaul's balanced attack. In each of the four games DePaul had four players score in double figures. The constant

Kevin Holland slips behind the defense and prepares to receive the pass against St. John's during DePaul's 79-69 victory. Holland averaged 5.8 points per game and 3.6 rebounds during the 1990-91 season.

David Booth
Forward — 1988-91

At first glance, David Booth did not look like a major college basketball player. His 190 pounds is stretched thin over a 6-foot-7 frame, and when he goes up against bigger, stronger foes, it looks like a mismatch. Oftentimes it is; in favor of Booth.

Despite the frail appearance, Booth is an iron man of sorts. In his first three years with the Blue Demons, Booth played in all 97 games and grew to be a team leader and fan favorite.

Booth showed spots of brilliance as a freshman in 1988-89. Despite weighing only about 165 pounds, Booth took the ball inside with success, scoring 9.9 points per game along with 4.4 rebounds. Possibly his finest performance came against Notre Dame when he scored 23 points, 7 rebounds, and 2 assists. DePaul finished the season at 21-12 and reached the NCAA tournament.

Booth stepped to the head of the scoring class as a sophomore. He started all 35 games in 1989-90, averaging 16.9 points and 6.1 rebounds as the Blue Demons posted a 20-15 record and went to the quarterfinals of the National Invitation Tournament.

Booth scored 37 points and collected 7 rebounds and 3 steals in an upset of Louisville that season. The performance earned him national player of the week honors from *Sports Illustrated*.

Booth improved even more as a junior. Spending more and more time in the paint, he led the team in both scoring and rebounding with 18.7 points and 6.8 rebounds per contest. He scored a career high 40 against UCLA and earned honorable mention All-America as the Blue Demons finished 20-9 in the NCAA field.

With his senior season still ahead, Booth stood fifth in career scoring with 1,463 points (tied with Curtis Watkins). He also stood twenty-first in career rebounds and among the career Top 10 in blocked shots and steals. By the end of his career, Booth may well join Mark Aguirre in the 2,000 club.

---

was Howard off the bench who rang up 17, 18, 12, and 17. Davis and Booth were both in double figures in three out of four games and averaged in double figures. Daughrity was in double figures twice, and Holland, Foster, Stern, and Niemann once.

The season closed with DePaul at 20-7 and put the Blue Demons in the Associated Press poll for the first time since the final poll of the 1986-87 campaign. The number 25 Blue Demons had gone 12-1 in their last thirteen games to earn a berth in the NCAA tournament. Their first round game would be in Dayton, Ohio, the site of the upset by St. Joseph's ten years to the day, against Georgia Tech.

Tech was a relatively young team with one veteran of note. The veteran, Kenny Anderson, was probably the best point guard in the nation. To beat Georgia Tech, the Blue Demons had to force the ball out of Anderson's hands. DePaul wasn't too successful. Anderson scored 31 points, and he received plenty of help, too. Jon Barry added 22 points, while Malcolm Mackey scored 12 points and had 8 rebounds. For the Blue Demons, Howard and Murphy each had 14 points, while Kevin Holland scored 11 points and had 10 rebounds in his final game as a Blue Demon.

DePaul finished the season at 20-9, its fifth straight 20-win season. David Booth averaged 18.7 points per game and 6.8 rebounds while earning honorable mention All-America. Stephen Howard was selected first team GTE Academic All-America after averaging 15.3 points and 6.3 rebounds. Senior Melvon Foster scored 6.9 points per game and averaged 2.8 assists. And Kevin Holland averaged 5.8 points and 3.6 rebounds.

16

A Family Business

From its northern inception at Howard Street to its southern end at Jackson Park or Englewood, the Howard el line in Chicago rumbles past houses and hospitals, apartments and vacant lots, parks and high rises, and store front after store front of family owned, family operated businesses.

There's a bar a block or so south of a North Side stop, a classic Chicago place with hardwood floors and neon signs touting Old Style and Budweiser. It's a place with plain wooden tables, plenty of stools at the bar, and a great lunch menu prepared by somebody everyone calls "momma."

A few more stops south, almost under the track, stands a cleaners. The couple that runs the place comes in early every morning. They eat lunch in the back, in shifts so that there's always someone at the counter to welcome the customer, and pull homemade white bread sandwiches from plain brown paper bags.

At Addison, the train rolls by America's most famous baseball park, Wrigley Field. In summer, the stop is crowded with fans and the street packed with vendors. The air is heavy with beer and sausages and little boys' dreams of the big leagues. In the winter, the air is a little lighter as snow falls quietly on Waveland and Sheffield and the Cubs hibernate.

On down the line, the train slips underground and runs through the heart of Chicago's Loop as the State Street subway before popping back up on the South Side. It flies by Chinatown, a block or so cut straight from San Francisco cloth and rolled flat by the Midwestern earth.

At Thirty-fifth Street, Comiskey Park rises on the western horizon, and on game nights the cheapest peanuts in the neighborhood are being sold by an older black man with weathered eyes named Zeke. Further south, there's an Italian beef and hot dog place just off the tracks. The same man's been running it since 1957. The first dollar bill is in a grease covered frame behind the counter. He works here every day, but Sunday, and cooks each order by hand.

Along the way, the train rolls quietly past one of the most successful family businesses. It's one without a storefront. One that doesn't even have a billboard.

It doesn't need regular hours. The summer heat can turn its bowels foul with humidity, and the winter cold can chill it like a refrigerator.

From the rumbling el a half block east, it doesn't look like a family business, but it is. Hidden behind the marble facade of a bow tie shaped building, the DePaul University Blue Demons men's basketball team, since 1942, has been the domain of the Meyer family.

Reared on Chicago's West Side, in St. Agatha's Parish near Thirteenth Street and Central Park Avenue, Ray Meyer came to DePaul University as a twenty-nine-year-old rookie head coach in April 1942. The Blue Demons were coming off a 10-12 record in 1941-42, their first losing season since 1927-28.

Coach Jim Kelly had already placed the team on the national map by leading the squad to a 17-0 record in 1933-34. Kelly led the squad to an 18-4 record in 1935-36, his last year at the helm, and managed the squad to the Olympic Finals before losing 54-53 to Washington for the right to play in the summer games in Berlin.

Tom Haggarty followed Kelly with 64 wins in four seasons and Bill Wendt coached the team to a 23-20 record in two seasons, including that 10-12 record in 1941-42, before handing the reins to Meyer.

Meyer knew well of DePaul. His high school coach at St. Patrick's Academy was Barney Varnes, a Blue Demons' star in the 1920s.

As a player, Meyer never faced DePaul. His three-year varsity career at Notre Dame was highlighted by the 1936 Helms Foundation National Championship and two years as team captain. He even coached as an assistant under George Keogan for two years, and when Keogan was sidelined by health problems, Meyer served as interim head coach for sixteen games, posting a 9-7 record.

Despite not playing DePaul during that time, Meyer knew what challenges lie ahead as he signed on as head coach on April 17, 1942. What Meyer never dreamed was that he'd spend forty-two years as head coach at DePaul, that he'd come to be known nationally as simply "The Coach," that he'd help change the face of the game of basketball, that he'd be elected to the Basketball Hall of Fame while still active on the bench, and that he was starting a family business that, fifty years later, continues to thrive.

The history of the DePaul basketball program is woven with the Meyer family. There was basketball at DePaul before, and one can assume that there will be basketball at DePaul again after the family leaves.

When Joey Meyer steps to the bench for the 1991-92 season, he begins the fiftieth year his family has coached the Blue Demons. It's a grand tradition of success he'll look to continue.

Year-by-Year Results

1923-24

Won 8, Lost 6
Percentage .571
Captain: Joe Hoban

DePaul		Opponents
W	Kent College	
W	Bauer & Black	
18	Valparaiso	20
24	Hamilton Club	13
27	Chicago Chiropractors	2
19	Loras	27
15	Luther	23
14	Wisconsin-LaCrosse	26
19	St. Mary's (MN)	22
14	Loras	10
27	Luther	9
30	American Col. of Phys. Ed.	15
L	St. Mary's (MN)	
37	Elmhurst	20

1924-25

Won 6, Lost 13
Percentage .316
Captain: Joe Hoban

DePaul		Opponents
12	Northern Illinois	9
13	Valparaiso	37
11	St. Louis	23
24	St. Thomas	16
23	Wisconsin-LaCrosse	25
8	YMCA College	36
13	Valparaiso	26
25	Elmhurst	11
17	St. Louis	29
29	Concordia	35
21	Lombard	42
19	Loras	21
40	Kent	19
15	Lombard	29
27	Loras	33
17	Wisconsin-LaCrosse	20
20	St. Mary's (MN)	24
W	YMCA College	
W	St. Mary's (MN)	

1925-26

Won 11, Lost 5
Percentage .688
Captain: Joe McInerney

DePaul		Opponents
33	St. Mary's (MN)	18
37	Loras	26
43	St. Louis	37
24	Concordia	22
42	Valparaiso	24
21	Northern Illinois	32
24	YMCA College	19
34	Northern Illinois	19
27	St. Viator's	22
22	St. Louis	38
25	American Col. of Phys. Ed.	21
22	St. Viator's	45
31	Loras	33
26	Wisconsin-LaCrosse	21
36	St. Mary's (MN)	20
26	Valparaiso	33

1926-27
Won 7, Lost 7
Percentage .500
Captain: Tom Cunningham

DePaul		Opponents
28	St. Louis	13
27	Augustana	20
21	Valparaiso	20
20	St. Viator's	24
26	St. Thomas	23
32	Detroit	29
30	St. Mary's (MN)	19
31	St. Louis	13
12	Loras	20
26	St. Thomas	27
25	St. Mary's (MN)	27
17	St. Viator's	29
24	Valparaiso	31
23	Chicago Ath. Assn.	27

1927-28
Won 2, Lost 5
Percentage .286
Captain: Tom Cunningham

DePaul		Opponents
L	Chicago Ath. Assn.	
W	Loras	
L	St. Ambrose	
31	St. Louis	14
10	St. Viator's	15
L	Concordia	
L	St. Ambrose	

1928-29
Won 5, Lost 4
Percentage .556
Captains: Tom Cunningham, George Reilly

DePaul		Opponents
21	Illinois "B"	16
24	St. Ambrose	25
39	Des Moines	28
21	St. Viator's	19
16	Des Moines	19
28	Illinois "B"	22
12	St. Viator's	20
20	St. Ambrose	16
18	Dayton	22

1929-30
Won 15, Lost 5
Percentage .750
Captain: Manning Powers

DePaul		Opponents
34	Valparaiso	21
22	North Dakota	14
38	South Dakota	19
21	Detroit	17
27	Loras	25
34	Colorado College	22
25	Wyoming	33
41	Utah	46
35	Utah	32
25	Nevada	24
37	San Francisco	33
31	St. Ignatius	33
35	Olympic Club	21
20	Athens AC	21
35	Santa Barbara	14
36	Pacific Coast Club	28
27	Hollywood AC	24
29	Arizona	16
38	Texas Mines	29
23	New Mexico	26

1930-31
Won 13, Lost 3
Percentage .813
Captain: John Ascher

DePaul		Opponents
40	Illinois "B"	27
36	Cornell College	15
12	St. Viator's	13
46	Illinois "B"	15
30	Southern Illinois	20
45	Rice	28
31	North Dakota	23
35	St. Thomas	25
21	Detroit	17
33	Centenary	15
28	St. Viator's	30
27	North Central	18
22	Loyola (IL)	15
33	McKendree	25
20	Loyola (IL)	24
48	St. Mary's (MN)	15

1931-32
Won 9, Lost 6
Percentage .600
Captain: Joe O'Connor

DePaul		Opponents
20	Southern California	18
28	St. Viator's	24
23	Carleton	27
33	Centenary	17
37	St. Thomas	14
24	St. Viator's	17
31	Catholic University	22
28	George Washington	35
21	St. John's	35
25	Niagara	30
25	Detroit	36
33	Detroit City College	32
26	Detroit	20
17	St. Viator's	18
35	McKendree	24

1932-33
Won 12, Lost 3
Percentage .800
Captain: Jim Doody

DePaul		Opponents
30	Elmhurst	14
39	Western Ontario	24
36	Western Ontario	20
29	St. Viator's	21
42	Beloit	22
38	St. Thomas	28
36	Western Michigan	32
25	North Central	26
46	Meiji	25
41	Grinnell	14
26	St. Viator's	23
39	Detroit City College	27
27	Western Michigan	46
24	Detroit	35
25	Detroit	19

1933-34
Won 17, Lost 0
Percentage 1.000
Captain: Ellsworth Weston

DePaul		Opponents
33	North Central	24
35	Nebraska	11
22	Minnesota	14
37	Arizona	26
43	Illinois Tech	35
35	Valparaiso	22
30	North Central	24
30	Missouri State	28
33	St. Louis	30
39	Western Michigan	36
47	St. Joseph's (IN)	22
38	Valparaiso	28
43	Illinois Tech	41
37	Western Michigan	29
30	Detroit	23
40	St. Louis	31
50	Detroit	41

1934-35
Won 15, Lost 1
Percentage .938
Captain: Frank Linskey

DePaul		Opponents
29	Illinois	26
52	Kalamazoo	14
35	Valparaiso	17
47	Missouri State	18
35	Beloit	9
37	Purdue	48
47	Grinnell	19
35	St. Louis	25
30	Northern Illinois	20
36	Western Michigan	32
30	North Central	20
54	Detroit	33
60	Valparaiso	28
31	Western Michigan	25
36	St. Louis	23
58	Detroit	25

1935-36
Won 18, Lost 4
Percentage .818
Captain: Ray Adams

DePaul		Opponents
51	St. Mary's (MN)	23
31	Hamline	24
45	University of Chicago	25
24	Purdue	28
24	Illinois	26
27	Wisconsin	22
42	Washburne	24
30	Drake	28
48	Minnesota	17
35	Indiana	31
40	St. Louis	16
53	Western Michigan	34
53	St. Louis	37
41	North Central	35
40	Detroit	33
33	Western Michigan	35
41	Detroit	29
W	Indiana State	
41	Indiana Central	36
36	Minnesota	30
33	Minnesota	27
*53	Washington	54

*Olympic Finals

1936-37
Won 15, Lost 6
Percentage .714
Captain: Ed Campion

DePaul		Opponents
34	North Dakota	36
41	Pittsburgh	37
27	Hamline	25
31	Illinois	25
45	Purdue	53
33	Wisconsin	17
25	Minnesota	34
40	St. Louis	23
35	University of Chicago	23
36	Evansville	25
33	Western Michigan	36
35	North Central	26
38	St. Louis	20
23	Michigan State	21
34	Detroit	19
35	St. John's	33
33	St. Joseph's (PA)	27
24	Detroit	29
41	Western Michigan	32
47	North Central	24
43	Loyola	46

1937-38
Won 12, Lost 10
Percentage .545
Captains: Pat Howlett, Tom Cleland

DePaul		Opponents
47	Valparaiso	37
28	University of Chicago	20
35	Illinois Wesleyan	11
28	Hamline	42
30	Wisconsin State	23
48	North Dakota	49
36	Wichita State	21
50	Purdue	60
46	St. Louis	19
37	Creighton	44
53	Centenary	26
38	St. Joseph's (PA)	37
29	Long Island	55
40	Loyola (IL)	53
40	Western Michigan	41
41	Illinois Wesleyan	39
31	St. Louis	29
34	St. Viator's	31
29	Hamline	39
36	Detroit	(ot) 38
53	Western Michigan	38
24	Detroit	40

1938-39
Won 15, Lost 7
Percentage .682
Captain: Bob Neu

DePaul		Opponents
55	Valparaiso	32
48	University of Chicago	(2 ot) 51
61	Arkansas State	32
36	Purdue	43
29	Iowa	34
31	Penn State	23
51	Santa Clara	57
46	Duquesne	40
38	Xavier	30
36	Villanova	29
40	St. John's	26
29	Butler	39
42	Toledo	36
26	Loyola (IL)	36
58	Illinois Wesleyan	19
37	South Dakota	35
39	Creighton	31
32	Wichita State	35
34	Kansas State	30
37	Nebraska	33
45	Illinois Wesleyan	38
39	Hamline	32

1939-40
Won 22, Lost 6
Percentage .786
Captain: Stan Szukala

DePaul		Opponents
44	Chicago Teachers	25
65	Arkansas State	17
37	Purdue	25
53	Hamline	33
33	Wisconsin State	29
42	Southern California	44
39	Oregon	37
46	Centenary	14
52	Santa Clara	50
56	Kansas State	30
46	Nebraska-Omaha	29
47	Detroit	37
32	University of Chicago	22
44	Detroit	40
37	Toledo	35
30	Indiana	51
53	Louisiana State	28
21	Loyola (IL)	15
33	Bradley	34
41	Toledo	39
43	Long Island	44
44	St. Joseph's (PA)	36
44	Long Island	36
49	Concordia	22
41	Bradley	39
*45	Long Island	38
*37	Colorado	51
*22	Oklahoma A&M	23

*NIT

1940-41
Won 13, Lost 8
Percentage .619
Captain: Ed Sachs, Elmer Gainer

DePaul		Opponents
52	Elmhurst	16
48	Kalamazoo	18
40	Chicago Teachers	31
50	Arkansas State	30
30	UCLA	23
37	Purdue	33
53	Butler	32
39	Santa Clara	43
45	Bradley	48
30	Long Island	44
52	St. Joseph's (PA)	50
45	Duquesne	36
37	University of Chicago	32
51	Toledo	55
37	Loyola (IL)	33
48	Creighton	60
40	Long Island	44
45	Toledo	47
40	Nebraska-Omaha	25
56	Concordia	32
41	Bradley	43

1941-42
Won 10, Lost 12
Percentage .455
Captain: Bob Wozny

DePaul	Opponent	Opponents
55	Concordia	24
47	Kalamazoo	22
35	Chicago Teachers	20
72	Arkansas State	26
43	University of Chicago	35
26	Purdue	30
27	Oregon	23
40	Oklahoma	26
48	Southern California	54
37	Toledo	50
43	West Texas	60
37	New York U.	38
44	Long Island	43
26	Kansas	43
51	Loyola (IL)	52
41	Toledo	43
34	Duquesne	35
33	Seton Hall	36
34	Georgetown	29
43	St. Joseph's (PA)	52
50	Bradley	37
36	Bradley	52

1942-43
Won 19, Lost 5
Percentage .792
Captain: Tony Kelly

DePaul		Opponent	Opponents
51	(A)	Navy Pier	28
42	(H)	Chicago Teachers	16
47	(H)	Glenview NTS	38
73	(H)	Navy Pier	32
45	(CS)	Purdue	37
49	(CS)	Southern California	47
49	(A)	Toledo	40
40	(A)	Duquesne	48
54	(A)	Marquette	46
67	(A)	University of Chicago	20
42	(CS)	Marquette	37
46	(A)	Loyola (IL)	38
57	(CS)	Western Michigan	44
45	(CS)	Michigan State	37
47	(CS)	Notre Dame	50
48	(CS)	Camp Grant	52
44	(CS)	Western Kentucky State	40
43	(A)	Camp Grant	48
53	(CS)	Kentucky	44
68	(CS)	Bradley	38
61	(A)	Bradley	42
52	(A)	Illinois Wesleyan	35
*46		Dartmouth	35
*49		Georgetown	53

*NCAA Tournament

1943-44
Won 22, Lost 4
Percentage .846
Captain: Dick Triptow

DePaul		Opponent	Opponents
65	(A)	Navy Pier	51
80	(H)	Concordia	31
88	(A)	Concordia	23
44	(H)	Glenview NTS	36
55	(CS)	Nebraska	14
85	(H)	Chicago Teachers	23
81	(CS)	Indiana	43
58	(H)	Navy Pier	37
64	(A)	St. Joseph's (PA)	56
*59	(A)	Long Island	38
59	(A)	Arkansas	30
78	(CS)	Chicago	26
55	(A)	Glenview NTS	50
57	(A)	Valparaiso	65
49	(CS)	Marquette	51
39	(CS)	Purdue	37
61	(CS)	Notre Dame	45
33	(CS)	Illinois	45
69	(H)	Valparaiso	38
56	(CS)	Western Kentucky	36
61	(CS)	Ohio State	49
48	(CS)	Wisconsin	35
80	(H)	Concordia	44
**68		Muhlenberg	45
**41		Oklahoma A&M	38
**39		St. John's	47

*Madison Square Garden
**NIT

1944-45

Won 21, Lost 3
Percentage .875
Captains: George Mikan, Dick Triptow

DePaul		Opponent	Opponents
65	(H)	Illinois Tech	46
53	(H)	Glenview NTS	31
62	(H)	Illinois Tech	45
61	(H)	Navy Pier	41
68	(CS)	Wyoming	29
66	(H)	Illinois Wesleyan	43
40	(CS)	Illinois	43
66	(H)	Radio Chicago	28
*74	(A)	Long Island	47
63	(A)	Illinois	56
65	(A)	Western Kentucky	37
85	(A)	Vaughan Hospital	33
45	(CS)	Hamline	41
49	(A)	Hamline	40
59	(CS)	Marquette	32
56	(CS)	Notre Dame	52
50	(CS)	Purdue	34
48	(CS)	Oklahoma A&M	46
56	(CS)	Great Lakes	64
65	(CS)	Western Kentucky	49
**76		Western Virginia	52
**97		Rhode Island	53
**71		Bowling Green	54
***44		Oklahoma A&M	52

*Madison Square Garden
**NIT
***Red Cross Benefit Game

1945-46

Won 19, Lost 5
Percentage .792
Captain: George Mikan

DePaul		Opponent	Opponents
71	(H)	Cicero Merchants	49
79	(A)	Joliet All-Stars	43
46	(A)	Oklahoma A&M	42
*59	(CS)	Bowling Green	54
*75	(CS)	Washington	50
*74	(CS)	Indiana State	56
82	(H)	Arkansas State	26
59	(CS)	Oregon State	40
37	(A)	Illinois	56
36	(A)	Minnesota	45
42	(A)	Notre Dame	43

DePaul		Opponent	Opponents
81	(A)	Western Kentucky	43
65	(A)	Murray State	43
58	(CS)	Michigan State	52
66	(CS)	Marquette	36
67	(CS)	Great Lakes	69
52	(CS)	Indiana State	42
**38	(CS)	Oklahoma A&M	46
**62	(CS)	Hamline	51
69	(CS)	Long Island	48
63	(CS)	Notre Dame	47
***75	(A)	Long Island	51
67	(A)	Bradley	46
65	(H)	Beloit	40

*DePaul Invitational
**Stadium Round Robin
***Madison Square Garden

1946-47

Won 16, Lost 9
Percentage .640
Captain: Gene Stump

DePaul		Opponent	Opponents
71	(H)	Chicago Teachers	40
67	(H)	Kalamazoo	61
39	(A)	Minnesota	54
45	(A)	Kentucky	65
48	(CS)	Rice Institute	44
73	(H)	St. Mary's (MN)	60
43	(CS)	Texas	61
60	(CS)	North Carolina	53
77	(H)	Illinois Wesleyan	45
41	(A)	Purdue	57
48	(A)	Loyola (CA)	38
50	(A)	Murray State	47
58	(A)	Niagara	51
52	(CS)	Michigan State	45
*37	(CS)	Oklahoma A&M	44
*47	(CS)	Bowling Green	59
54	(A)	St. Ambrose	41
53	(CS)	Kentucky	47
45	(CS)	Marquette	52
66	(CS)	Bradley	50
45	(A)	Notre Dame	80
41	(CS)	Kansas	58
61	(CS)	Notre Dame	50
55	(CS)	Loyola (IL)	51
83	(H)	Lawrence Tech	50

*Stadium Round Robin

1947-48

Won 22, Lost 8
Percentage .733
Captains: Ed Mikan, Whitey Kachan

DePaul			Opponents
46	(H)	Chicago Teachers	30
86	(H)	St. Norbert	39
72	(H)	Kalamazoo	33
50	(A)	Kentucky	74
71	(CS)	Oklahoma	61
44	(A)	Minnesota	46
50	(CS)	Loyola (IL)	43
54	(A)	John Carroll	53
84	(H)	Morningside	34
47	(CS)	Holy Cross	40
60	(A)	Evansville	50
46	(A)	Notre Dame	52
*69	(A)	St. John's	(2 ot) 66
56	(A)	Niagara	53
52	(CS)	Michigan State	42
32	(CS)	Oklahoma A&M	31
51	(CS)	Kentucky	68
63	(A)	Michigan State	49
65	(CS)	Marquette	49
73	(H)	Lawrence Tech	47
51	(H)	Regis	37
50	(CS)	Notre Dame	46
56	(A)	St. Louis	(ot) 58
67	(CS)	Bradley	48
47	(H)	St. Joseph's (IN)	33
52	(CS)	St. Louis	42
48	(CS)	Loyola	49
**75		North Carolina State	64
**59		New York	73
**59		Western Kentucky	61

*Madison Square Garden
**NIT

1948-49

Won 16, Lost 9
Percentage .640
Captain: Chuck Allen

DePaul			Opponents
70	(H)	Illinois Tech	34
70	(H)	Chicago Teachers	28
36	(A)	Kentucky	67
60	(CS)	Illinois	50
61	(H)	Illinois Wesleyan	57
50	(CS)	Minnesota	67
51	(A)	Illinois	89
44	(CS)	Loyola	56
63	(H)	Centenary	40
72	(A)	Baldwin-Wallace	54
43	(A)	Oklahoma City	41
39	(A)	Oklahoma A&M	32
59	(A)	Notre Dame	38
53	(A)	Niagara	57
61	(A)	St. John's	58
45	(CS)	Kentucky	56
26	(CS)	Oklahoma A&M	37
82	(H)	St. Joseph's (IN)	46
47	(CS)	Indiana	46
55	(CS)	Loyola (IL)	45
67	(H)	Northern Illinois	49
49	(CS)	Notre Dame	54
69	(CS)	Denver	50
88	(H)	St. Norbert	65
51	(CS)	Ohio State	63

1949-50

Won 12, Lost 13
Percentage .480
Captain: Sam Vukovich

DePaul			Opponents
73	(H)	St. Norbert	45
70	(A)	Ohio State	68
70	(H)	Illinois Wesleyan	63
41	(CS)	LaSalle	49
55	(A)	Indiana	61
59	(CS)	Loyola (IL)	53
47	(A)	Kentucky	49
52	(CS)	Southern California	57
65	(A)	Bradley	68
41	(A)	Oklahoma A&M	40
62	(CS)	Ohio State	70
53	(A)	Notre Dame	58
*88	(A)	Boston College	55
**74	(A)	St. John's	68
53	(CS)	Kentucky	86
45	(CS)	Oklahoma A&M	53
74	(A)	St. Joseph's (IN)	64
51	(CS)	San Francisco	53
67	(CS)	Cincinnati	59
56	(CS)	Bradley	67
63	(A)	John Carroll	55
68	(CS)	Notre Dame	58
47	(CS)	Loyola	61
73	(A)	Lawrence Tech	53
55	(CS)	Bowling Green	73

*Boston Garden
**Madison Square Garden

1950-51
Won 13, Lost 12
Percentage .520
Captain: Bato Govedarica

DePaul			Opponents
84	(H)	St. Norbert	70
79	(A)	Quincy	57
53	(A)	Oklahoma A&M	(2 ot) 60
63	(CS)	Bradley	72
92	(H)	Illinois Wesleyan	62
68	(CS)	Illinois	69
79	(H)	St. Mary's (MN)	(ot) 72
78	(A)	Northern Illinois	57
68	(A)	Illinois	65
53	(A)	Cincinnati	52
55	(A)	Kentucky	63
75	(A)	St. Norbert	64
*59	(A)	Manhattan	62
52	(CS)	Loyola	51
63	(A)	Lawrence Tech	65
57	(CS)	Oklahoma A&M	73
60	(CS)	Beloit	94
85	(H)	St. Joseph's (IN)	48
68	(CS)	Notre Dame	54
55	(A)	Notre Dame	61
57	(CS)	Kentucky	60
101	(H)	North Central	70
78	(CS)	Bowling Green	80
94	(CS)	Ohio State	67
55	(A)	Loyola	58

*Madison Square Garden

1951-52
Won 19, Lost 8
Percentage .704
Captains: Ron Feiereisel, Stan Hoover

DePaul			Opponents
91	(H)	St. Norbert	45
88	(H)	Gustavus Adolphus	61
74	(A)	North Central	63
87	(H)	Chicago Teachers	58
64	(A)	Minnesota	57
69	(A)	Northern Illinois	74
95	(H)	Samuel Houston	47
87	(H)	Illinois Wesleyan	47
60	(A)	Kentucky	98
61	(A)	Illinois	70
88	(H)	Morningside	54
84	(H)	St. Ambrose	62
49	(A)	Oklahoma A&M	52
97	(H)	Milwaukee Teachers	44
81	(H)	Fort Leonard Wood	70
80	(CS)	Beloit	57
84	(H)	Fort Sheridan	46
69	(CS)	Illinois	65
99	(H)	Glenview NTS	64
62	(CS)	Cincinnati	48
66	(A)	Manhattan	65
53	(CS)	Oklahoma A&M	50
70	(A)	Notre Dame	76
63	(CS)	Loyola (IL)	68
56	(A)	Fort Sheridan	32
61	(CS)	Kentucky	63
77	(CS)	Notre Dame	78

1952-53
Won 19, Lost 9
Percentage .679
Captain: Ron Feiereisel

DePaul			Opponents
97	(H)	Gonzaga	90
84	(H)	Lewis	48
82	(H)	St. Ambrose	61
70	(H)	Illinois Wesleyan	56
86	(H)	St. Norbert	58
51	(A)	Oklahoma A&M	62
79	(H)	Southern Illinois	69
* 63		LaSalle	61
* 64		Manhattan	73
* 81		Miami (OH)	78
83	(H)	Taylor	69
75	(A)	St. Louis	82
93	(H)	Lawrence Tech	63
76	(A)	Bradley	91
103	(H)	Quincy	85
68	(CS)	LaSalle	62
68	(A)	Cincinnati	67
58	(CS)	Oklahoma A&M	47
83	(CS)	Notre Dame	56
85	(H)	Elmhurst	43
68	(A)	Loyola (IL)	43
66	(A)	Temple	71
69	(CS)	Duquesne	77
75	(CS)	Bradley	69
67	(A)	Notre Dame	93
** 74		Miami (OH)	72
** 80		Indiana	82
** 70		Pennsylvania	90

*Holiday Basketball Tournament
Madison Square Garden
**NCAA Tournament

1953-54
Won 11, Lost 10
Percentage .524
Captains: Jim Lamkin, Dan Lecos

DePaul			Opponents
81	(H)	Ripon	36
73	(H)	Illinois Wesleyan	63
102	(H)	Wisconsin State	47
90	(H)	St. Norbert	47
82	(H)	Manchester (IN)	59
98	(H)	Illinois-Normal	68
65	(A)	Illinois	79
81	(H)	St. Mary's (MN)	65
* 55		Holy Cross	69
* 61		Fordham	65
99	(H)	Quincy	62
63	(A)	Kentucky	81
94	(H)	Lewis	42
61	(CS)	Illinois	71
53	(CS)	Notre Dame	59
69	(A)	Bradley	80
70	(CS)	St. Louis	86
71	(A)	Notre Dame	86
61	(CS)	Kentucky	76
81	(H)	Lawrence Tech	75
80	(CS)	Bradley	(ot) 76

*Sugar Bowl Tournament

1954-55
Won 16, Lost 6
Percentage .727
Captains: Jim Lamkin, Frank Blum

DePaul			Opponents
98	(H)	Kalamazoo	46
94	(CS)	Minnesota	93
92	(H)	Illinois-Normal	55
84	(H)	Minnesota	94
72	(H)	Quincy	22
112	(H)	Taylor	69
76	(A)	Michigan State	75
109	(H)	Lawrence Tech	60
103	(H)	Manchester (MN)	74
88	(H)	John Carroll	55
101	(H)	Elmhurst	60
59	(A)	Kentucky	92
104	(H)	St. Ambrose	62
65	(A)	Bradley	62
72	(CS)	Michigan State	88
89	(H)	Illinois Wesleyan	78
70	(CS)	Manhattan	71
76	(H)	St. Norbert	61
82	(CS)	Bradley	70
72	(CS)	Kentucky	76
81	(CS)	Notre Dame	77
61	(A)	Notre Dame	72

1955-56
Won 16, Lost 8
Percentage .667
Captain: Ron Sobieszczyk

DePaul			Opponents
82	(H)	Illinois Wesleyan	66
78	(A)	Minnesota	82
86	(H)	Milwaukee Teachers	68
84	(CS)	Penn State	62
69	(A)	Kentucky	71
* 68	(CS)	Duquesne	64
* 59	(CS)	San Francisco	82
79	(A)	Illinois	97
84	(H)	Wayland (TX)	56
72	(A)	Ohio State	83
102	(H)	Illinois-Normal	77
77	(A)	Notre Dame	74
71	(CS)	Paris (France)	45
91	(CS)	Bradley	76
71	(A)	St. Louis	89
66	(A)	Illinois	80
98	(H)	Lawrence Tech	58
99	(CS)	Brandeis	71
84	(H)	Manchester (IN)	74
81	(CS)	Kentucky	79
91	(H)	Lewis	77
80	(CS)	Notre Dame	74
86	(A)	Manhattan	70
** 63		Wayne	72

*DePaul Invitational
**NCAA Tournament

1956-57
Won 8, Lost 14
Percentage .364
Captain: Dick Heise

DePaul			Opponents
80	(H)	Illinois Wesleyan	62
60	(A)	Marquette	(ot) 61
67	(H)	Dayton	59
78	(A)	Purdue	83
81	(H)	Bowling Green	87
71	(H)	Wichita State	61
*68		Wake Forest	74
*73		Iowa	(ot) 72
*79		Utah	86
67	(H)	Louisville	86
81	(A)	Memphis State	85
70	(A)	Duquesne	76
70	(H)	Miami (OH)	80
76	(H)	Western Kentucky	(ot) 80
58	(A)	Dayton	75
97	(H)	St. Louis	95
74	(H)	Portland	69
87	(H)	Illinois-Normal	77
75	(H)	Baldwin-Wallace	70
80	(A)	Notre Dame	95
76	(A)	Louisville	97
73	(H)	Notre Dame	85

*Dixie Classic Tournament

1957-58
Won 8, Lost 12
Percentage .400
Captain: Chuck Henry

DePaul			Opponents
71	(H)	Nebraska Wesleyan	45
70	(A)	Illinois	75
69	(A)	Bowling Green	82
55	(A)	Creighton	67
60	(H)	Purdue	55
60	(H)	Dayton	69
62	(H)	Creighton	56
63	(H)	Duquesne	54
62	(H)	Louisville	60
61	(A)	Notre Dame	79
79	(H)	Portland	(ot) 76
65	(H)	Illinois-Normal	58
66	(H)	Indiana	76
62	(A)	Western Kentucky	77
62	(H)	Baldwin-Wallace	67
53	(A)	Dayton	62
64	(H)	Miami (OH)	69
69	(H)	Canisius	63
55	(A)	Louisville	73
71	(H)	Notre Dame	75

1958-59
Won 13, Lost 11
Percentage .542
Captain: McKinley Cowsen

DePaul			Opponents
63	(H)	Christian Brothers	57
89	(H)	Baldwin-Wallace	48
71	(A)	Purdue	89
73	(H)	Bowling Green	70
77	(A)	Evansville	86
67	(H)	Miami (OH)	74
70	(A)	Duquesne	59
60	(H)	Dayton	62
69	(H)	Notre Dame	66
89	(H)	Valparaiso	64
76	(A)	Western Michigan	65
69	(A)	Indiana	75
80	(H)	Western Kentucky	70
89	(H)	Marquette	80
69	(A)	Dayton	88
65	(H)	Western Michigan	63
70	(H)	Louisville	63
67	(A)	Notre Dame	76
66	(A)	Louisville	83
73	(A)	Canisius	67
69	(A)	Marquette	82
*57		Portland	56
*70		Kansas State	102
*65		Texas Christian	71

*NCAA Tournament

1959-60
Won 17, Lost 7
Percentage .708
Captain: McKinley Cowsen

DePaul			Opponents
95	(H)	Illinois Wesleyan	50
83	(H)	Western Ontario	56
74	(A)	Bowling Green	68
85	(H)	North Dakota	43
87	(H)	Purdue	65
77	(H)	Ohio	54
75	(H)	Marquette	55
77	(H)	Baldwin-Wallace	43
74	(H)	Louisville	75
65	(A)	Western Kentucky	86
70	(H)	Notre Dame	73
82	(A)	Valparaiso	64
81	(A)	Miami (OH)	79
78	(H)	Indiana	82
74	(H)	Army	69
85	(A)	Louisville	76
70	(A)	Dayton	66
58	(A)	Notre Dame	70
65	(A)	Marquette	63
82	(H)	Creighton	65
66	(H)	Dayton	67
*69		Air Force	63
*59		Cincinnati	99
*67		Texas	61

*NCAA Tournament

1960-61
Won 17, Lost 8
Percentage .680
Captain: Bill Haig

DePaul			Opponents
72	(H)	Baldwin-Wallace	56
62	(H)	Illinois Wesleyan	58
83	(H)	North Dakota	62
62	(H)	Bowling Green	60
81	(H)	Marquette	78
72	(H)	Miami (OH)	70
81	(H)	Western Michigan	60
55	(H)	Western Ontario	50
75	(A)	Dayton	64
69	(A)	Ohio	60
78	(H)	Louisville	70
58	(A)	Notre Dame	61
60	(A)	Western Michigan	85
78	(A)	Indiana	81
92	(H)	Christian Brothers	71
65	(A)	Western Kentucky	71
64	(A)	Marquette	87
101	(H)	Tampa	68
77	(A)	Providence	81
69	(A)	St. Bonaventure	78
75	(A)	Louisville	67
78	(H)	Notre Dame	57
89	(H)	Youngstown	55
84	(H)	Dayton	83
* 67		Providence	73

*NIT

1961-62
Won 13, Lost 10
Percentage .565
Captain: M.C. Thompson

DePaul			Opponents	
66	(A)	Minnesota		56
102	(H)	Lawrence Tech		79
72	(H)	North Dakota		51
79	(H)	Denver		50
70	(H)	South Carolina		60
68	(H)	Providence		63
* 60	(A)	St. Bonaventure		70
* 96	(A)	Syracuse		59
68	(H)	Marquette		75
78	(H)	Christian Brothers		56
89	(H)	Indiana		98
80	(A)	Notre Dame		88
81	(H)	Louisville		82
88	(H)	Dayton	(2 ot)	90
79	(H)	Baldwin-Wallace		49
86	(H)	Western Kentucky		78
79	(A)	Louisville	(3 ot)	78
69	(H)	St. Bonaventure		88
83	(A)	Marquette		99
51	(A)	Bowling Green		83
77	(H)	Western Ontario		59
87	(H)	Notre Dame		80
61	(A)	Dayton		77

*Motor City Tournament

1962-63
Won 15, Lost 8
Percentage .652
Captain: M.C. Thompson

DePaul			Opponents
73	(H)	NE State College	45
92	(H)	Aquinas College	72
76	(H)	Minnesota	74
79	(H)	Marquette	72
91	(A)	Western Michigan	(ot) 90
82	(A)	Detroit	77
89	(H)	Baldwin-Wallace	71
70	(H)	Western Ontario	45
62	(A)	Notre Dame	82
83	(H)	Notre Dame	69
56	(A)	Dayton	57
75	(A)	Indiana	76
55	(H)	Bowling Green	53
78	(H)	Louisville	73
59	(A)	Providence	77
67	(A)	St. Bonaventure	71
81	(A)	Marquette	87
83	(H)	Gannon	48
84	(H)	Christian Brothers	55
69	(A)	Louisville	(ot) 71
88	(H)	Western Kentucky	86
68	(H)	Dayton	66
*51		Villanova	63

*NIT

1963-64
Won 21, Lost 4
Percentage .840
Captains: Emmette Bryant, Dennis Freund

DePaul			Opponents
80	(H)	North Dakota	56
78	(H)	Idaho State	67
98	(H)	California-Davis	59
105	(H)	Lawrence Tech	56
82	(H)	Providence	64
90	(H)	Marquette	69
*102	(A)	Canisius	79
* 86	(A)	Xavier	80
99	(A)	Western Kentucky	82
86	(A)	Notre Dame	73
111	(H)	Portland	83
89	(H)	Dayton	83
75	(A)	Indiana	76
79	(H)	Louisville	83
90	(H)	Notre Dame	75
68	(A)	Memphis State	99
72	(A)	Marquette	69
98	(H)	Western Ontario	58
81	(H)	St. Bonaventure	76
85	(H)	American	59
70	(A)	Louisville	66
84	(H)	Duquesne	65
80	(A)	Bowling Green	89
79	(A)	Dayton	73
** 66		New York U.	79

*Queen City Tournament
**NIT

1964-65
Won 17, Lost 10
Percentage .630
Captain: Jim Murphy

DePaul			Opponents
80	(H)	NE Missouri State	60
80	(H)	Christian Brothers	59
86	(H)	North Dakota	58
89	(H)	Middle Tenn. State	68
78	(A)	Indiana	91
69	(A)	Louisville	70
91	(H)	Seattle	77
* 52		Florida State	44
* 84		Brigham Young	75
* 67		Oklahoma City	60
72	(H)	Marquette	54
99	(H)	Memphis State	70
118	(H)	Western Ontario	44
63	(A)	Dayton	59
69	(A)	Duquesne	73
94	(H)	Bowling Green	64
97	(H)	Niagara	59
70	(A)	Providence	72
67	(A)	Villanova	85
59	(A)	Notre Dame	62
67	(A)	Marquette	61
77	(H)	Portland	64
67	(H)	Notre Dame	83
64	(H)	Dayton	71
** 99		Eastern Kentucky	52
** 78		Vanderbilt	(ot) 83
** 69		Dayton	75

*Oklahoma City Tournament
**NCAA Tournament

1965-66
Won 18, Lost 8
Percentage .692
Captains: Don Swanson, Tom Meyer

DePaul			Opponents
77	(H)	Illinois Wesleyan	55
82	(A)	Marquette	69
87	(H)	Louisville	62
114	(H)	Christian Brothers	75
82	(A)	Iona	37
96	(H)	St. Joseph (NM)	74
102	(H)	Baldwin-Wallace	65
* 64		Florida	72
* 80		Alabama	64
74	(A)	North Dakota	85
70	(H)	Dayton	81
120	(H)	Western Ontario	51
97	(H)	Notre Dame	71
81	(A)	Niagara	61
84	(H)	Loyola (CA)	60
100	(H)	Indiana	79
69	(A)	St. Bonaventure	73
76	(H)	Marquette	70
77	(A)	Bowling Green	62
57	(H)	Providence	61
79	(H)	Duquesne	69
79	(A)	Notre Dame	71
73	(A)	Dayton	76
101	(H)	Steubenville	67
73	(H)	Villanova	76
** 65		New York U.	88

*Gator Bowl Tournament
**NIT

1966-67
Won 17, Lost 8
Percentage .680
Captains: Mike Norris, Errol Palmer

DePaul			Opponents
82	(H)	North Dakota	47
85	(H)	St. John's (MN)	64
79	(H)	Southern California	82
89	(H)	Baldwin-Wallace	39
69	(A)	Villanova	61
* 75		Stanford	88
* 77		Massachusetts	85
* 93		Arizona	59
64	(H)	Bellarmine	63

DePaul			Opponents
65	(A)	Marquette	68
76	(H)	St. Bonaventure	73
72	(H)	Notre Dame	76
73	(H)	Bowling Green	72
65	(A)	Dayton	81
78	(H)	Niagara	65
70	(A)	Indiana	72
79	(H)	Marquette	74
56	(A)	Notre Dame	49
71	(H)	Xavier	60
114	(H)	Aquinas	64
67	(A)	Duquesne	77
77	(H)	Wisconsin-Milwaukee	48
97	(H)	Detroit	62
67	(A)	Providence	68
84	(H)	Dayton	79

*Oklahoma City Tournament

1967-68
Won 13, Lost 12
Percentage .520
Captain: Bob Mattingly

DePaul			Opponents
111	(H)	Augustana	79
89	(H)	Central Missouri State	72
103	(H)	St. John's (MN)	55
67	(H)	Iowa State	63
77	(H)	Loyola (CA)	82
88	(H)	Tennessee Tech	68
75	(H)	Bellarmine	62
50	(A)	Marquette	72
82	(H)	Wisconsin-Milwaukee	69
67	(A)	St. Bonaventure	77
68	(H)	Notre Dame	75
79	(A)	Niagara	72
70	(A)	Dayton	65
93	(H)	Illinois Wesleyan	77
57	(H)	Northern Illinois	55
79	(H)	Indiana	78
78	(A)	Xavier	97
53	(H)	Marquette	58
85	(A)	Notre Dame	(ot) 91
48	(H)	Villanova	57
60	(H)	Providence	71
69	(H)	Duquesne	79
58	(H)	Dayton	70
111	(A)	Detroit	(2 ot) 107
61	(A)	Bowling Green	89

1968-69
Won 14, Lost 11
Percentage .560
Captain: Al Zetsche

DePaul		Opponents	
95	(H)	Doane	62
94	(H)	NE Missouri State	64
93	(H)	St. Joseph's (IN)	78
100	(H)	California Western	65
107	(H)	Illinois Wesleyan	84
* 64		St. Joseph's (PA)	74
* 95		Rhode Island	86
* 83		Penn State	63
81	(H)	Northern Illinois	79
72	(H)	Marquette	77
60	(A)	Notre Dame	66
86	(H)	Xavier	77
83	(H)	Dayton	86
57	(A)	Villanova	81
66	(A)	Indiana	87
62	(A)	Providence	83
83	(H)	Niagara	74
63	(H)	Notre Dame	85
111	(H)	Wisconsin-Milwaukee	79
56	(A)	Marquette	66
72	(H)	St. Bonaventure	(ot) 71
86	(H)	St. Leo	74
68	(A)	Duquesne	87
85	(H)	Bellarmine	75
57	(A)	Dayton	63

*Quaker City Tournament

1969-70
Won 12, Lost 13
Percentage .480
Captain: Ken Warzynski

DePaul			Opponents
97	(A)	Michigan Lutheran	76
86	(H)	Southwest Louisiana	61
90	(H)	John F. Kennedy	55
84	(H)	East Tennessee St.	77
101	(H)	Parsons	79
93	(H)	St. Mary's (CA)	89
104	(H)	Nevada	71
78	(H)	Providence	79
85	(H)	St. Joseph's (IN)	86
84	(H)	Harvard	90
73	(A)	Xavier	71
60	(H)	Marquette	72
73	(A)	Notre Dame	96
75	(A)	Dayton	79
59	(A)	St. Bonaventure	83
75	(H)	Indiana	70
88	(H)	Northern Illinois	73
87	(H)	Missouri-St. Louis	74
73	(A)	Niagara	79
76	(H)	Duquesne	100
60	(A)	Marquette	79
90	(H)	Wisconsin-Milwaukee	72
63	(H)	Dayton	74
76	(A)	Northern Illinois	87
90	(H)	Villanova	102

1970-71
Won 8, Lost 17
Percentage .320
Captain: Joe Meyer

DePaul			Opponents
100	(H)	Virginia Commonwealth	77
68	(H)	St. Bonaventure	79
77	(A)	Northwestern	91
86	(H)	Parsons	71
* 85		Kentucky	106
* 68		Kansas State	78
94	(H)	Spring Hill	65
** 72		Louisiana State	91
** 69		Oklahoma City	73
** 57		San Francisco	77
88	(H)	Illinois Wesleyan	71
85	(H)	St. Joseph's (IN)	71
59	(A)	Villanova	99
71	(H)	Dayton	76
51	(A)	Marquette	73
72	(H)	Niagara	83
74	(A)	Duquesne	90
80	(A)	Drake	93
55	(H)	Marquette	84
76	(H)	Notre Dame	107
81	(H)	Wisconsin-Milwaukee	66
60	(A)	Dayton	92
64	(A)	Providence	74
87	(H)	Mankato	74
84	(H)	Xavier	76

*Kentucky Invitational Tournament
**All-College Tournament (Oklahoma City)

1971-72
Won 12, Lost 11
Percentage .522
Captains: Al Burks, Harry Shields

DePaul			Opponents
108	(H)	Rocky Mountain	84
87	(A)	Niagara	108
66	(A)	St. Bonaventure	80
64	(H)	Providence	75
93	(H)	Parsons	75
83	(H)	Dubuque	61
82	(H)	St. Joseph's (IN)	70
75	(A)	Dayton	72
79	(H)	Wisconsin-Green Bay	67
61	(A)	Marquette	70
75	(H)	Eastern Illinois	68
83	(H)	Villanova	94
80	(H)	Wisconsin-Milwaukee	79
61	(H)	Marquette	79
67	(A)	Southern Carolina	91
78	(A)	Notre Dame	93
*74		Northwestern	72
90	(H)	Lewis	82
65	(H)	Duquesne	70
62	(A)	Xavier	71
66	(A)	Toledo	(ot) 70
94	(H)	NC-Charlotte	83
94	(H)	Drake	76

*Played at Chicago Stadium

1972-73
Won 14, Lost 11
Percentage .560
Captains: Al Burks, Harry Shields

DePaul			Opponents
79	(H)	St. Mary's (MN)	54
88	(H)	Northwestern	80
75	(A)	Drake	86
87	(H)	Winona State	57
70	(H)	St. Bonaventure	68
89	(H)	San Diego State	75
80	(A)	Providence	107
93	(H)	Long Island	61
82	(H)	St. Joseph's (IN)	64
76	(H)	Eastern Illinois	58
59	(A)	Marquette	60
86	(H)	Westmont	69
67	(H)	Notre Dame	72
59	(H)	Manhattan	68
66	(A)	South Carolina	84
74	(H)	Dayton	82
71	(A)	Duquesne	85
55	(H)	Marquette	70
69	(H)	Xavier	67
89	(A)	Villanova	80
70	(A)	NC-Charlotte	74
102	(H)	Lewis	70
62	(H)	Wisconsin-Green Bay	63
87	(H)	Niagara	81
67	(H)	Toledo	65

1973-74
Won 16, Lost 9
Percentage .640
Captain: Mike Gillespie

DePaul			Opponents
82	(H)	St. Mary's (MN)	72
67	(H)	Washington State	45
65	(A)	Northwestern	76
91	(H)	Rocky Mountain	73
*61	(A)	Tennessee	96
*93	(A)	Utah State	102
94	(H)	California State	63
75	(H)	Providence	93
**75	(A)	Brown	69
**52	(A)	Massachusetts	55
89	(A)	St. Joseph's (IN)	71
88	(A)	Niagara	77
79	(A)	St. Bonaventure	77
59	(A)	Marquette	63
76	(H)	Marshall	68
99	(H)	Lewis	73
71	(A)	Dayton	85
72	(A)	Notre Dame	101
57	(H)	Marquette	70
77	(A)	Xavier	70
65	(H)	Villanova	63
55	(H)	Wisconsin-Green Bay	44
89	(H)	St. Leo	52
94	(H)	Duquesne	85
83	(A)	Marshall	80

*Volunteer Classic
**Basketball Hall of Fame Tournament

1974-75

Won 15, Lost 10
Percentage .600
Captains: Greg Boyd, Jim Bocinsky, Bill Robinzine

DePaul			Opponents
64	(A)	UCLA	79
77	(H)	St. Mary's (CA)	70
80	(A)	Gonzaga	73
69	(A)	Washington State	83
89	(H)	St. Bonaventure	72
50	(H)	Rhode Island	48
75	(H)	San Jose State	(ot) 73
71	(A)	Providence	85
104	(H)	Marshall	77
77	(H)	Northwestern	63
60	(A)	Marquette	61
63	(H)	Niagara	64
90	(H)	Manhattan	75
85	(H)	Wisconsin-Green Bay	59
95	(H)	Lewis	69
109	(H)	St. Mary's (MN)	68
86	(H)	Dayton	80
96	(A)	Marshall	107
69	(H)	Marquette	72
74	(A)	Virginia Tech	87
94	(H)	St. Xavier	71
64	(A)	Duquesne	66
75	(H)	Notre Dame	70
88	(A)	Cincinnati	96
89	(H)	Indiana State	66

1975-76

Won 20, Lost 9
Percentage .690
Captain: Andy Pancratz

DePaul			Opponents
85	(H)	St. Ambrose	67
*100	(A)	Memphis State	91
* 67	(A)	Arizona State	74
83	(H)	Drake	72
78	(A)	Louisville	76
92	(H)	Lewis	67
65	(A)	Northwestern	57
** 73	(A)	George Washington	57
** 67	(A)	Detroit	74
70	(A)	Louisiana State	67
91	(H)	Providence	66
100	(H)	Loyola (IL)	77
72	(H)	Marquette	79
61	(A)	Niagara	81
82	(A)	St. Bonaventure	101

DePaul			Opponents
102	(H)	St. Xavier	70
68	(A)	Notre Dame	89
84	(H)	Dayton	72
89	(H)	Duquesne	75
70	(A)	Rhode Island	71
71	(A)	Indiana State	(ot) 62
118	(H)	Marshall	62
73	(H)	Virginia Tech	65
53	(A)	Marquette	64
70	(H)	Cincinnati	60
72	(H)	Villanova	63
67	(H)	Wisconsin-Green Bay	60
*** 69		Virginia	60
*** 66		Virginia Military	(ot) 71

*Sun Devil Classic
**Motor City Classic
***NCAA Tournament

1976-77

Won 15, Lost 12
Percentage .556
Captains: Ron Norwood, Joe Ponsetto

DePaul			Opponents
69	(A)	UCLA	76
75	(A)	Northwestern	(ot) 73
89	(H)	St. Mary's (CA)	75
66	(A)	Wisconsin	68
77	(H)	Gonzaga	53
74	(A)	Maryland	92
42	(A)	Indiana	50
77	(H)	Army	66
68	(H)	Niagara	58
86	(A)	Bradley	80
85	(H)	St. Bonaventure	74
66	(A)	Loyola (IL)	72
50	(A)	Wisconsin-Green Bay	57
82	(H)	Illinois Wesleyan	63
74	(A)	Dayton	67
93	(H)	Bradley	73
64	(H)	Marquette	85
75	(H)	Creighton	84
72	(A)	Duquesne	84
73	(A)	Providence	84
94	(H)	Loyola (IL)	76
77	(A)	Marquette	(2 ot) 72
93	(H)	Eastern Michigan	75
93	(A)	Marshall	74
63	(A)	St. Louis	70
88	(H)	Valparaiso	72
68	(H)	Notre Dame	76

1977-78

Won 27, Lost 3
Percentage .900
Captains: Dave Corzine, Joe Ponsetto

DePaul			Opponents
93	(H)	Butler	65
94	(H)	Evansville	71
89	(H)	Bradley	85
89	(H)	Wichita State	84
85	(A)	Wisconsin	62
83	(H)	Northwestern	79
67	(A)	Louisiana State	68
96	(A)	Centenary	77
* 82	(A)	Penn State	67
*100	(A)	Yale	52
92	(H)	Western Michigan	61
93	(H)	Loyola (IL)	73
91	(A)	Eastern Michigan	83
80	(A)	Bradley	66
74	(A)	Marquette	80
74	(H)	Dayton	70
100	(H)	St. Louis	81
78	(H)	Providence	68
85	(A)	Creighton	(3 ot) 82
63	(H)	Oral Roberts	57
83	(H)	Duquesne	58
69	(A)	Notre Dame	(ot) 68
55	(H)	Wisconsin-Green Bay	49
73	(A)	Loyola (IL)	63
54	(A)	Air Force	41
89	(A)	Valparaiso	62
96	(H)	Illinois State	84
** 80		Creighton	78
** 90		Louisville	(2 ot) 89
** 64		Notre Dame	84

*Kodak Classic
**NCAA Tournament

1978-79

Won 26, Lost 6
Percentage .813
Captains: Gary Garland, Curtis Watkins

DePaul			Opponents
85	(A)	UCLA	108
74	(A)	Evansville	55
108	(H)	Northern Illinois	86
96	(H)	Eastern Michigan	68
81	(A)	Butler	62
92	(A)	Wichita State	95
84	(H)	Wisconsin	78
90	(H)	Northwestern	83
51	(A)	Bradley	50
88	(H)	Creighton	70
77	(H)	Georgia Tech	71
86	(H)	Air Force	66
84	(A)	Providence	75
80	(H)	Loyola (IL)	73
64	(A)	Dayton	68
87	(A)	Illinois State	69
80	(A)	Western Michigan	82
75	(A)	Oral Roberts	72
77	(A)	Loyola (IL)	73
82	(H)	Centenary	66
85	(A)	Ball State	76
69	(H)	Villanova	66
104	(H)	Valparaiso	76
61	(H)	Marquette	60
88	(H)	UAB	77
76	(H)	Notre Dame	72
99	(H)	Loyola (IL)	101
* 89		USC	78
* 62		Marquette	56
* 95		UCLA	91
* 74		Indiana State	76
* 96		Pennsylvania	93

*NCAA Tournament

1979-80

Won 26, Lost 2
Percentage .929
Captains: Clyde Bradshaw, Jim Mitchem

DePaul		Opponent	Opponents
90	(H)	Wisconsin	77
66	(H)	Texas	60
57	(A)	Northern Illinois	(ot) 55
99	(A)	UCLA	94
57	(A)	Eastern Michigan	55
* 81	(A)	Northwestern	75
* 92	(A)	Loyola (IL)	85
68	(H)	Bradley	61
92	(A)	Missouri	79
80	(A)	Loyola (IL)	75
96	(H)	Ball State	79
92	(A)	Marquette	85
61	(H)	Lamar	59
93	(H)	Maine	79
78	(H)	Louisiana State	73
57	(A)	UAB	54
105	(H)	Evansville	94
84	(A)	Creighton	73
102	(H)	North Texas State	71
65	(H)	Dayton	63
95	(A)	Valparaiso	71
103	(H)	Butler	79
92	(H)	La Salle	75
105	(A)	Wagner	89
94	(H)	Loyola (IL)	87
74	(A)	Notre Dame	(2 ot) 76
97	(H)	Illinois State	81
** 71		UCLA	77

*Chicagoland Cage Classic
**NCAA Tournament

1980-81

Won 27, Lost 2
Percentage .931
Captains: Mark Aguirre, Clyde Bradshaw

DePaul		Opponent	Opponents
* 86		Louisville	80
74	(H)	Gonzaga	56
88	(H)	Santa Clara	71
93	(H)	Northern Illinois	56
63	(A)	Texas	65
92	(A)	North Texas State	86
** 71		Loyola (IL)	67
** 62		Northwestern	54
93	(H)	UCLA	77
*** 72		Georgetown	67
*** 85		San Diego State	69
78	(H)	Furman	65
85	(A)	Maine	77
62	(H)	Old Dominion	63
93	(H)	St. Louis	67
90	(H)	Wagner	75
69	(A)	La Salle	62
54	(A)	Illinois State	50
91	(H)	Syracuse	69
69	(H)	Detroit	58
77	(H)	UAB	66
83	(H)	Creighton	57
61	(A)	Evansville	53
78	(H)	Marquette	71
89	(A)	Butler	64
105	(A)	Loyola (IL)	95
84	(A)	Dayton	64
74	(H)	Notre Dame	64
**** 48		St. Joseph's (PA)	49

*Tip-Off Classic
**Chicagoland Cage Classic
***Cabrillo Classic
****NCAA Tournament

1981-82

Won 26, Lost 2
Percentage .929
Captains: Terry Cummings, Skip Dillard

DePaul			Opponents
78	(A)	Illinois-Chicago	53
73	(H)	Purdue	67
69	(A)	Gonzaga	56
80	(A)	Santa Clara	58
88	(H)	Western Michigan	46
75	(A)	UCLA	87
90	(H)	Maine	67
75	(H)	Louisville	68
74	(H)	Illinois State	58
55	(A)	Northern Illinois	46
86	(H)	Penn State	60
96	(H)	St. Mary's	72
71	(H)	Dayton	69
76	(A)	Creighton	67
92	(H)	South Carolina	59
70	(A)	Old Dominion	60
79	(H)	UAB	68
99	(A)	St. Louis	80
92	(A)	Syracuse	87
46	(H)	St. Joseph's	(ot) 44
67	(A)	Marquette	66
59	(H)	Evansville	58
98	(H)	Loyola (IL)	80
83	(H)	Ohio	61
74	(A)	Detroit	70
75	(A)	Furman	74
81	(A)	Notre Dame	69
*75		Boston College	82

*NCAA Midwest Regional

1982-83

Won 21, Lost 12
Percentage .636
Captain: Brett Burkholder

DePaul			Opponents
* 79		Davidson	39
* 73		Arizona State	(ot) 72
70	(H)	UCLA	(ot) 73
67	(H)	South Florida	55
62	(A)	Illinois State	72
63	(H)	Western Michigan	42
69	(H)	Northern Illinois	45
105	(H)	Fairleigh Dickinson	64
63	(A)	Purdue	65
68	(H)	Creighton	66
78	(H)	Pepperdine	73
48	(H)	Gonzaga	49
76	(A)	Loyola	82
58	(A)	Louisville	63
56	(H)	Dayton	52
51	(H)	Princeton	41
56	(A)	UAB	54
55	(H)	St. Joseph's	54
78	(H)	Detroit	53
65	(A)	Georgetown	71
83	(A)	Evansville	82
62	(A)	Ohio University	(2 ot) 63
52	(A)	St. John's	64
55	(H)	Notre Dame	53
51	(A)	South Carolina	52
74	(H)	Marquette	62
60	(H)	Pan American	49
71	(A)	Dayton	80
** 76		Minnesota	73
** 65		Northwestern	63
** 75		Mississippi	67
** 68		Nebraska	58
** 60		Fresno State	69

*Crush Classic
**NIT Championship

1983-84

Won 27, Lost 3
Percentage .900
Captains: Tyrone Corbin, Jerry McMillan

DePaul			Opponents
73	(A)	Northern Illinois	58
69	(H)	Ohio University	45
69	(H)	Illinois State	66
84	(H)	Western Michigan	60
63	(H)	Georgetown	61
*77		Alabama	76
*50		Texas Tech	47
68	(H)	Purdue	61
59	(A)	Creighton	(ot) 57
78	(H)	Biscayne College	50
81	(A)	Pepperdine	73
76	(A)	St. Mary's	74
98	(H)	UAB	63
59	(A)	South Florida	50
50	(H)	Princeton	39
84	(A)	UCLA	68
59	(H)	St. John's	(ot) 57
45	(A)	St. Joseph's	58
62	(A)	Notre Dame	54
93	(H)	Loyola	77
71	(A)	Dayton	72
79	(H)	Dayton	59
73	(H)	Louisville	63
96	(H)	Evansville	65
65	(H)	South Carolina	56
66	(A)	Detroit	47
62	(H)	Pan American	29
64	(H)	Marquette	49
**75		Illinois State	61
**71		Wake Forest	(ot) 73

*Suntory Ball (Tokyo, Japan)
**NCAA Tournament

1984-85

Won 19, Lost 10
Percentage .655
Captains: Tyrone Corbin, Kenny Patterson

DePaul			Opponents
59	(H)	Northern Illinois	58
80	(H)	UCLA	61
77	(H)	Chico State	37
84	(A)	Illinois State	71
95	(H)	Notre Dame	83
78	(A)	Penn State	61
57	(A)	Georgetown	77
64	(A)	Western Michigan	65
61	(H)	Northwestern	56
87	(H)	Creighton	58
76	(H)	St. Mary's	53
59	(A)	UAB	66
69	(H)	Houston	58
64	(H)	Old Dominion	58
71	(A)	Notre Dame	66
72	(H)	Eastern Washington	50
64	(A)	Dayton	65
56	(A)	Princeton	42
73	(A)	Louisville	77
63	(H)	Dayton	67
90	(H)	Pepperdine	65
71	(A)	Loyola	78
80	(A)	St. John's	93
77	(H)	Indiana State	65
87	(H)	LaSalle	60
69	(H)	Marquette	52
65	(A)	Pan American	55
64	(A)	Marquette	68
*65		Syracuse	70

*NCAA Tournament

1985-86

Won 18, Lost 13
Percentage .581
Captains: Marty Embry, Lemone Lampley

DePaul			Opponents
63	(A)	Northern Illinois	61
93	(H)	St. Francis (NY)	48
61	(H)	Illinois State	54
70	(H)	Western Michigan	59
84	(A)	Houston	78
70	(A)	Northwestern	67
70	(H)	Georgetown	85
56	(A)	Purdue	71
*64		Navy	67
*63		Texas	62
66	(H)	Dayton	52
70	(H)	Pepperdine	57
54	(H)	Notre Dame	70
75	(H)	Cleveland State	90
70	(H)	UAB	61
90	(H)	Loyola (IL)	55
96	(H)	Northern Iowa	53
64	(A)	Dayton	77
73	(H)	Evansville	41
65	(A)	Marquette	(ot) 70
53	(A)	Old Dominion	66
53	(H)	Louisville	72
61	(A)	Creighton	74
48	(A)	Indiana State	44
81	(H)	St. John's	72
59	(A)	Notre Dame	70
63	(A)	UCLA	65
95	(H)	Marquette	87
**72		Virginia	68
**74		Oklahoma	69
**67		Duke	74

*Cotton States Classic
**NCAA Tournament

1986-87

Won 28, Lost 3
Percentage .903
Captains: Dallas Comegys, Andy Laux

DePaul			Opponents
78	(H)	Northern Illinois	51
63	(H)	North Carolina-Wilmington	44
61	(A)	Illinois State	53
93	(A)	Western Michigan	61
75	(A)	Louisville	68
74	(H)	Creighton	64
72	(H)	Old Dominion	61
72	(H)	Northwestern	54
92	(A)	Pepperdine	75
80	(A)	Dayton	64
81	(H)	Furman	64
59	(H)	Notre Dame	54
84	(A)	Loyola (IL)	65
81	(H)	South Florida	55
61	(H)	Indiana State	49
78	(A)	Evansville	68
71	(A)	Georgetown	74
70	(H)	Weber State	51
58	(A)	LaSalle	54
84	(H)	North Carolina State	62
88	(H)	Dayton	65
88	(A)	Marquette	76
83	(A)	Alabama-Birmingham	71
88	(H)	Monmouth (NJ)	53
96	(A)	Iona	82
84	(H)	Georgia Tech	67
62	(A)	Notre Dame	73
68	(H)	Marquette	59
*76	(H)	Louisiana Tech	62
*83	(H)	St. John's	(ot) 75
*58	(N)	Louisiana State	63

*NCAA Tournament

1987-88

Won 22, Lost 8
Percentage .733
Captains: Kevin Edwards, Kevin Golden, Andy Laux

DePaul		Opponent	Opponents
76	(H)	Pepperdine	(ot) 84
88	(H)	Niagara	(ot) 87
76	(H)	Illinois State	55
94	(H)	Western Michigan	64
73	(H)	Notre Dame	(ot) 69
88	(A)	Weber State	65
89	(A)	Washington	73
64	(A)	Northwestern	64
93	(H)	Texas-San Antonio	82
68	(A)	Hartford	61
64	(H)	Georgetown	74
72	(H)	Dayton	79
77	(A)	Notre Dame	71
93	(H)	Loyola (IL)	77
95	(A)	Old Dominion	88
81	(H)	Marquette	66
66	(A)	North Carolina State	71
64	(A)	Indiana State	56
70	(A)	Georgia Tech	71
86	(H)	Bradley	80
63	(H)	Evansville	65
92	(H)	Iona	56
65	(A)	St. John's	51
81	(H)	Jackson State	69
101	(A)	Miami (FL)	82
92	(A)	Dayton	77
77	(H)	Louisville	58
77	(A)	Marquette	65
* 83	(N)	Wichita State	62
* 58	(N)	Kansas City	66

*NCAA Tournament

1988-89

Won 21, Lost 12
Percentage .636
Captains: Stanley Brundy, Terence Greene

DePaul		Opponent	Opponents
* 77	(N)	Nevada-Las Vegas	86
* 70	(N)	Ohio State	72
* 89	(N)	Chaminade	68
66	(H)	Maine	46
78	(A)	Illinois State	77
75	(H)	Washington	79
82	(A)	Niagara	75
120	(H)	American	85
64	(A)	Georgetown	74
** 73	(H)	North Carolina A&T	52
**115	(H)	Loyola Marymount	111
† 62	(N)	Mississippi State	60
† 60	(N)	Seton Hall	83
67	(H)	North Carolina	87
67	(A)	Louisville	81
89	(H)	Eastern Illinois	75
122	(H)	Loyola Marymount	108
64	(A)	Marquette	72
69	(A)	Loyola (IL)	70
85	(A)	Bradley	82
67	(A)	South Florida	59
85	(H)	Duquesne	63
81	(H)	N. Carolina State	74
78	(A)	Dayton	50
89	(H)	Miami (FL)	79
64	(H)	St. John's	67
88	(H)	Texas-San Antonio	55
‡ 62	(A)	Fordham	61
60	(A)	Notre Dame	67
91	(H)	Marquette	79
73	(H)	Notre Dame	70
§ 66	(N)	Memphis State	63
§ 70	(N)	Nevada-Las Vegas	85

*Maui Classic
**Old Style Classic
†USF&G Sugar Bowl Tournament
‡Madison Square Garden
§NCAA Tournament

1989-90

Won 20, Lost 15
Percentage .571
Captains: James Hamby, Kevin Holland

DePaul			Opponents
*71	(H)	Ohio State	53
*70	(H)	North Carolina State	63
*52	(A)	St. John's	53
*53	(N)	Nevada-Las Vegas	88
64	(H)	Hartford	56
62	(H)	LaSalle	83
49	(A)	Houston	65
**69	(H)	Western Illinois	72
51	(A)	North Carolina	70
73	(H)	Dayton	84
71	(H)	Marquette	62
91	(A)	Florida International	67
55	(H)	Weber State	47
71	(H)	Loyola (IL)	56
68	(A)	Duquesne	55
64	(H)	Georgetown	74
73	(H)	Niagara	58
55	(A)	Marquette	77
87	(A)	Detroit	82
66	(H)	Louisville	62
76	(H)	Miami (FL)	48
77	(A)	UCLA	87
51	(H)	Fordham	38
71	(A)	North Carolina State	80
66	(A)	Miami (FL)	49
68	(H)	Alabama-Birmingham	74
63	(A)	Notre Dame	62
74	(A)	St. John's	77
59	(H)	Bradley	48
79	(H)	Texas	89
69	(H)	Northern Illinois	51
64	(H)	Notre Dame	59
+89	(H)	Creighton	72
+61	(H)	Cincinnati	59
+47	(A)	St. Louis	54

*Dodge Preseason NIT
**First Chicago Christmas Classic
+ NIT

1990-91

Won 20, Lost 9
Percentage .690
Captain: Kevin Holland

DePaul			Opponents
88	(H)	Czechoslovakia	65
111	(H)	Marathon	75
84	(H)	Hartford	73
117	(H)	Florida Int'l.	65
85	(A)	Pepperdine	64
*96	(H)	Illinois State	78
75	(A)	Louisville	94
90	(H)	UCLA	92
**56	(H)	Wisconsin-Green Bay	57
**70	(H)	Oklahoma State	72
†75		North Carolina	90
†81		Central Florida	(ot) 78
81	(A)	Dayton	73
68	(H)	Marquette	63
76	(H)	Houston	62
61	(A)	Northern Illinois	70
80	(A)	Texas	90
92	(H)	Drake	71
75	(H)	Duquesne	62
84	(A)	Marquette	56
72	(A)	Georgetown	63
81	(H)	Detroit	74
80	(A)	Bradley	69
102	(A)	Loyola (IL)	67
73	(A)	Niagara	58
77	(A)	Notre Dame	(ot) 80
66	(A)	Miami (FL)	53
79	(H)	St. John's	69
75	(H)	Miami (FL)	58
80	(H)	Notre Dame	56
‡70		Georgia Tech	87

*First Chicago Christmas Classic
**Old Style Classic
†Red Lobster Classic
‡NCAA Tournament